YORK NOTES

Children's Literature

Lucy Pearson

with Peter Hunt

Longman
is an imprint of

Harlow, England • London
Sydney • Tokyo • Singapo
Cape Town • Madrid • Mex

York Press

YORK PRESS
322 Old Brompton Road, London SW5 9JH

PEARSON EDUCATION LIMITED
Edinburgh Gate, Harlow CM20 2JE, United Kingdom
Tel: +44 (0)1279 623623 Fax: +44 (0)1279 431059
Website: www.pearsoned.co.uk

First edition published in Great Britain in 2011

© Librairie du Liban *Publishers* 2011

The right of Lucy Pearson to be identified as author
of this work has been asserted by her in accordance
with the Copyright, Designs and Patents Act 1988.

ISBN 978–1–4082–6662–5

British Library Cataloguing in Publication Data
A CIP catalogue record for this book can be obtained from the British Library

Library of Congress Cataloguing-in-Publication Data
Pearson, Lucy (Lucy R.)
  Children's literature / Lucy Pearson. -- 1st ed.
    p. cm. -- (York notes companions)
  Includes bibliographical references and index.
  ISBN 978-1-4082-6662-5 (pbk. : alk. paper)
  1. Children's literature, English--History and criticism. 2. Children's literature,
  American--History and criticism. I. Title. II. Series.
PR990.P43 2011
820.8'09282--dc22
                                          2011004706

10 9 8 7 6 5 4 3 2 1
14 13 12 11

Phototypeset by Chat Noir Design, France
Printed in Malaysia, CTP-PJB

Contents

Contents

Part One
Introduction

Most readers will encounter children's literature in some form or other: nursery rhymes, fables, picture books and stories are shared with children in cultures across the world. In the West, characters from children's books such as Harry Potter, the Gruffalo and the Cat in the Hat are recognisable cultural icons. Paradoxically, this cultural ubiquity has often caused children's literature to be dismissed as an unsuitable object for serious study: can books which are 'just' for children really be complex and important enough to merit consideration by academics? Since the 1970s, however, the importance of thinking critically about children's literature has been recognised by university departments and, since the turn of the millenium, children's literature has become an increasingly popular option on undergraduate courses. In the chapters that follow, this book looks in detail at some representative texts and explores the history, culture and critical debates with which they are associated.

The chapters are divided into two main sections. In Part Three: 'Texts, Writers and Contexts', each chapter is organised around a major genre or category of children's literature, such as fantasy or picture books. The historical development of the genre and some of its key components are briefly explored, with reference to three main authors. This author-specific approach is supplemented by consideration of other relevant authors where this provides further insight into the history and scope of the genre. Each chapter in this part then concludes with an extended commentary on a single text, which exemplifies some of the features and techniques discussed in the foregoing chapter through a close textual analysis.

Part Four: 'Critical Theories and Debates' takes a broader look at major critical issues and approaches to the discipline. Beginning with the question of what it means to read children's books from a critical perspective, the first chapter in this section examines some of the key critical schools in children's literature scholarship. The second chapter examines approaches to one contested area – gender – in detail, while the third explores the issue of ideology more broadly, touching on postcolonialism, religion, war and censorship, and considering the place of such issues in children's literature. How far can or should children's books engage with controversial issues in the real world? How do writers for children negotiate the balance of power between author and reader, when the relationship between adult and child creates a pre-existing inequality? The final chapter looks to the future: in the rapidly changing technological, political and social contexts of the modern world, where will children's literature fit in? What kinds of books can we expect to emerge in the coming decades? This section offers a glimpse of the different kinds of debate which children's literature scholarship offers.

These main sections of the book are framed by Part Two: 'A Cultural Overview', which gives a brief account of the social, political and philosophical events which have helped to shape children's literature, and Part Five: 'References and Resources', which includes a timeline of significant historical and literary events, and some annotated suggestions for further reading. These sections provide some broader context for the material discussed in Parts Two and Three.

The Boundaries of Children's Literature

Children's literature is almost the only category of literature defined nearly exclusively by its intended audience. While some categories, such as women's literature or African-American literature, are aimed at particular groups, they are also primarily created by members of those groups. By contrast, apart from a few notable exceptions – S. E. Hinton's *The Outsiders* (1967) and Christopher Paolini's *Eragon* (2003), for example, written when their authors were still in their teens – 'children's' books are predominantly written by adults for children. As Part Four: 'Criticising Children's Literature' shows, this anomaly has led some critics to question whether a true 'children's literature' can really exist at all. The issue is further complicated because many texts read by children were not originally intended for them: Daniel Defoe's adult novel *Robinson Crusoe* (1719) has found a lasting place in the children's literature canon, while books such as Virginia Andrews's gothic saga *Flowers in the Attic* (1979) and Dave Pelzer's autobiographical account of childhood abuse *A Child Called It* (1995) have attracted many adolescent readers (despite the best efforts of adults to discourage them).

Even when we accept a definition of children's literature which is predicated on the fact that the books concerned are intended for, or widely read by, children, difficulties of definition still remain. Notions of when childhood begins and ends, what children can do or understand, and what children need vary widely across time and place. Is there a recognisable 'childness' which links a middle-class child in Victorian Britain, a child soldier in Rwanda during the 1990s and a low-income child in twenty-first century urban America? Even within cultures, the boundaries of childhood are fluid. In contemporary Britain, does childhood end at ten (the age of criminal responsibility in England and Wales), at sixteen (the age of sexual consent) or at eighteen (when civic rights and responsibilities such as voting are conferred)? As Part Three: 'Real Lives' and Part Three: 'Young Adult Fiction' show, disagreements about what childhood is and when it begins and ends have significantly affected the discourse around children's literature. Scholars such as Peter Hunt have questioned whether it is meaningful to consider historical texts as children's literature at all: when the language, references and style of a book are no longer accessible to a child reading today, and can only be enjoyed or understood by specialist academics, is it really still a book for children?[1] For the purposes of this volume, children's literature is defined as literature intended for readers aged between one and eighteen at the time it was written.

Because children's literature is defined in terms of its intended audience, it covers a much wider range than any other field of literature. Whereas Romantic literature, for example, is generally understood to comprise a specific set of texts delineated by historical period, geographical origin and generic similarities, 'children's literature' has no historical, geographical or generic boundaries. Prose, poetry, drama and illustration are all represented in books for children, as is almost every conceivable genre: Hilaire Belloc's satirical and humorous poems *Cautionary Tales for Children* (1907); Shirley Hughes's beautifully illustrated *Dogger* (1977), about a small boy losing his favourite toy; and Patrick Ness's dystopian novel *The Knife of Never Letting Go* (2008), a disturbing exploration of politics, oppression and war, can all be classed as children's literature. Almost every culture has some literature for children, and children in the English-speaking world, for instance, are familiar with characters from other countries, such as Pinocchio (Italy), Pippi Longstocking (Sweden), Tintin (Belgium) and Asterix (France); it is therefore difficult to draw clear geographical boundaries for the subject.

Studying children's literature is further complicated by the range of possible approaches to the discipline. The fields of education, child development, sociology, librarianship, book history and psychology, as well as literature, have all contributed important work on children's literature. Indeed, it is almost impossible to consider children's literature without reference to these other fields: as Part Two: 'A Cultural Overview' shows, books for children have been consciously used to promote and pursue different social ideologies, educational theories and ideas about childhood. This book takes a primarily literary critical approach, but the influence of other fields is acknowledged where it touches directly on the issues under discussion.

The wide scope of children's literature poses particular challenges for a book such as this one, which aims to present the history, literary characteristics and critical debates associated with the subject. Inevitably, the selection of texts and topics discussed represents only a tiny sample of the field as a whole: the aim is not to offer a comprehensive survey, but to provide the reader with an understanding of some key issues and texts as a starting point for more in-depth study. The historical portions of this volume introduce a few of the books which have become widely accepted as part of the 'canon' of children's literature as it is studied on university courses. In contemporary children's literature, it is more difficult to identify 'canonical' texts, and more recent texts have been selected on the basis that they are representative of current trends and techniques, and for their popularity in the current market. Many of the twentieth- and twenty-first-century books discussed have been recipients of prizes such as the Carnegie Medal, awarded annually by the Chartered Institute of Library and Information Professionals (CILIP) to an 'outstanding' book for children; although prizes do not infallibly reflect the literary merit or importance of a book, they do indicate a certain degree of cultural prominence at the time of publication.

This book focuses on literature written in English, with a particular emphasis on British authors, although some texts from other countries are also included.* Historically, children's literature has developed in parallel in Britain and the United States of America, and many texts have crossed the Atlantic in both directions; for this reason American authors are also well represented. For the purposes of brevity, the focus is on prose fiction; poetry and illustration are

---

* In these instances, the nationality of authors from outside Britain is stated in the text.

discussed in dedicated chapters, and drama is omitted.* This focus reflects the dominance of children's novels both in the marketplace and in much critical work on children's literature. The historical range of this book and the state of the contemporary marketplace mean that writers of colour are underrepresented within the canon; one of the challenges inherent in producing an introduction to earlier work is to avoid reproducing some of the ideological biases which shaped previous eras.

Looking Forward: The Literature and the Discipline

The wide scope of children's literature and the diversity of possible approaches to its study present particular challenges to a book of this type, and to students coming to the subject for the first time. However, the breadth of the subject also makes it exciting and full of possibility. Scholars who bring expertise from fields such as child development, film studies, cultural studies and librarianship help to provide new and stimulating ways of thinking about texts. At the same time, the form and boundaries of children's literature are in a constant state of flux as they respond to the changing world.

Each generation has feared the demise of books for children: during the 1960s, the growing dominance of television caused fears that the book would be ousted by TV programmes, while in the 1980s, the emergence of the video game caused similar anxieties. Today's parents, who grew up in the 1980s, now worry that the variety of technology and online media available to their children threatens the popularity of reading. It is certainly the case that, as we move into a new technological age, children are increasingly likely to

---

* Drama written specially for children poses particular difficulties for study: while many live productions are put on for children each year, relatively few of these are published and – apart from some notable exceptions such as J. M. Barrie's *Peter Pan* (1904) – there is no established 'canon' of drama for children. The issue is further complicated by the necessity of considering television and film productions for children: while these can certainly be considered as texts, they fall too far outside the realm of 'children's literature' to be easily included in the present work.

download books and read them on portable devices, engage with media which mix text, pictures and sound, and play computer games which require them to actively participate in the creation of narrative. As Part Four: 'The Future of Children's Literature' shows, however, the changing social and technological context for children's literature is far from a threat. On the contrary, children's literature has historically risen to the challenges posed by social change, and has often been at the cutting edge of 'future' narrative techniques. The rapidly changing context for contemporary children's books makes this a particularly exciting time to study children's literature. As we seek to understand contemporary trends and to predict future developments, an appreciation of the way in which children's literature has developed in the past becomes increasingly important. While it can only present a small selection of the wide range of material available, this book offers readers an entrance into this exciting area of study.

Lucy Pearson

Note

1   Peter Hunt, *Criticism, Theory and Children's Literature* (Oxford: Blackwell, 1991), p. 61.

Part Two
A Cultural Overview

'Before there could be children's literature', John Rowe Townsend wrote in 1965, 'there had to be children.'[1] Townsend was drawing upon the influential view of childhood put forward by the French historian Philippe Ariès, who argued that the concept of childhood as a distinctive period of life did not emerge in Western Europe until the seventeenth century. Prior to this point, Ariès argued, children were seen as 'miniature adults' once past the stage of babyhood – a perspective which was progressively displaced as economic and cultural changes altered conceptions of the family and helped to develop new attitudes towards the child. Historians of childhood have challenged Ariès's theories, identifying significant flaws in his methodology, and contemporary scholars have largely rejected the notion that children in the West prior to the seventeenth century were essentially regarded as adults.[2] However, Ariès's progressive view of childhood has had an important influence on histories of children's literature, which until recently have tended to depict it as dependent upon the emergence of a specific historical concept of childhood, and to present a linear progression towards literature which more fully 'recognised' the particular nature of children and childhood.

This narrative has been increasingly challenged by recent scholarship: Nicholas Orme has argued that a specialist children's literature had emerged 'by 1400 at the latest', while Matthew Grenby comments that 'whichever definition we use, we find that children's literature has no easily discernible starting point.'[3] Nevertheless, as Grenby notes, the mid-eighteenth century saw a significant shift in both the amount and the nature of the literature being produced especially for children, and developments in children's literature have historically been closely related to changes in cultural perceptions of childhood. Ariès's most important legacy has been in establishing childhood as culturally constructed: while most scholars now reject the idea that there was *no* concept of childhood prior to the seventeenth century, they can agree that ideas about what exactly constitutes childhood and what children want or need have varied widely across historical periods, as well as across different countries and cultures. The changing perception of children and childhood has particular relevance to the evolving nature of children's literature: while the political, economic and social contexts in which children's books have been produced have all had an important influence on the literature, perhaps the most important context for a history of children's literature is a history of the child.

Although a number of scholars have identified texts which can be classed as 'children's literature' dating from the Middle Ages and even earlier, the context in which literature was produced and consumed in these societies makes the line between literature for children and for adults significantly blurred. Low levels of literacy outside the clergy and the time and expense involved in producing texts prior to the widespread adoption of the printing press meant that relatively few children would have had access to books at all, still less to books written and produced especially for them. Those texts which were produced for children in particular tended to be largely didactic in nature. Some of the earliest examples of children's texts were 'horn books': simple reading primers which consisted of a single sheet of paper, usually showing the alphabet and the Lord's Prayer, pasted onto a wooden or leather board and protected by a thin sheet of animal horn. There is plenty of evidence that children did have access to some texts which might more properly be described as 'literature' and which were designed for enjoyment rather than simply education, such as Chaucer's *Canterbury Tales* (*c.* 1387–1400), the *Gesta Romanorum* (a collection of legends and saints' lives compiled near the beginning of the fourteenth century) and popular romances, but these texts were primarily intended for adult audiences. Similarly, we can assume that children were able to share in and enjoy stories which circulated orally, such as popular ballads about figures like Robin Hood, Arthurian legends, folk tales and fairy stories, but there is little evidence to show whether any of this oral tradition was aimed explicitly at children. In fact, some of the tales now closely associated with children's literature – folk tales and fairy tales – almost certainly originated as stories for an adult audience or for a mixed one: Jack Zipes argues that even those stories which were directed particularly at children, such as warnings about dangerous animals, were not considered 'children's tales'.[4] While children were certainly reading and enjoying literature during the Middle Ages and before, therefore, it is difficult to identify many texts produced especially with children's interests or needs in mind. Although we may not give credence to Ariès's idea that there was no concept of childhood at all, it is certainly evident that children were expected to share many of the interests of their elders, if only because the high cost of books was a disincentive to producing many specialist texts for readers outside the clergy.

The 'Birth' of Children's Literature

In the seventeenth century, many more texts written especially for children began to appear. Although the large number of specialist texts for children indicates a perceived difference between the needs and interests of children and those of adults (a distinction which is often considered to be a prerequisite for children's literature), it is notable that the religious impetus of most of these texts reflects a belief in the fundamental similarity between adults and children. The Puritan writers who were responsible for most of the children's texts of this period were motivated by the belief that humanity is born into sin, and that even babies need to embrace Christian doctrine in order to expiate their innate sinfulness. Authors including the well-known writer and preacher John Bunyan – best known for his adult text *Pilgrim's Progress* (1678), which also found popularity with child readers – and James Janeway wrote texts designed to impress the importance of Christian belief and the possibility of salvation upon their young readers. Some of these texts were widely circulated, such as James Janeway's highly influential *A Token for Children* (1671–2; discussed in more detail in Part Three: 'Real Lives'), which depicts the lives and deaths of a series of children who have found salvation. Janeway's stories are heavily didactic, focusing on elaborate deathbed scenes in which his unfortunate protagonists urge family and friends to repent their sins before it is too late. Nevertheless, as Matthew Grenby points out, Janeway did offer child readers something to enjoy: while the long sermons his child protagonists deliver are designed to convey Christian doctrine, they also offer child readers the pleasing fantasy of enjoying moral and spiritual superiority over their elders.[5] John Bunyan's *Book for Boys and Girls* (also called *Country Rimes for Children* or *Divine Emblems*, 1686) is (to modern eyes) even more appealing: a miscellany of poems mostly relating to different animals which are glossed with a moral and religious message. In 'Of the Boy and the Butterfly', for example, Bunyan sketches an image of a child at play:

> He hollo's, runs, and cries out, Here, Boys, here,
> Nor doth he Brambles or the Nettles fear.
> He stumbles at the Mole-Hills, up he gets,
> And runs again, as one bereft of wits.[6]

Bunyan disparages the child's energies, which are expended 'only for a silly Butter-fly' (l. 12), and draws a comparison between this fruitless endeavour and the energies of those who seek to gain worldly things; however, the exuberance of the boy is in itself appealing (indeed, one might wonder whether child readers would not be led to feel that such 'fruitless' endeavours are pleasurable in themselves). This is a depiction of the child which is recognisable to a modern eye: playful, impetuous and noisy! Texts like this illustrate that even heavily didactic early children's texts contain elements often identified as characteristics of children's literature, such as imaginative scenarios and recognisable child characters. There is some evidence that popular literature included even more texts which aimed to entertain child readers. One such example is *The History of Tom Thumb the Little* (1621), which recounts the adventures of the diminutive character Tom Thumb. Only one copy of the booklet survives, indicating the ephemeral nature of such popular texts: while few examples remain of folk tales and fairy tales for children before the eighteenth century, the existence of books such as this suggests that children may well have had access to a much greater spread of imaginative popular texts.

The notion that 'true' children's literature emerged only with a certain concept of childhood is an oversimplification; nevertheless, the mid-eighteenth century did see significant developments which brought children's books closer to the kinds of texts we recognise as children's literature today. The publication in 1744 of *A Little Pretty Pocket-Book* – issued by publisher John Newbery – is usually seen as a landmark in the history of children's literature. Patricia Demers describes Newbery's collection of rhymes and fables, 'intended for the Instruction and Amusement of little Master Tommy and pretty Miss Polly', as 'the embodiment of the enlightened eighteenth-century view of literature for the young'.[7] The book's promise of delight as well as instruction is characteristic of the books published for children during this period: whereas the majority of texts aimed explicitly at children during the seventeenth century are primarily focused on the education of their readers, Newbery's book is one of a whole host of texts which place an equal emphasis on the pleasure of reading. In the same year that Newbery published *A Little Pretty Pocket-Book*, Thomas and Mary Cooper issued *Tommy Thumb's Pretty Song-Book*, the earliest surviving collection of nursery rhymes, which contains many rhymes still familiar to children today, including 'Baa

Baa, Black Sheep', 'Ladybird, Ladybird, Fly Away Home' and 'Mary Mary, Quite Contrary'.* A few years before this Thomas Boreman began publishing his series of 'Gigantick Histories' (1740–3), entertaining descriptions of the sights of London made even more appealing to children by the small size of the books, which were just a few inches in height. Many critics have seen this shift towards more texts focused on pleasure as a crucial prerequisite for a 'true' children's literature, based on the idea of children with different interests and needs rather than on the pragmatic desire to educate and shape young citizens. Perhaps even more significantly, *A Little Pretty Pocket-Book* and its eighteenth-century contemporaries represent the emergence of children's publishing as a distinctive industry in its own right; Newbery's firm was to continue publishing for the rest of the century, and it was joined by many competitors. Peter Hunt characterises the rest of the eighteenth century as 'a battle between the religious/educational and commercial interests for the market in children's books';[8] while moral and educational tales continued to play an important role (including on the lists of publishers such as Newbery), commercial publishers were increasingly motivated to make their texts more appealing in order to compete in an active market.

The emergence of books like *A Little Pretty Pocket-Book* and the flourishing of children's publishing in the mid-eighteenth century reflect some key social and cultural changes in British society. Diminishing rates of child mortality contributed to a new focus on children and the family: as the expectation that children would die in infancy became less pronounced, a greater emphasis on loving relationships between parents and children emerged. Georgiana, Duchess of Devonshire, was one of a number of high-profile women whose public personas were for the first time constructed around

---

* The 1644 edition of *Tommy Thumb's Pretty Song-Book* is marked as volume 2, so we can assume that it was preceded by another collection, but no copies of volume 1 have survived. The fact that we only know of the earlier volume because of the second part – which survives in only two copies – is indicative of the degree to which histories of early children's literature are necessarily partial.

their roles as loving and involved mothers: whereas wealthy women of previous generations had typically left the care of their children to wet nurses, Sir Joshua Reynolds's painting *Georgiana, Duchess of Devonshire, with Her Daughter* (1784) depicts Georgiana playing with her baby daughter, emphasising her maternal nature.* This shift in attitudes to the family was in part produced by socio-economic changes which were allowing greater social mobility: wealthy middle-class families – who had through economic necessity traditionally been more involved with their children than the upper classes – were gaining social prominence and thereby disseminating new models for child-rearing. These wealthy families also represented a new economic demographic, providing publishers like John Newbery with a lucrative new market. Many eighteenth-century children's texts show the influence of this middle-class, socially mobile demographic, focusing on the possibility of worldly rather than spiritual advance. The famous *History of Goody Two-Shoes* (1765), another landmark text published by John Newbery, features a pious heroine on the Puritan model who sets an example to the adults around her; Goody Two-Shoes is rewarded by social rather than spiritual elevation, beginning as a pauper with only one shoe and rising to lady of the manor.

Locke and Rousseau

Influential in the shift towards children's literature aimed at amusing child readers as well as instructing them were the ideas of the philosopher John Locke, notably his *Essay Concerning Human Understanding* (1690) and *Some Thoughts on Education* (1693). Locke presented children as a *tabula rasa* (blank slate), emphasising the importance of education and socialisation in forming the

---

* Portraits like this are, of course, an unreliable guide to how people behaved in actuality. However, the appearance of paintings which presented children and parents as loving and playful demonstrates a new cultural focus on the idea of childhood, even if the change in people's private lives was less dramatic.

character. Locke's assertion that character was formed gradually placed greater emphasis on the importance of experiences during childhood, and by extension the importance of providing children with reading material designed to shape them appropriately. In addition, he advocated the use of entertainment as a means of instructing children, an idea which is clearly evident in Newbery's *Little Pretty Pocket-Book*, which promised 'instruction with delight'. The influence of Locke is also discernible in Sarah Fielding's *The Governess* (1749), which demonstrates the role of education and storytelling in the formation of young girls' characters. The first 'school story' – a genre with a long and successful history in English-language children's literature – *The Governess* follows the development of a group of schoolgirls as they exchange stories with one another. Each story is calculated to teach the girls a particular virtue or moral lesson, and the 'fictional' narratives they tell are accompanied by their accounts of their own life stories, which illustrate the ways in which the girls have been shaped by their previous education and experiences. By the end of the book, the education the girls have received through the storytelling has helped to shape them into a harmonious and virtuous society. The text exemplifies Locke's ideas about the importance of childhood experiences in shaping both the individual and society.

Locke also helped to promulgate a belief in the importance of rationality in children's books: since childhood was of central importance in shaping the character, Locke argued, exposure to fantastical and frightening notions such as the existence of the supernatural could have a long-lasting and damaging effect on the child. This emphasis on the rational and realistic caused many writers to shy away from including fantastical elements in their work for children: in *The Governess*, for example, Sarah Fielding includes fairy stories among the tales told by her child protagonists, but uses the frame narrative to emphasise the unreality of these tales and their moral messages. While the eighteenth century saw the first editions of fairy tales aimed directly at children – Charles Perrault's *Histories, or Tales of Past Times, Told by Mother Goose* (1697) appeared in an

English translation in 1729 – tensions about the possible effects of fantasy on child readers remained prevalent well into the nineteenth century.

Locke's ideas contributed significantly to the work of philosopher Jean-Jacques Rousseau, whose *Émile, or On Education* (1762) was to have a profound influence on ideas about childhood and children's literature. Like Locke, Rousseau presented childhood as a crucial period of life. In contrast to the seventeenth-century view of humanity as innately sinful, Rousseau argued for the existence of an innate human goodness which – he suggested – was corrupted by society. In *Émile*, he presented a model for the education of an ideal citizen, emphasising the importance of allowing children to learn through experience. Rousseau suggested that his fictional child Émile should be given only one book, Daniel Defoe's *Robinson Crusoe* (1719), which depicts the adventures of a castaway on a desert island and exemplifies the growth of character in a setting divorced from 'civilisation'. Ironically, given his emphasis on learning through experience rather than from books, Rousseau's ideas were to inspire many texts for children which aimed to provide the kind of education through experience which Rousseau advocated. Johann Sebastian Wyss developed the Robinson Crusoe model with his *Swiss Family Robinson* (1812–13; discussed in Part Three: 'Adventure Stories'), in which an entire family rather than a single man is marooned on an island. Maria Edgeworth, one of the most well-known and successful children's writers of the early nineteenth century, was also heavily influenced by Rousseauian ideas: her story 'The Purple Jar' (1801; discussed in Part Three: 'Real Lives') famously exemplifies the way in which parents could apply Rousseau's notion of learning through experience. Almost seventy years later, Louisa May Alcott adopted a similar approach in *Little Women* (1868), in which the four March girls learn to become 'little women' through experiences both humorous – such as the episode when their mother allows them to try the experiment of 'all play and no work' – and tragic – the older girls' neglect of their duty to the poor results in fragile Beth's exposure to scarlet fever.

The Romantic Child and the Birth of Fantasy

Writers such as Edgeworth and Alcott demonstrate that Rousseau's philosophy lent itself to the tradition of the moral tale, which remained an important component of children's literature throughout the nineteenth century. However, Rousseau's belief in the innate morality of childhood and the importance of allowing children freedom to explore nature and develop naturally, rather than exposing them to the corruptive influence of society, also played an important role in fostering a children's literature which was less closely focused on morality and education. The association of childhood with nature and innocence was to become increasingly important towards the end of the eighteenth century and into the nineteenth. The image of the innocent and natural child is important to the work of the Romantics, notably in Wordsworth's 'Intimations of Immortality from Recollections of Early Childhood' (1807), in which he portrays the child* 'trailing clouds of glory', reiterating Rousseau's notion of society as a corruptive force in his assertion that 'Shades of the prison house begin to close / Upon the growing boy'.[9] The Romantic image of childhood as a prelapsarian state (comparable to the state of humanity before the fall from Eden) has played a significant role in conceptions of childhood from the nineteenth century to the present day. Edenic images of childhood are central to Robert Louis Stevenson's *A Child's Garden of Verses* (1885; discussed in Part Three: 'Rhymes and Rhythms'), while well-known texts such as Frances Hodgson Burnett's *The Secret Garden* (1911) and Kenneth Grahame's *The Wind in the Willows* (1908) present a return to nature as integral to self-development and healing.

---

* Similar portrayals of the child are evident in William Blake's *Songs of Innocence and of Experience* (1789–94), where they are employed more directly as social comment: in poems such as 'The Chimney Sweeper', industrial society is portrayed not only as morally corruptive but also as abusive.

The idea of the child as both innocent and natural was a central component of nineteenth-century approaches to childhood. As the nineteenth century progressed, children were increasingly focused upon and idealised, partly because falling birth rates and still-high levels of childhood mortality made individual children more precious. Much Victorian literature for adults utilised the image of the child for both political and sentimental purposes. Charles Dickens's portrayals of poor children in *Oliver Twist* (1838) and *The Old Curiosity Shop* (1841) show child heroes who are uncorrupted by the society around them, despite being exposed to poverty and criminality. Little Nell, the child heroine of *The Old Curiosity Shop*, is the epitome of the Victorian sentimental child: her struggles against poverty were followed avidly by Victorian audiences, both adults and children, when they appeared in serial form in 1840 and 1841, while American readers famously greeted incoming ships bearing the final instalment of the serial with the cry 'Does Little Nell live?' Her eventual tragic death made a huge impact on Victorian audiences: Irish MP Daniel O'Connell burst into tears on reaching the end of the story, and flung the book out of the window of the train in which he was travelling.* The strong focus on children and childhood within adult literature was accompanied by a greater cultural focus on real children, reflected in legislation and social initiatives aimed at protecting the kind of impoverished children who frequently featured in the pages of Dickens's novels. The Education Act of 1870 established the principle of universal schooling for children aged between five and twelve, while successive Factory Acts limited the hours and conditions under which children could work. The National Society for the Prevention of Cruelty to Children, founded in 1884, further highlighted the plight of poor children, while Barnado's 'Ragged School' for orphans, founded in 1867, sought to provide practical help. Much children's literature of the period

---

* Not all readers found the sentimentality of Dickens's narrative so compelling, however; Oscar Wilde acerbically remarked that 'one would have to have a heart of stone to read the death of Little Nell without laughing.' Quoted in Laurence W. Mazzeno, *The Dickens Industry: Critical Perspectives 1836–2005* (New York: Camden House, 2008), p. 40.

directly engaged with the social inequities addressed by philanthropic legislation: stories about the poorest class of children were a popular genre, while Charles Kingsley's *The Water Babies* (1863) was instrumental in highlighting the abuses suffered by child chimney sweeps and helped to bring about the Climbing Boys Act of 1875, which sought to curb the worst of these abuses.

Fantasies of Childhood: The 'First Golden Age'

The increasing cultural focus on children and childhood during the Victorian period set the stage for a radical expansion in children's literature in the 1860s, widely considered to mark the beginning of the 'first golden age' of children's literature. Lewis Carroll's *Alice's Adventures in Wonderland* (1865; discussed in Part Three: 'Alternative Worlds') is a landmark text which epitomises the move towards a new era in children's literature. Drawing on the traditions of fantasy and nonsense which had already developed, Carroll produced a fresh and groundbreaking novel which helped to establish fantasy as a major mode in English-language children's literature. The fairy-tale tradition which emerged in the eighteenth century had continued to grow into the nineteenth, with writers such as Hans Christian Andersen producing modern fairy tales for children as well as retellings of traditional tales. Many Victorian fantasy books followed the example of their predecessors in using fantasy as a vehicle for moral and religious messages: *The Water Babies* is a religious fantasy as well as a social commentary, while George Macdonald's *At the Back of the North Wind* (1871) is a complex religious allegory. By contrast, Lewis Carroll embraced the nonsensical and fantastical for its own sake; although it is not true to say that *Alice's Adventures in Wonderland* is solely focused on delight, it both resists and satirises the didactic tradition of children's literature. It is also notable for the way in which it allies itself with the child, adopting a child's point of view and eliding the gap between adult narrator and child reader. This child-centred writing does not,

19

however, imply simplicity: on the contrary, by offering children a confusing and destabilising text which draws on mathematics and philosophy, satirises popular modes of literature and education, and explores the unequal power relations between adult and child, Carroll demands a great deal from child readers. Peter Hunt suggests that the book's true legacy is that it 'liberated child readers from simplicity'.[10]

The period from the publication of *Alice's Adventures in Wonderland* to the beginning of the First World War saw an outpouring of children's literature. The popularity of *Alice* helped to foster the already growing trend for fantasy in children's literature, and some of the best-known children's fantasies appeared during this period. J. M. Barrie's play *Peter Pan*, which engaged with the tensions surrounding the idealisation of childhood and fantasy, premiered in 1904, and Kenneth Grahame's *The Wind in the Willows* demonstrated the possibilities of the animal story in 1908. A totally different brand of fantasy was introduced by Edith Nesbit in 1902 with *Five Children and It*, which blends realism and fantasy in the story of five very ordinary children who are granted the power to wish for whatever they like by an irascible 'sand fairy'. Nesbit is also notable for her realistic fiction, in particular her series of stories about the Bastable children, beginning with *The Story of the Treasure Seekers* (1899). The more child-centred focus which is a key component of the texts produced during this golden age of children's literature is intrinsic to Nesbit's work, which adopts a child's viewpoint both literally – the Bastable books are narrated by Oswald Bastable, one of the child characters – and in the sense that children's concerns and interests are foregrounded. The way in which Nesbit handles the adventures of her child characters illustrates the increasing dominance of ideas about the importance of play, freedom and experience in childhood: both the Bastable stories and the series of fantasy novels which begins with *Five Children and It* feature the child characters engaged in imaginative adventures which frequently lead them away from 'good' behaviour. However, whereas many contemporary examples of realistically naughty child characters had typically shown significant consequences for bad behaviour – as in Susan Coolidge's *What Katy Did* (1872), in which Katy's refusal to abide by her aunt's instruction not to swing on a new swing results in her crippling back injury – Nesbit allows her child characters to emerge from their adventures largely unscathed. In *The Wouldbegoods* the children's misadventures come about as a direct result of their resolve to do good works after the manner of the moral tales with which they are familiar from their own reading; Nesbit therefore both highlights the shortcomings of this particular brand of morality and implies that good intentions mitigate bad behaviour. This moral ambiguity signals Nesbit's place in the process of liberating child readers from simplicity which Peter Hunt suggests was initiated by *Alice's Adventures in Wonderland*.

Warfare and Retreat: The Early Twentieth Century

The early twentieth century saw a period of relative quiescence in children's literature. The two world wars had significant practical and cultural effects on children's books: many children's writers, illustrators and editors were conscripted, and wartime shortages of paper limited the number of books which could be published, encouraging publishers to restrict their output to already established and well-known writers. Nicholas Tucker suggests that the uncertainty of the war also led to a more conservative outlook on the part of the public, who sought familiar texts rather than new writers.[11] As a result, a handful of writers dominated the period from the beginning of the First World War up until the 1950s: Arthur Ransome and Enid Blyton offered an essentially cosy image of middle-class childhoods in books in which children enjoyed adventures far removed from the everyday hardships experienced by many real children during the war years and interwar period. Noel Streatfeild's family and 'career' novels – notably *Ballet Shoes* (1936) – similarly offered child readers an image of safety and security. Although these texts appear to be removed from the context of war and international conflict which overshadowed Britain during the first half of the twentieth century, they can be seen to respond to the context in which they were written in some important ways. Streatfeild's books, which were among the bestselling and most highly regarded texts in Britain during this period, mirror some of the instability of war through their focus on fractured and disrupted families. In *Ballet Shoes*, Streatfeild depicts a female 'created' family composed of the three adopted Fossil children – Pauline, Petrova and Posy – and their guardian Garnie. The children's adopted father, Great Uncle Matthew, has embarked on an expedition from which he has not returned, so that the family is deprived both of a father figure and of financial stability, forcing Garnie to take in lodgers and all three children to seek ways of earning support for the family, most notably by learning ballet and dancing in public performances. The wish-fulfilment element of Streatfeild's novel – the fantasy of becoming an acclaimed and successful dancer – is therefore built around a situation which would have been all too familiar to many families in the wake of the First World War: the absence of a male parent and the necessity for women to seek paid employment. This scenario was to gain even more immediate resonance for child readers shortly after the book was published: only three years after the first appearance of *Ballet Shoes*, a new generation of children were deprived of their fathers by war. The sense of danger and conflict connected with the two world wars is even more evident in J. R. R. Tolkien's *The Hobbit* (1937; discussed in Part Three: 'Alternative Worlds'), the precursor to Tolkien's successful *Lord of the Rings* (1954–5). The theme of leaving the safety and security of home to face conflict and danger abroad has obvious parallels with the experience of war, while the subsequent books in the series (published for adults rather than children) address the conflict between good and evil more explicitly. While books dealing directly with the topic of war and its impact on children's lives were slow to appear, therefore, the influence of the war years was discernible in the books published during this period.

Postwar Narratives: The 'Second Golden Age'

The aftermath of war helped to create a new international focus on children and childhood. Adults had created an international situation which had produced two world conflicts in the course of a single lifetime: the inherent possibility for change represented by children and childhood therefore held particular cultural significance. Children's literature offered the opportunity to shape a new generation who could correct the mistakes of their parents and build international peace, an aim directly stated by the International Board on Books for Young People (IBBY), founded in 1952, which sought 'to promote international understanding through children's books'.[12] Political and social policy in Britain in the postwar years reflects a new emphasis on the importance of childhood and education: beginning with the 1944 Education Act, which widened access to secondary education, there was a series of reforms aimed at improving children's standards of living and access to education. Economic growth during the 1950s further contributed to a new focus on children and childhood: Hugh Cunningham argues that parents increasingly began to believe that their children could have better lives than those of previous generations, and to work to achieve this.[13]

The sense of childhood as an important and formative period of life was reflected and reinforced by new ideas about child development, notably the work of British psychiatrists Donald Winnicott and John Bowlby, and of American paediatrician Benjamin Spock, whose childcare manual *The Pocket Book of Baby and Child-Care* (1946) was a bestseller.[14] Like the work of Locke in the eighteenth century, such theories encouraged parents to invest in their children both emotionally and financially. The state was also more willing to invest in child citizens: the 1950s and 1960s saw increasing social funding of schools and libraries, creating a new market for children's books in these institutions. All these factors combined to produce a 'second golden age' of children's literature which stretched from the 1950s to the 1970s. Like the first golden age, this period was characterised by a host of landmark fantasy novels, beginning in 1950 with the first book in C. S. Lewis's 'Narnia' series, *The Lion, the Witch and the Wardrobe* (discussed in Part Three: 'Alternative Worlds'). Like Tolkien's Middle Earth, Lewis's fantasy world is in part a response to the experience of war, focusing closely on conflict and ideas of good and evil. The same themes are evident in much of the fantasy which was to succeed Lewis: Susan Cooper, Alan Garner and Diana Wynne Jones all emerged during this period as notable fantasy writers whose work reflected some of the darkness which had overshadowed their wartime childhoods.

Lucy Boston's 'Green Knowe' series (1954–6) displays many of the associations between childhood, innocence and nature which were evident in the work of the first golden age, but also shows the influence of war. Her child characters retreat to a rural idyll in the form of the ancient house Green Knowe, which provides a haven from the often difficult reality of the outside world, where the children experience loneliness, isolation and displacement in boarding schools or as refugees – an experience common to many children during the war years. The device of the manor house, which enables its child residents to slip between different times, offers the possibility of restoring a connection with history fractured by war. A concern with negotiating both history and identity was also a key component of much historical fiction during the 1950s. Most notably, Rosemary Sutcliff's series, which starts with *The Eagle of the Ninth* (1954–80), and is set in the final years of the Roman occupation of Britain, deals with issues of individual and national identity and with the process of reconstruction after the demise of an established way of life – all themes which had obvious relevance in the postwar years.

The world wars continued to be an important influence on children's literature for the rest of the twentieth century. As the experience of war receded into history, children's books began to address it more directly – a trend which is discussed in Part Three: 'Real Lives'. The continuing threat of the Cold War also had a significant presence in children's literature from the end of the Second World War until the dissolution of the Soviet Union in 1991. In particular, the fear of nuclear warfare – which reached a height during the Cuban Missile Crisis of 1962, when the United States appeared to be on the brink of nuclear war with the Soviet Union and Cuba, and reintensified during the 1980s, when the UK and the United States commissioned new nuclear armaments – was reflected in a number of books which depicted the aftermath of nuclear catastrophe. Robert C. O'Brien's *Z for Zachariah* (1975), Nicholas Fisk's *A Rag, a Bone and a Hank of Hair* (1980) and Hugh Scott's *Why Weeps the Brogan* (1989) all grapple with the possibility of human survival in the event of nuclear war.

Society and Ideology in Children's Books

While the impact of world conflict had a significant influence on children's literature in the mid-twentieth century, the second golden age was also closely connected with contemporary developments. The 1960s and 1970s saw radical changes in almost every aspect of British and American culture and society. Of particular relevance to children's literature is a changing social consciousness which drew more attention to marginalised groups who had previously been underrepresented socially, politically and culturally. Until the 1960s, white, middle-class childhoods had dominated in children's literature. An increasingly affluent and educated working class, along with a socially progressive agenda which sought to create a more inclusive society, helped to create a demand for books which reflected a broader demographic of child readers. The extension of compulsory education and the growing sense of adolescence as a distinctive period of life created a demand for books which could cater to the new 'teenage' demographic (a phenomenon discussed more fully in Part Three: 'Young Adult Fiction'). Increasingly, children's books began to feature working-class characters and to use more vernacular language: Robert Westall's *The Machine Gunners*

(1975) portrays working-class children who speak in their local Tyneside dialect and employ swear words as well as slang terms. High levels of immigration in Britain in the 1960s also worked to change the demographic of child readers: increasingly, urban British children came from a variety of ethnic and cultural backgrounds. Children's books began to reflect this diversity, both in the form of books which included non-white characters and tackled issues of race and racism (as in the work of Bernard Ashley, discussed in Part Three: 'Real Lives'), and through the success of writers of colour such as John Agard and Grace Nichols (discussed in Part Three: 'Rhymes and Rhythms'), who brought the language and culture of black Britons to children's poetry and prose. In the United States, the growing civil-rights movement helped to fuel the desire for a more representative children's literature, and a number of notable African-American authors began their careers during this period. Virginia Hamilton won a host of awards for her groundbreaking work, which combined myth and legend with realistic depictions of contemporary African-American life in novels such as *Zeely* (1967), *The Planet of Junior Brown* (1971) and *M. C. Higgins, the Great* (1975).

The increasingly inclusive nature of children's literature during the 1960s and 1970s reflects the degree to which a new socially progressive consciousness was informing ideas about childhood and children's literature. The desire for social and cultural change represented in the political activism of the feminist movement and the civil-rights movement found particular expression in children's literature: in the attempt to create a new social ideology, books which encouraged young people to question the status quo and offered them alternative paradigms were a natural focus. The rapid pace of change during this period also heightened the sense that children and young people needed books which could help them make sense of the world in which they lived. Whereas fantasy was the dominant mode of the 1950s, the 1960s and 1970s saw important developments in realism and a new vogue for books which dealt with issues such as bullying, racism, sex and relationships, and family problems. Idyllic images of childhood did continue, but they were increasingly disrupted by an awareness of the difficulties and dangers of childhood in the modern world.

The End of the Twentieth Century

Social realism continued to be an important mode into the 1980s and 1990s, as the changing nature of Western childhoods continued to pose new challenges for children's authors. A greater social preoccupation with issues such as sexual abuse, self-harming behaviours and drug abuse was reflected in children's literature. The increasing prevalence of books tackling difficult social issues signals a growing ambivalence about the nature of childhood itself. During the first half of the twentieth century, themes such as sex and violence were excluded from children's books, which tended to cater for a presumed child reader who was both sheltered from such issues and innocent of them. By contrast, books such as Cynthia Voigt's *When She Hollers* (1994), about a young woman who decides to fight back – with a knife if necessary – against years of sexual abuse, reconfigure childhood as space which can be and often is dangerous and threatened.

The image of the innocent child was further disrupted by an increasing realisation that children themselves could be the agents of desire and of violence. In Britain, this shift was precipitated (or perhaps simply emphasised) by the murder of two-year-old James Bulger in 1993 by two ten-year-old boys. The murder, which attracted immense media coverage, provoked intense national debate over the nature of childhood and the degree to which children can or should be considered 'innocent'. While many commentators sought to explain the crimes of the two perpetrators as a result of social failings, others presented them as intrinsically evil, a viewpoint which is reminiscent of the seventeenth-century characterisation of children as 'born into' sin. These debates found direct expression in children's literature, notably in Anne Fine's award-winning book *The Tulip Touch* (1996), in which the attention-seeking games of neglected child Tulip descend into dangerous and criminal behaviour. Fine's novel bore the tag line 'No one is born evil. No one', and it implies that Tulip's actions are dictated by her experiences of neglect and abuse, and by the failure of society to protect her from these experiences. Nevertheless, the book raises difficult questions for both child and adult readers about the nature of childhood.

Children's literature during the 1980s and 1990s was strongly and visibly affected by commercial constraints. The affluence of the 1950s and 1960s, and the high levels of social funding which had made schools and libraries a significant force in the children's book market, were replaced by recession and by conservative governments in both Britain and America who emphasised the values of the market and the importance of the limited state. As a consequence, children's publishers – which had proliferated during the 1960s and 1970s – were faced with a restricted and difficult market. Tom Engelhardt and Jack Zipes have argued that this situation created a much more commercially focused children's publishing which was oriented around the idea of the child (and accompanying adult) as a consumer rather than a reader.[15] This shift was reflected in an increasingly brand-oriented publishing which relied heavily on series rather than individual titles and authors. While series publishing has always existed, it is certainly the case that series became an important and prominent part of the children's market during this period. Francine Pascal's 'Sweet Valley High' books (1983–2003), which featured a pair of beautiful, blonde twins living an affluent lifestyle in Southern California, and the 'Point Horror' franchise (1986–present) were among the most prominent of these series. Both series were written by multiple authors (although all the 'Sweet Valley High' were published under the name of Francine Pascal) and relied on strong formulas and brand recognition rather than innovation. The dominance of series like these contributed to the belief that children's literature suffered a decline during the 1980s and 1990s: while many groundbreaking and innovative works were published during this period, it is certainly true that the perceived importance of children's literature waned during this period.

Magic and Crossing Over: The 'Third Golden Age'?

Since the mid-1990s, the relative decline of children's literature has been dramatically reversed, to the extent that some commentators have argued for the existence of a 'third golden age' of children's literature. The publication of Philip Pullman's *Northern Lights* (1995) and J. K. Rowling's *Harry Potter and the Philosopher's Stone* (1997) marks the beginning of a new cultural interest in children's literature which – as in the first and second golden ages – is closely connected with fantasy texts. The resurgence in interest in children's literature which has taken place since the mid-1990s is closely connected with economic prosperity and high levels of social investment: the Labour government elected in 1997 invested heavily in schools and libraries, and in reading initiatives such as Bookstart, which provides all children born in the UK with free books.*

The social and political emphasis on children's literature reflects a renewed focus on the importance of childhood itself; however, one notable feature of the third golden age of children's literature has been the way in which it has broken down the barriers between adult and children's literature. Both Philip Pullman and J. K. Rowling have been published in editions aimed directly at the adult market, and both authors have attracted a large adult audience. More broadly, the children's and young adult markets have increasingly challenged age-based classification. The work of British writer David Almond epitomises the fluidity of much modern children's literature: Almond's best-known book, *Skellig* (1998), is marketed at the pre-teen and early teen audience, but has appeal for older readers, while many of his other books straddle the boundary between adult and children's literature.

The difficulty of classifying children's literature according to the age of its audience perhaps reflects a broader shift in the perception

---

* Bookstart is a charitable project, not a government initiative, and receives considerable funding from commercial sponsors. However, it is also promoted and partially funded by the state.

of childhood in the Western world at the end of the twentieth century and the beginning of the twenty-first. Children are often more competent and confident than their parents in negotiating the new technological developments with which they are surrounded. At the same time, the arenas to which these technologies give them access – the Internet and the digital world – lack many of the boundaries between adult and child which characterised most of the twentieth century. Children can access content made by and meant for adults, and can interact online in adult spaces. While such interactions raise anxieties about the potential for abuse, and in particular the ability of adults to pose as children in order to befriend potential victims, they also offer children the opportunity to claim more agency and to take on the role of adults. New digital media also offer children more potential control over narrative and storytelling. Whereas the series novels of the 1980s positioned the child as consumer – returning to a familiar and consistent brand – media such as role-playing games require children to take on the role of creator, directing their own movements and determining their own storylines. The growing visibility and activity of fan communities online also offer children and young people an opportunity to tell their own stories: many young people write fan fiction and produce art and videos based on existing narratives and media properties.

Cory Doctorow's *Little Brother* (2008) reflects both the possibilities and the anxieties relating to the interaction of children with new technologies. The book deals with the experiences of a group of teenagers who are arrested after their proximity to a terrorist attack raises suspicions that they may have been involved. The potential criminality of the teenagers is identified through their facility with technology – the protagonist Marcus Yallow is an accomplished hacker – and when their mistreatment at the hands of the authorities politicises the group, they utilise their skills to resist government control by creating an illicit, unmonitored wireless network. The book deals with a number of contemporary anxieties, including terrorism and the fear of surveillance culture, but it is also notable for its depiction of young people as independent agents whose connection with technology both exposes them to the adult world, and empowers them to resist and control it. Thus it epitomises the changing perception of children in the twenty-first century. Appropriately, the book also engages with new developments in publishing: Doctorow made the book freely available on his website in multiple electronic formats as well as publishing a conventional paper edition. The boundaries of childhood and children's literature as we progress into the twenty-first century are expanding both conceptually and practically.

Notes

1   John Rowe Townsend, *Written for Children: An Outline of English-Language Children's Literature*, 2nd edn (Harmondsworth: Kestrel, 1983), p. 17.

2   Harry Hendrick summarises the impact of Ariès on historical approaches to childhood and explores the shortcomings of Ariès's work in 'Children and Childhood', *ReFresh: Recent Findings of Research in Economic and Social History*, 15 (autumn 1992), pp. 1–4.

3   Nicholas Orme, *Medieval Children* (New Haven, CT: Yale University Press, 2001), p. 271; Matthew Grenby, 'Children's Literature: Birth, Infancy, Maturity', in Janet Maybin and Nicola J. Watson (eds), *Children's Literature: Approaches and Territories* (Basingstoke: Palgrave Macmillan/Open University, 2009), pp. 39–56, p. 43.

4   Jack Zipes, 'Origins: Fairy Tales and Folk Tales', in Maybin and Watson (eds), *Children's Literature: Approaches and Territories*, pp. 26–39, p. 26.

5   Matthew Grenby, *Children's Literature* (Edinburgh: Edinburgh University Press, 2008), pp. 5–6.

6   John Bunyan, 'Of the Boy and the Butterfly', in Patricia Demers (ed.), *From Instruction to Delight: An Anthology of Children's Literature to 1850* (Oxford: Oxford University Press, 2004), pp. 71–2, ll. 7–10.

7   Demers (ed.), *From Instruction to Delight*, p. 121.

8   Peter Hunt, *An Introduction to Children's Literature* (Oxford: Oxford University Press, 1994), p. 29.

9   William Wordsworth, 'Ode: Intimations of Immortality from Recollections of Early Childhood', in Antonia Till (ed.), *The Collected*

Poems of William Wordsworth (Ware: Wordsworth Editions, 1995), pp. 701–4, ll. 68–9.

10   Peter Hunt, *Children's Literature* (Oxford: Blackwell, 2006), p. 50.

11   Nicholas Tucker, 'Setting the Scene', in Kimberley Reynolds and Nicholas Tucker (eds), *Children's Book Publishing in Britain since 1945* (Aldershot: Scolar Press, 1998), pp. 1–19.

12   IBBY publication, quoted in Patricia Crampton, 'Will It Travel Well?', *Signal*, 17 (May 1975), pp. 75–80, p. 75.

13   Hugh Cunningham, *The Invention of Childhood* (London: BBC Books, 2006), pp. 214–15.

14   Henry Jenkins, 'The Sensuous Child: Dr. Benjamin Spock and the Sexual Revolution', in Henry Jenkins (ed.), *The Children's Culture Reader* (New York: New York University Press, 1998), pp. 209–30.

15   Tom Engelhardt, 'Reading May Be Harmful to Your Kids: In the Nadirland of Today's Children's Books', *Harper's Magazine*, June 1991, pp. 55–62; Jack Zipes, 'The Cultural Homogenization of American Children', in *Sticks and Stones: The Troublesome Success of Children's Literature from Slovenly Peter to Harry Potter* (London: Routledge, 2000), pp. 1–23.

Part Three
Texts, Writers and Contexts

Alternative Worlds: Carroll, Lewis and Wynne Jones

Fantasy is closely associated with children's literature. Fairy tales and fables have long been regarded as especially suitable for children – although they were not originally written especially for them – and today are considered firmly part of the children's literature canon. In Britain especially, fantasy has occupied a special place in the history of children's literature. Both the so-called golden ages of British children's literature saw an outpouring of new fantasy works: some commentators have argued that the emergence of fantasy books such as Lewis Carroll's *Alice's Adventures in Wonderland* (1865), which foregrounded imagination, adventure and playfulness, was integral to the development of a 'true' children's literature. Carroll's work ushered in the first golden age of children's literature, which saw the publication of a host of works still popular today: J. M. Barrie offered children entry into Neverland in *Peter and Wendy* (1911), Kenneth Grahame gave them access to the startlingly human antics of Ratty, Mole and Badger in *The Wind in the Willows* (1908), and Charles Kingsley plunged them into underwater adventures with *The Water Babies* (1863).* Fantasy was similarly dominant during the 1950s,

---

* *Peter and Wendy* was of course to become better known as *Peter Pan*. The year 1911 marks the first publication of the story in novel form: it had begun life as part of an extended episode in a story for adults, *The Little White Bird* (1902), and subsequently found success on the stage before being published as a novel.

1960s and 1970s, which are widely agreed to have formed a second golden age: C. S. Lewis opened a wardrobe door into Narnia (1950–6), Philippa Pearce enabled children to step back in time through *Tom's Midnight Garden* (1958), and Alan Garner called old myths into the modern age in *The Owl Service* (1967). The fantasy genre has retained its hold over contemporary children's literature: the success of J. K. Rowling's 'Harry Potter' series (1997–2007), Philip Pullman's 'His Dark Materials' (1995–2000) and Stephenie Meyer's 'Twilight' saga (2005–8) illustrates that the genre continues to grow and evolve.

As the variety of the texts so far mentioned suggests, fantasy is a genre that is diverse and difficult to define. All fiction contains an element of fantasy, in the sense that it offers an imaginary account of people and events; however, most critics have identified fantasy as dealing with events that could not, rather than did not, happen. Even this definition is ambiguous: Matthew Grenby has pointed out that ideas of what is possible and what is impossible or supernatural vary according to time, place and point of view.[1] Modern readers would usually class stories of witchcraft and magic as fantasy, but to a medieval audience they would have seemed within the realms of the possible. In Philip Pullman's 'His Dark Materials' trilogy, the cosmology of the Christian Church is presented as a carefully constructed fantasy, but millions of people around the world consider the existence of God to be not only a possibility, but a certainty.

Even within a definition of fantasy as a genre which deals with the impossible or supernatural, the degree of fantasy can vary considerably. Talking animals are certainly fantastical, but, whereas Kenneth Grahame and Beatrix Potter both endowed their animal characters with human dress, manners and abodes, Richard Adams's rabbits in *Watership Down* (1972) retain the habits and behaviours of real wild rabbits, except for the fact that they can talk and reason: they are no more real than Peter Rabbit or Benjamin Bunny, but they appear less improbable. The alternative worlds created by J. R. R. Tolkien and Ursula Le Guin are fully realised and distinct from the world in which we live, but C. S. Lewis and J. K. Rowling's magical worlds are both annexes of our own, and in Stephenie Meyer's 'Twilight' series vampires and werewolves exist as part of an ordinary American town. In some stories the fantasy element is uncertain: if fantastical elements are presented as a dream, as in *Alice's Adventures in Wonderland,* or as the imaginative experience of a character, then are they really fantasy, or simply a reflection of real-life experience? In Penelope Lively's *A Stitch in Time* (1976) the reader is never entirely sure whether the echoes of the past heard by the protagonist Maria are really ghosts of some kind, or simply products of her intensely realised imagination, while William Mayne's *A Game of Dark* (1971) leaves open the possibility that Donald's experiences in another world are a psychological manifestation of his anguish over his relationship with his ill father. Fantasy can encompass psychological realism, light-hearted escapism, humour, political satire, adventure and much more. While fantasy texts have been consistently important to the history of children's literature, therefore, the kinds of books offered under this heading have varied considerably according to the concerns of the time, the age of the children at whom the texts are aimed, and the interests of the author.

The Dangers of Fantasy

Although fantasy has had a strong presence in children's literature, it has not always been regarded as valuable or suitable for children. Much early children's literature had a strong religious and moral emphasis, and used stories which could be closely related to children's real-life experiences to inculcate appropriate values and behaviour (see Part Three: 'Real Lives'). In this context, fantastical stories were often viewed as overly frivolous, or even as harmful. While the animosity of early children's literature towards fantasy has sometimes been overstated, writers of the eighteenth and early nineteenth century frequently betray concerns over the potential effects of fantasy on their readers. Fairy tales in particular drew criticism. Sarah Trimmer (1741–1810), one of the most influential eighteenth-century writers of and about children's literature, complained:

> the terrific images, which tales of this nature present to the imagination, usually make deep impressions, and injure the tender minds of children, by exciting unreasonable and groundless fears. Neither do the generality of tales of this kind supply any moral instruction level to the infantine capacity.[2]

Trimmer's objections sprang partly from the graphic content of some fairy tales – she was particularly critical of the gory illustrations for 'Blue Beard' in an 1804 edition of *Nursery Tales* – but she also emphasised the 'liveliness' of children's imaginations and the consequent danger that they would fail to distinguish between fantasy and reality. While Trimmer herself wrote fantasy stories for children – her *Fabulous Histories* (1786), better known as *The History of the Robins*, was an anthropomorphic fantasy about a family of robins – she took care to advise her readers that they should be considered 'not as containing the real conversations of birds (for that it is impossible we should ever understand) but as a series of fables',[3] and the primary function of the stories was to deliver a strong moral message to her readers. The animus against fairy tales was by no means universal, and many of Trimmer's contemporaries defended them and decried the influence of the new rational children's literature epitomised by Trimmer and her fellows. Nevertheless, as late as 1895 Agnes Repplier was moved to defend fairy tales against the kind of criticisms voiced by Sarah Trimmer, arguing that they were 'brave old tales which are [children's] inheritance from a splendid past'.[4] As this chapter will show, the tension surrounding fairy tales and fantasy for children was to last well into the twentieth century.

Adventures in Wonderland: Lewis Carroll

Agnes Repplier's defence of fairy tales at the end of the nineteenth century indicates the enduring influence of the rational and didactic children's literature epitomised by Sarah Trimmer. By the time Repplier wrote her 'Battle of the Babies', however, the forces of rationalism had already suffered a critical blow: the publication in 1865 of *Alice's Adventures in Wonderland* marks the beginning of a golden age of children's literature in which fantasy played a central role. Over a century later, this iconic text retains its status and continues to inspire adaptations, imitations and parodies, most recently in the 2010 film by Tim Burton, which depicts the adventures of a teenage Alice in 'Underland'. The gap between the interests and knowledge of modern children and those of their nineteenth-century predecessors, which creates a significant barrier for modern child readers, has led Peter Hunt to question whether Carroll's books can still be considered as children's literature; nevertheless, they have undoubtedly played an important role in shaping children's literature as we know it today.[5]

Alice's Adventures in Wonderland was famously written for a real child: Alice Liddell, the daughter of Dean Liddell at Christ Church College, Oxford, where Lewis Carroll (real name Charles Dodgson) was lecturer of mathematics. Carroll's relationship with the real Alice has been the subject of much speculation: his intimate friendship with Alice and other young girls, and his interest in photographing his young friends (often in the semi-nude) are inevitably viewed with suspicion by a modern audience. The exact nature of Carroll's relationship with Alice Liddell is impossible to establish – and, as Humphrey Carpenter suggests, is arguably unimportant to the books themselves – but his close relationships with and idealisation of young girls reflect some aspects of Victorian society which are important to the text. As discussed in Part Two: 'A Cultural Overview', the nineteenth century saw children and childhood attain a new cultural dominance. An increased emphasis on the importance of childhood was accompanied by a greater focus on education, which helped to fuel the appetite for moral tales and didactic literature which persisted to the end of the nineteenth century. At the same time, the influence of the Romantics positioned the child as both natural and innocent, emphasising children's freedom from social and rational constraints. Both aspects of Victorian childhood are evident in *Alice's Adventures in Wonderland*. Alice herself is portrayed as the product of a conventional Victorian nursery, reliant on rigidly defined social codes and on a heavily didactic education, both of which are wickedly parodied by Carroll. Wonderland represents an escape from these constraints and a move towards a more imaginative and liberated childhood. Mary Thwaite characterises the liberating elements of the fantasy as intrinsic to Carroll's text and other Victorian fantasy works for children, arguing that 'the child, at last, was put to the centre, and his [sic] need to wonder and laugh and roam and to live in a world of his own making was recognised.'[6] However, it should be noted that, while Wonderland represents an escape from the constraints of Alice's everyday life, it is also a confusing and often threatening realm, not the purely pleasurable world which Thwaite's analysis implies.

The child-centred nature of *Alice's Adventures in Wonderland* is strongly evident in Lewis Carroll's narratorial voice, which is less didactic and more sympathetic to the child reader than those of Carroll's predecessors and contemporaries. Whereas many earlier texts for children had addressed the child in an overtly didactic manner which clearly privileged the voice and values of the adult world over those of the child, Carroll closed the gap between narrator and reader, creating the impression of addressing the child on her own terms. Throughout the text, Alice's own thoughts and comments on her experiences are allowed to dominate, without any overt moralising gloss from the narrator. Where the narratorial voice does interject, it frequently serves to heighten the sense of absurdity, as in the 'Eat me' episode. When the cake Alice eats makes her grow to more than nine feet tall, Alice berates herself for crying: "'You ought to be ashamed of yourself,'" said Alice, "a great girl like you" (she might well say this), "to go on crying in this way!"'[7] The narrator's comment resembles the kind of moral judgement common in other books of the period, which frequently took the opportunity to draw readers' attention to examples of correct behaviour, but in this case it is an absurd comment on the fact that Alice is literally great (in the Victorian sense of large). Carroll's narratorial voice is therefore complicit with the child reader, poking fun at typical adult behaviour.

The absurdity and incomprehensibility of the adult world underlies much of the fantasy in Wonderland. While a superficial viewing might suggest that Carroll was merely focused on creating a sense of the bizarre and wonderful, many critics have pointed out that Alice's experiences in Wonderland are in fact simply an exaggerated version of what young children experience in daily life: from the point of view of a child, the peculiar rules and concerns of the inhabitants of Wonderland are scarcely less incomprehensible than those of adults in the everyday world. Alice is repeatedly puzzled or frustrated by her attempts to make sense of the people and creatures she experiences, as in her encounter with the Mad Hatter:

> 'What a funny watch!' she remarked. 'It tells the day of the month, and doesn't tell what o'clock it is!'
>
> 'Why should it?' muttered the Hatter. 'Does *your* watch tell you what year it is?'
>
> 'Of course not,' Alice replied very readily: 'but that's because it stays the same year for such a long time altogether.'
>
> 'Which is just the case with mine,' said the Hatter.
>
> Alice felt dreadfully puzzled. The hatter's remark seemed to her to have no sort of meaning in it, and yet it was certainly English. (p. 62)

Alice's attempts to understand the rules of Wonderland mimic the experiences of a child attempting to understand adult life and behaviour; they also subversively undermine the rationale of the real world by suggesting that incomprehensible adult rules might be equally nonsensical. In fact, both *Alice's Adventures in Wonderland* and its sequel *Through the Looking Glass* fundamentally disrupt rationality and linguistic meaning. The nonsense verses with which the text is interspersed are all parodies of well-known Victorian poems which would have been familiar to Alice and her child contemporaries: Alice is puzzled to hear the Mad Hatter recite 'Twinkle twinkle little bat' (p. 63), and when she tries to recite Isaac Watts's didactic verse 'How doth the little busy bee', she is disconcerted to find herself recounting the activities of a little crocodile instead (p. 19). The constantly shifting status of words in the text contributes to the sense of existential uncertainty which characterises both *Alice's Adventures in Wonderland* and *Through the Looking Glass*. Alice is continually forced to re-examine her own identity and sense of self. In Wonderland, she changes size so frequently that she begins to wonder whether she has become someone else altogether, concluding 'I must have been changed for Mabel!' (p. 19). In *Through the Looking Glass*, Tweedledum and Tweedledee cause her to question whether she exists at all, suggesting that she is nothing but a character in the Red King's dream: '"If that there King was to wake," added Tweedledum, "you'd go out – bang! – just like a candle!"' (p. 168). Alice dismisses the notion, but the existential question has additional weight for the reader, who is aware that she is, after all, a character in Carroll's 'dream'.

Although Wonderland is confusing and unpredictable, both of Carroll's texts essentially follow a *Bildungsroman* form in which Alice progresses from immaturity and inexperience to autonomy and maturity.* Alice's uncertainty about her own identity diminishes as she gains experience: by the end of her adventures she is able to resist

---

* The *Bildungsroman* or 'education novel' is a novel which traces the early educational, moral or spiritual development of its hero, following their journey into maturity. For obvious reasons, it is a popular form in children's literature.

the bizarre interpretations of the adults in Wonderland, sweeping away the Queen of Hearts and her court with the exclamation 'You're nothing but a pack of cards!' (p. 109). In *Through the Looking Glass*, Alice is able to assume an adult position when she is recognised as 'Queen Alice'; she uses her authority to reject the strange behaviour of the Red and White Queens, asserting her own version of 'mature' behaviour over those of the 'adults' within the text. It is notable that by the time she is able to assert herself against the Queen of Hearts, she has 'grown to her full size' (p. 109): while her successor Peter Pan was to want 'always to be a little boy and to have fun',[8] *Alice's Adventures in Wonderland* ultimately asserts the value of growing up.

After Alice: The Golden Age and the Shadow of War

Although *Alice's Adventures in Wonderland* was a landmark text, contemporaries of Lewis Carroll such as George Macdonald and Charles Kingsley had already begun to establish fantasy as an important genre in children's literature. In the wake of Carroll's success, the genre became even more firmly associated with children's literature. The end of the nineteenth century and the beginning of the twentieth saw a golden age of children's fantasy which included J. M. Barrie's *Peter Pan*, Kenneth Grahame's *Wind in the Willows* and E. Nesbit's *Five Children and It* (1902). The First World War, however, heralded a decline in the amount of fantasy published for children. This was in part a result of a decline in British children's literature as a whole: the two world wars had a heavy impact on children's publishing, resulting in the loss of many children's authors, illustrators and publishers and in a severe shortage of paper and other materials. Fewer children's books were published, and publishers focused their efforts on a few popular authors. In the context of conflict and upheaval it is unsurprising that the two most successful authors in this period were Arthur Ransome and Noel Streatfeild, both of whom portrayed largely idyllic childhoods in a realist mode which offered child readers a safe, familiar world. However, the war years were to inspire a new outpouring of children's fantasy, which formed a major part of the second golden age of British children's literature in the 1950s, 1960s and 1970s.

J. R. R. Tolkien's *The Hobbit*, published in 1937, heralded the beginning of a new era of fantasy in children's literature. The adventures of the timid, ordinary hobbit Bilbo Baggins introduced readers to Tolkien's vividly realised Middle Earth, which was later to provide a setting for his influential novel for adult readers, *The Lord of the Rings* (1954–5). Whereas Alice's confusing and unpredictable adventures in Wonderland had been contrasted against the regularity of an everyday Victorian childhood, Middle Earth is both entirely consistent and entirely separate from the real world. The internal consistency of Middle Earth reflects Tolkien's view of fantasy, which he argued depends on the creation of:

> a Secondary World which your mind can enter. Inside it, what [the storyteller] relates is true: it accords with the laws of that world […] The moment disbelief arises, the spell is broken.[9]

In Middle Earth, the magical ring Bilbo Baggins steals from Gollum will make anyone who wears it invisible – but it also consistently works to awaken feelings of greed and avarice in the wearer. Under the laws of Tolkien's world, it is not possible to gain one effect without the other, unless a satisfactory explanation is put forward for the change in rules – thus, while the essentially placid character of hobbits is given as an explanation for Bilbo's ability to resist the corrupting influence of the ring, he is not immune to it. Tolkien's theory of secondary worlds was both successful – *The Hobbit* and *The Lord of the Rings* continue to be bestsellers – and influential, inspiring many imitators. The internal consistency of fantasy has been used with great effect by writers such as Ursula Le Guin, who explores the issues of power and responsibility through a carefully worked-out system of magic in her 'Earthsea' series (1968–2001). Rather than functioning as a *deus ex machina*, magic in Le Guin's Earthsea is subject to clear rules of cause and effect.* 'Rain on Roke may be drouth [drought] on Osskil', a teacher warns the hero, Ged, when teaching him how to work magic which changes the weather, and Ged's failure to appreciate the need to preserve the balance of power unleashes great evil.[10] Other fantasy writers have successfully resisted Tolkien's requirement of a fully realised fantasy world, however: Diana Wynne Jones (discussed below) is one of a number of authors whose use of the fantasy genre involves intentionally disrupting readers' belief in the secondary world.

The world wars disrupted the development of children's literature, but they can also be seen as instrumental in creating fantasy in the twentieth century. Tolkien was part of a generation indelibly marked by the horrors of the First World War, and *The Hobbit* includes a number of elements which can be related to his wartime experiences: notably, the most frightening episodes take place underground in dark tunnels which owe a clear debt to the trenches. Tom Shippey has argued that Tolkien was one of a number of British writers whose experiences of war caused them to turn to fantasy 'because they felt that the theme of human evil was not one which could be rendered adequately or confronted directly through the medium of realistic fiction alone'.[11] Themes of conflict and evil are an important component of Tolkien's Middle Earth, and of many other fantasy worlds of the postwar era: C. S. Lewis's 'Narnia' stories (discussed below), Susan Cooper's 'Dark Is Rising' sequence (1965–77) and Alan Garner's *The Weirdstone of Brisingamen* (1960) all use fantasy in order to stage conflicts between the forces of good and evil. Cooper's description of 'the powers of the Dark, which are reaching out now steadily and stealthily over all this world'[12] evokes a postwar sensibility which had been marked by the twin shadows of conflict and Holocaust. In the final book in the series, *Silver on the Tree* (1977), the connection between the conflicting light and dark is even more explicitly related to the political context of the period: the

---

* A *deus ex machina* is a plot device which provides a contrived solution to an apparently insoluble problem.

assertion that 'the Dark can only reach people at extremes – blinded by their own shining ideas, or locked up in the darkness of their own heads'[13] reflects Susan Cooper's experience of a world which had been severely affected by the extremism of both Nazism and Communism.

Through the Wardrobe: C. S. Lewis

The influence of the world wars is clearly discernible in the work of Tolkien's friend and contemporary C. S. Lewis. The first published and best-known book in the series, *The Lion, the Witch and the Wardrobe* (1950) locates itself directly within the context of the Second World War:

> Once there were four children whose names were Peter, Susan, Edmund and Lucy. This story is about something that happened to them when they were sent away from London during the war because of the air-raids.[14]

When the four Pevensie children travel through the back of a wardrobe into the land of Narnia, they emerge into a world which is as marked by conflict as the one from which they have come: Maria Tatar suggests that they 'end up fighting the war by proxy against the armies of the White Witch'.[15] The 2005 film adaptation of the book highlights this aspect of the text by including scenes of the Blitz in London at the beginning of the film, which form a counterpart to the (vastly expanded) battle scenes in Narnia at the end. In the books themselves, however, it is the question of evil rather than the issue of conflict in itself which is most clearly addressed in the text. The youngest brother, Edmund, betrays the Pevensies to the evil White Witch, who is holding the land of Narnia in thrall. While the religious elements of Edmund's betrayal have received much attention, the way in which he justifies his action also resonates with the wartime setting of the story:

> You mustn't think that even now Edmund was quite so bad
> that he actually wanted his brother and sisters to be turned
> into stone […] but he managed to believe, or pretended to
> believe, that she wouldn't do anything very bad to them.
> 'Because,' he said to himself, 'all these people who say nasty
> things about her are her enemies, and probably half of it isn't
> true. She was jolly nice to me, anyway, much nicer than they
> are.' (pp. 82–3)

Given that the book was published only five years after the end of the
Second World War, it is impossible not to draw parallels with Nazi
collaborators. The combination of resentment, denial and greed
which contributes to Edmund's decision to betray his family (and
consequently the whole of Narnia) enables readers to grasp some of
the factors which led to the rise of Nazi rule. The book has
sometimes drawn criticism for its black-and-white portrayal of good
and evil, but the characterisation of Edmund provides some
interesting shades of grey, highlighting the fact that evil can spring
from very ordinary motivations.

The growing prominence of fantasy during the nineteenth
century was associated with a move away from heavily moral and
didactic texts, and towards a children's literature more focused on
pleasure. The Narnia books, however, are a particularly clear example
of the way in which fantasy continued to play an educative role. Like
C. S. Lewis's earlier adult series, the books have a strong Christian
message. *The Lion, the Witch and the Wardrobe* is an allegorical
retelling of the Passion of Christ: the salvation of Narnia ultimately
rests on the sacrifice and resurrection of the talking lion Aslan, whose
identity as a Christ-figure is reiterated several times during the course
of the series. The lessons that the Pevensies and the other children
who visit Narnia learn on their adventures have implications for their
lives in our world. This is perhaps most clearly evident in the
transformation of Eustace in *The Voyage of the Dawn Treader* (1952).
At the beginning of the book Eustace is not an attractive character:

he liked bossing and bullying, and though he was a puny little person who couldn't have stood up even to Lucy, let alone Edmund, in a fight, he knew that there are dozens of ways to give people a bad time if you are in your own home and they are only visitors.[16]

In the course of the story, Eustace's greed causes him to be turned into a dragon, and it is only after he recognises that he has been 'an unmitigated nuisance' (p. 82) that Aslan helps him to become 'reborn' as a human being, in a highly symbolic episode that culminates in Eustace being washed clean by Aslan. When he returns from Narnia 'everyone soon started saying how Eustace had improved' (p. 189). The clear message for the child reader is that Eustace's spiteful and bullying behaviour is neither right nor rewarding for Eustace himself.* While the medium of fantasy helps to disguise the didactic purpose, this purpose certainly remains important to the text.

C. S. Lewis uses the fantasy elements of Narnia to convey some specific ideas, but the fantasy setting is also vital to his attempt to convey something more than basic moral and educational messages. Lewis argued that fairy tales offered the child reader 'the dim sense of something beyond his reach [which] far from dulling or emptying the actual world, gives it a new dimension of depth'.[17] His attempt to convey to the child reader some sense of the underlying meaning and mysteries of the Christian faith is a crucial component of the Narnia books. It is most evident – and most effective – in the chapter of *The Lion, the Witch and the Wardrobe* which follows Aslan's sacrifice at the hands of the White Witch. Lucy and Susan carry out a vigil next to his body, waiting in the night and the cold. When the sun rises, they hear a deafening cracking sound:

---

* The particular characteristics of Eustace's nastiness are extremely revealing of Lewis's own particular prejudices: Eustace's left-wing, progressive, atheist parents are portrayed as primarily responsible for his poor character.

> The rising of the sun had made everything look so different –
> all colours and shadows were changed – that for a moment
> they didn't see the important thing. Then they did. The Stone
> Table was broken into two pieces by a great crack that ran
> down it from end to end; and there was no Aslan. (p. 146)

The scene brilliantly conveys the sense of mystery, horror and wonder which underlies the story of the Passion. While Lewis's use of Christian doctrine in the Narnia books has been controversial, he does succeed in conveying the sense of something beyond the reader's reach which he identifies as a key component of the best fantasy.[18]

Writing the Unthinkable: Fantasy and the Unconscious

The idea that fantasy allows writers to address themes too subtle or too difficult to confront in realist fiction was an important element in critical approaches to fantasy in the mid-twentieth century. While some critics continued to focus on the imaginative and pleasurable aspects of fantasy, arguing that it was an inherently escapist genre, new ideas about child development increasingly characterised fantasy as both useful and necessary. Psychologists and psychoanalysts such as Bruno Bettelheim increasingly presented fantasy as essential to healthy psychological development. In his influential work *The Uses of Enchantment* (1976), Bettelheim argued that fantasy offered children a safe context within which they could deal with destructive and frightening emotions and ideas, stating that 'without fantasies to give us hope, we do not have the strength to meet the adversities of life. Childhood is the time when these fantasies need to be nurtured.'[19] The link between fantasy and psychological development is prominent in several children's fantasies of the mid-twentieth century. In Catherine Storr's *Marianne Dreams* (1958), the frustrations of a young girl confined to her bed by illness are manifested in increasingly dark and realistic dreams: resolving the problems she faces in the fantasy world is intertwined with overcoming her real feelings of frustration and resentment.* Similarly, in William Mayne's *A Game of Dark* (1971), Donald's struggle with his inability to love his ill father are played out through a fantasy world in which he is a squire who must slay a marauding worm. When he finally overcomes the worm, the two worlds meet:

> He was now in two worlds. One of them was the hillside and the green grass. The other was the house in Hales Hill, and the bed he had slept in and the thin wall he leaned against there, and both were actual, and he could choose which to be in. One was silent, and in the other the dreadful breathing continued. [...] he knew that the man in the other room was his father, whom he knew now how to love.[20]

The close connection between Donald's real life, where he is unable to act, and the fantasy world in which conflict is manifested in a battle which he can fight, illustrates the way in which fantasy can work to offer the child reader a sense of agency. Similarly, in Philip Pullman's 'His Dark Materials' trilogy (1995–2000), Will is unable to combat his mother's depression in our world, but his passage into the alternative world of Cittagazze with Lyra enables him to see and fight the Spectres which are its underlying cause. Fantasies like this offer child readers the opportunity to work through issues that are too painful to address directly.

Changing Worlds: Fantasy and Ideology

Fantasy authors have used the genre to create texts focused on the psychological or moral development of their readers; they have also used fantasy as a vehicle for changing society. The scope fantasy offers for exaggerating real-life situations, inverting the normal order or

---

* The psychological elements of *Marianne Dreams* are not merely incidental: Catherine Storr was a practising psychiatrist.

posing the question 'what if?' makes it an ideal genre within which to challenge existing social norms or highlight particular social or cultural issues.

Some texts use fantasy as a medium for justice. *The Water Babies*, by Lewis Carroll's contemporary Charles Kingsley, was partly concerned with exposing the plight of child sweeps, who were frequently mistreated and often died as a result of their work. Chimney sweep Tom is abused and exploited by his master Mr Grimes until he falls into a river and drowns. He is reborn as a 'water baby' and embarks on a journey during which he receives various moral lessons. Near the end of Tom's journey, he comes upon his former master trapped in a chimney pot: a just punishment for Grimes's maltreatment of his child apprentices and one which highlights the need for action against such abuses in the real world.

During the 1960s and 1970s, a growing consciousness of issues such as sexism and racism (discussed in more detail in Part Three: 'Real Lives') was manifested in fantasy texts which aimed to encourage child readers to consider alternative ideologies. Bob Leeson addresses issues of race and culture in *The Third-Class Genie* (1975), in which a schoolboy accidentally summons a genie from an appropriately modern beer can. When the genie temporarily exhausts his powers and is stranded outside his can, his schoolboy master is faced with the problem of how to deal with the presence of a black man without passport or papers, and is brought face-to-face with some of the racial tensions his black schoolfriends encounter. The book encourages readers to examine their own prejudices and highlights some of the problems with the racial status quo. Ursula Le Guin similarly worked to changed attitudes about race in her 'Earthsea' books, which challenge the white hegemony of much fantasy by portraying the hero and most of the other main characters as people of colour. In the final two books of the series, Le Guin also challenged gender bias by subverting the masculine dominance which she had (unconsciously) established in the earlier books of the stories. Reflecting on her decision to 'politicise' the world of Earthsea by consciously addressing issues of gender, Le Guin commented: 'The politics of Fairyland are ours.'[21] The scope fantasy allows for addressing real-life concerns is perhaps one reason the genre has continued to grow and develop since it rose to prominence in the nineteenth century. By moving outside the constraints of how the world 'really' is, writers are able to offer new ways of thinking about how it might be.

Moving Narratives: Diana Wynne Jones

One of the most creative and thought-provoking authors of modern fantasy is Diana Wynne Jones, who has published over forty works of fantasy since the publication of her first book for children, *Wilkins' Tooth*, in 1973. Jones's work spans a wide range of fantasy modes and genres, age groups and narrative techniques; she has written about alternative worlds in her 'Chrestomanci' series (1977–2006), time-slips in *A Tale of Time City* (1987) and *The Time of the Ghost* (1981), and fantasy encounters in the everyday world in *Wilkins' Tooth* and *Archer's Goon* (1984). Many of her books respond to or adapt older fantasy works: *Eight Days of Luke* (1975) is based on Norse myth, *Howl's Moving Castle* (1986) is based around traditional fairy-tale motifs, and the events of *Hexwood* (1993) are set in motion when a young man asks a computer to make him a role-playing game based around 'Hobbits on a Grail Quest'.[22] Although she has never attained the prominence or popularity of authors such as C. S. Lewis or J. K. Rowling, Jones's books have a large and loyal following and have had an influential effect on modern children's fantasy.

Diana Wynne Jones's earliest fantasy works were primarily 'low' fantasy: books set principally in the 'real' world into which the fantasy elements intrude. Like the nineteenth-century fantasist Edith Nesbit, who established a new mode of fantasy with *Five Children and It* and its sequels, Jones derives a good deal of humour from the collision between fantasy and reality. This technique is particularly successful in *The Ogre Downstairs* (1974). At the start of the book, Caspar, Johnny and Gwinny appear to have totally ordinary problems: their mother's remarriage to a strict and intolerant stepfather (the 'Ogre' of the title) has brought with it a new set of household rules and two unlikeable stepbrothers. When the chemistry kit their stepfather has given them turns out to be magical, however, they are plunged into increasingly peculiar situations as they try to explore the possibilities of the chemistry set without revealing it to the rest of the family. Discovering a powder that makes you float in the air is exciting, but problematic when you are supposed to be tucked up in bed:

> Gwinny was lying on her back near the middle of the ceiling now. Johnny raised the dripping mop and aimed it for the part of Gwinny's legs where he thought the chemicals had splashed. But it was not easy to aim a long, top-heavy mop. He hit Gwinny plumb on the backside. She shrieked, 'Stop it! It's cold!' and went floundering and scrambling and bobbing out of reach, like an upside-down pink crab, with a muddy splotch on the back of her nightdress.[23]

Much of the fun of *The Ogre Downstairs* lies in the way in which Jones shows the real-life consequences of magic, which often turns out to be much more inconvenient or dangerous than at first appears. However, like many contemporary children's books, it is also concerned with contemporary issues and problems: the emotional centre of the novel is the way in which the children come to terms with their new family situation as the chemistry set forces them to a greater understanding of their stepfamily. When Caspar inadvertently swaps bodies with his stepbrother Malcolm, he comes to realise that many aspects of their situation are hard on Malcolm:

> 'But think how he jeers,' Caspar told his conscience. And his conscience smartly returned that one by reminding him that Malcolm's face was not good at showing feelings, and asking Caspar what he would do himself if he were too proud to beg someone to be friends. (p. 85)

The Ogre Downstairs is the work of Jones that is most closely and obviously concerned with real-life problems, but many of her other books deal directly or indirectly with real issues. Family is a central concern in her books, which frequently portray imperfect or downright unlikeable adult figures: in *Fire and Hemlock* (1985), Polly's parents are going through a difficult divorce; David in *Eight Days of Luke* (1975) is forced to live with his unlikeable and unloving relatives; and in *The Time of the Ghost* (1981) the four girls are so neglected by their parents that nobody notices when one of them goes missing.* Diana Wynne Jones's fantasy is, like that of Lewis Carroll, in part a commentary on the often confusing and threatening aspects of childhood.

While many of Diana Wynne Jones's books are clearly set in the real world, she has also written 'high' fantasy set in completely realised fantasy worlds. As in her 'low'-fantasy books, however, she is intimately concerned with realistic characters and experiences. Her most conventionally 'high'-fantasy series, the 'Dalemark Quartet' (1975–93), owes something to the 'swords and sorcery' tradition set in motion by Tolkien: set in a vaguely medieval world, it includes magical powers, a quest for precious objects, several battles and a set of heroes who progress from humble roots to greatness. In Diana Wynne Jones's hands, however, these elements are more realistic and more nuanced than in many other works in this genre. She pokes gentle fun at some of the more improbable elements of high-fantasy books, which frequently show their inexperienced protagonists adapting almost instantly to a life of travelling and warfare: in *The Crown of Dalemark* (1993), Mitt ends the first day of his quest sitting in a bowl of vinegar after becoming so saddle-sore he can hardly walk. Jones's keen understanding of high-fantasy tropes and clichés is also hilariously shown in *The Tough Guide to Fantasyland* (1996), an encyclopedia of common fantasy terms and tropes which includes entries such as:

* *The Time of the Ghost* is closely based on Jones's own childhood – a fact which partially explains her interest in writing about peculiar and often problematic families.

> **Self-Knowledge** is, on rare occasions, a QUEST OBJECT. It
> is seldom found, and then only by PRINCES. Tourists
> [readers] are not expected to acquire it.[24]

Contrary to this entry, all Diana Wynne Jones's books – including
the high fantasies – are deeply concerned with self-knowledge in a
way which frequently impacts on the reader as well as the protagonist
of the book. In the course of the Dalemark Quartet, the reader's
perception of almost every character introduced in the first book has
radically changed by the fourth – and not always for the better.
Characters' own views of themselves are also radically altered: at the
start of *Drowned Ammet* (1977), both Mitt and the reader believe in
his self-appointed role as a freedom fighter, but by the end of the
story Mitt realises 'he had it in him to be far worse than Al [who has
taken Mitt prisoner earlier in the book].'[25] Similarly, in *The Lives of
Christopher Chant* (1988) Christopher starts out as a charming little
boy, and for most of the book the reader shares his assumption that
he is a likeable person. It is only when he visits World Eleven in order
to rescue his teacher from the evil Dright that Christopher realises he
might not be quite as nice as he has believed:

> Every one of the people was staring at Christopher with
> contempt and dislike. Christopher put his face into the same
> expression and stared back. And he realised his face was rather
> used to looking this way. He had worn this expression most of
> the time he had lived at the Castle. It gave him an unpleasant
> shock to find that he had been quite as horrible as these Eleven
> people.[26]

Since the book is told from Christopher's point of view, the
unpleasant shock has almost as much effect on the reader, throwing
the previous events of the book into a new light. In other books
Jones achieves this effect by the use of multiple narrators, whose
different accounts of the same events highlight the subjectivity of any
given narrative. In *The Merlin Conspiracy* (2003), the collection of

herbs Roddy collects to perform a spell are nothing but 'a shoddy bunch of flowers'[27] from the point of view of Nick, who narrates the other half of the story; this is only the smallest of a complex set of different perspectives on the same events which almost result in disaster for the whole universe. Diana Wynne Jones's use of multiple narrators and the ways in which she shows characters re-evaluating their own perceptions of the narrative provide a means of exploring the possibilities of the fantasy worlds she creates. More importantly, however, they force readers to constantly re-evaluate their own perceptions and opinions; as Farah Mendelssohn puts it, Jones 'continually asks us to consider the reliability of whoever is guiding us through the dark woods'.[28]

Like many of the other fantasy writers of the twentieth century, Diana Wynne Jones was strongly affected by the experience of war. Whereas J. R. R. Tolkien and C. S. Lewis were adults during wartime and had seen active service, Jones was a small child during the Second World War. She has stated, 'I think I write the kind of books I do because the world suddenly went mad when I was five years old', and her fantasies certainly convey a sense of dislocation from normality.[29] Many of her stories focus on the way 'ordinary' things are highly subjective: in *The Merlin Conspiracy* the character Maxwell Hyde publishes mystery stories set in his own world of Blest on Earth:

> I publish on Thule, Tellans, lots of places too. Everyone in those places is apt to go on about how convincing my alternate-world setting is, but of course it's only Blest. Quite ordinary to me – and to Blest people too, worse luck. I hardly sell at all in Blest. (p. 253)

Like Lewis Carroll in *Alice's Adventures in Wonderland*, Jones makes the point that the fantastical and absurd is largely a matter of perspective: a message which has deeper resonance in today's multicultural society, when child readers are more likely to encounter unfamiliar cultures and ideas.

Extended Commentary: Wynne Jones, *Howl's Moving Castle* (1986)

The idea that normal rules are purely a matter of perspective is one which Diana Wynne Jones uses to great effect in *Howl's Moving Castle*, one of her best-known titles. The opening of the book places it firmly in the fairy-tale tradition:

> In the land of Ingary, where such things as seven-league boots and cloaks of invisibility really exist, it is quite a misfortune to be born the eldest of three. Everyone knows you are the one who will fail first, and worst, if the three of you set out to seek your fortunes.[30]

The familiarity of fairy-tale elements such as seven-league boots makes the fantastical ordinary, not only because in Ingary they 'really exist', but also because the reader can be expected to recognise these elements just as readily as they recognise stories about cars and telephones. At the same time, however, Jones undermines the fantasy by drawing attention to the fact that she is working with established narrative tropes: whereas Tolkien argued that fantasy is dependent on sustaining the reader's belief in the secondary world, Jones intentionally breaks the illusion of reality by reminding the reader that she is telling a story, a strategy which is referred to as 'metafiction'. The metafictive effect of the novel is deepened by the fact that the characters within the story are equally aware of the narrative 'rules' of fairy tales: Sophie, the eldest child who is the heroine of the story, 'read a great deal, and soon realised how little chance she had of an interesting future' (p. 10). Jones further plays with generic conventions by linking the book closely to Frank L. Baum's popular fantasy *The Wonderful Wizard of Oz* (1900): Sophie encounters a Wicked Witch, a scarecrow, a little dog and a man without a heart, but none of them take on exactly the role readers familiar with Baum's work might expect.

Having established that Sophie is destined to have a boring and unsuccessful life, Jones immediately upturns this narrative convention by having her fall victim to a witch's curse which turns her into an elderly lady. Sophie sets out to seek her fortune, but she continues to adhere to the narrative rules she thinks she knows from fairy tales. In the tradition of quest narratives in which the hero (and it generally is a hero) frequently meets magical beings on his journey, Sophie's journey is punctuated by apparently ordinary encounters with a scarecrow and a dog caught in a hedge. Unlike Dorothy in *The Wonderful Wizard of Oz*, she appears to gain little by offering them her aid:

> 'There's two encounters,' she said, 'and not a scrap of magical gratitude from either. [...] I'm surely due to have a third encounter, magical or not. In fact, I insist on one.' (p. 36)

By referring directly to the expectations raised by the generic conventions, Diana Wynne Jones cleverly manipulates the reader. On one hand, familiarity with fairy-tale tropes might lead the reader to agree with Sophie that her encounters ought to have magical implications. On the other hand, since the same expectations require the eldest child to lead a dull life, both Sophie and the reader are misled into believing that her experiences only *resemble* the magical encounters of fairy tale, and are actually perfectly ordinary. By the end of the novel, our expectations are challenged again, as the scarecrow and the dog prove to be more magical than they at first appear.

As in many of Jones's books, *Howl's Moving Castle* highlights the subjective nature of fantasy. Whereas the Narnia books and *Alice's Adventures in Wonderland* emphasise the fantasy elements of the alternative world by focusing on the perspective of a visitor from our world, Sophie is a native of Ingary and consequently perceives it as perfectly ordinary. While staying in the magical moving castle belonging to Wizard Howl, however, she makes her own journey into an alternative world, where she encounters Howl's family gathered round a set of magical boxes:

The main magic box had a glass front like the one downstairs, but it seemed to be showing writing and diagrams more than pictures. All the boxes grew on long, floppy white stalks that appeared to be rooted in the wall at one side of the room. (p. 149)

The alert reader will, of course, recognise the 'magic boxes' as a television and games console. From Sophie's point of view, ours is the fantasy world, while she reflects that the computer game about an 'enchanted castle' (p. 151) is strangely familiar.

Like many fantasy novels, *Howl's Moving Castle* follows many of the conventions of the *Bildungsroman*: it follows Sophie's path towards self-awareness and maturity, culminating in her achieving both success and love when she marries the Wizard Howl. However, much of the story is not about the inevitability of Sophie's narrative journey, but about her ability to choose her own path. As a girl, she is heavily influenced by the expectations she believes are attached to being the eldest: when her stepmother offers her an apprenticeship in the family hat shop, Sophie 'simply felt resigned' (p. 14) and she gradually becomes the quiet and dull person she believes she is supposed to be. When the Witch of the Waste turns her into an old woman she is liberated from these expectations. The rules attached to being an old woman are very different from those attached to being an eldest daughter: Sophie comforts herself with the reflection that 'Perhaps she was a little mad, but then old women often were' (p. 35). In fact, Sophie is not mad, but she is liberated by her new role, and she becomes increasingly more self-confident (and indeed opinionated and bossy). By the end of the book, Sophie is back to her normal shape – but it becomes apparent that the role she was playing as an old woman was much closer to the 'real' Sophie than the one she takes on at the start of the book.

Sophie's expectations about narrative and the way these shape her own sense of self tie into a broader theme about storytelling and the power of words in *Howl's Moving Castle*. Throughout the book, the things that Sophie says turn out to be true: when she tells a hat she is trimming 'You have a heart of gold and someone in a high position will see it and fall in love with you' (pp. 17–18), she is surprised to find that exactly this happens to the person who buys the hat. It is gradually revealed that this is more than a coincidence: Sophie is a witch whose words have power. Jones uses this trope in several other books: in *The Spellcoats* (1973) Tanaqui gradually realises that the story she is telling about her adventures has the power to determine their outcome, while in *Fire and Hemlock* Thomas Lynn's stories to Polly frequently (and often uncomfortably) come true. This device serves to make the reader more aware of the power of the stories we tell ourselves, and implies that we ought consequently to be careful about which stories we choose to tell.

There is a great deal of humour in Diana Wynne Jones's manipulation of generic conventions and reader expectations in *Howl's Moving Castle*, but in this and in her other books there is much more going on under the surface than at first appears. By playing with reader expectations so explicitly, Jones forces readers to think more carefully about their expectations and assumptions. Fantasy has often been accused of being escapist, but the complexities of Jones's narrative demand a critical and self-aware reader: the revelation that Sophie's magical powers have invested the dog and the scarecrow at the beginning of the book with life and autonomy sheds new light on this episode and encourages us to read more closely in the future. Sophie's realisation that she does not have to comply with the expectations set up by the fairy-tale genre is in fact deeply subversive, suggesting to child readers that they do not have to conform to the expectations of the adult world and are free to choose their own stories. As Part Three: 'Real Lives' will show, stories for children have often been used to impose a certain interpretation of the world on their readers: Diana Wynne Jones suggests that all interpretations are subject to criticism and change.

Notes

1   Matthew Grenby, *Children's Literature* (Edinburgh: Edinburgh University Press, 2008), p. 145.

2   Sarah Trimmer, quoted in Virginia Haviland (ed.), *Children and Literature: Views and Reviews* (New York: Lothrop, Lee and Shepard, 1973), p.3.

3   Sarah Trimmer, *Fabulous Histories: The History of the Robins* (London: Grant and Griffith, 1848), pp. 1–2.

4   Agnes Repplier, 'Battle of the Babies (1895)', in Haviland (ed.), *Children and Literature*, pp. 33–6, p. 36.

5   Peter Hunt (ed.), 'Introduction' to *Alice's Adventures in Wonderland and Through the Looking Glass* (Oxford: Oxford University Press, 2009), pp. vii–xliii, p. xliii.

6   M. F. Thwaite, *From Primer to Pleasure: An Introduction to the History of Children's Books in England, from the Invention of Printing to 1900* (London: The Library Association, 1963), p. 81.

7   Lewis Carroll, *Alice's Adventures in Wonderland and Through the Looking Glass*, ed. Peter Hunt (Oxford: Oxford University Press, 2009), p. 17.

8   J. M. Barrie, *Peter Pan* (Oxford: Oxford University Press, 2006), p. 36.

9   J. R. R. Tolkien, 'Children and Fairy Stories', in Sheila Egoff and G. T. Stubbs (eds), *Only Connect: Readings on Children's Literature* (New York: Oxford University Press, 1969), pp. 111–20, p. 114.

10   Ursula Le Guin, *A Wizard of Earthsea* (London: Puffin, 2010), p. 56.

11   Tom Shippey, 'Tolkien as a Post-War Writer', in Patricia Reynolds and Glen H. GoodKnight (eds), *Proceedings of the J. R. R. Tolkien Centenary Conference* (Altadena, CA: Mythopoeic Press, 1995), pp. 84–93, p. 86.

12   Susan Cooper, *The Dark Is Rising* (Harmondsworth: Puffin, 1976), p. 53.

13   Susan Cooper, *Silver on the Tree* (Harmondsworth: Puffin, 1979), p. 156.

14   C. S. Lewis, *The Lion, the Witch and the Wardrobe* (London: Fontana Lions, 1986), p. 9.

15   Maria Tatar, quoted in Grenby, *Children's Literature*, p. 154.

16   C. S. Lewis, *The Voyage of the Dawn Treader* (London: Fontana Lions, 1986), p. 7.

17   C. S. Lewis, 'On Three Ways of Writing for Children', in Egoff and Stubbs (eds), *Only Connect*, pp. 207–20, p. 215.

18   Charles Butler, *Four British Fantasists: Places and Culture in the Children's Fantasies of Penelope Lively, Alan Garner, Diana Wynne Jones, and Susan Cooper* (Oxford: Scarecrow Press, 2006), p. 203.

19   Bruno Bettelheim, *The Uses of Enchantment: The Meaning and Importance of Fairy Tales* (Harmondsworth: Penguin, 1991), p. 121.

20   William Mayne, *A Game of Dark* (Harmondsworth: Puffin, 1974), pp. 125–6.

21   Ursula K. Le Guin, *Earthsea Revisioned* (Cambridge, MA: Green Bay Publications, 1993), p. 25.

22   Diana Wynne Jones, *Hexwood* (London: Collins, 2000), p. 340.

23   Diana Wynne Jones, *The Ogre Downstairs* (London: Harper Trophy, 2002), p. 17.

24   Diana Wynne Jones, *The Tough Guide to Fantasyland* (London: Gollancz, 2004), p. 183.

25   Diana Wynne Jones, *Drowned Ammet* (Oxford: Oxford University Press, 2003), p. 238.

26   Diana Wynne Jones, *The Lives of Christopher Chant* (New York: Harper Trophy, 2001), p. 577.

27   Diana Wynne Jones, *The Merlin Conspiracy* (London: Collins, 2003), p. 118.

28   Farah Mendelssohn, quoted in Grenby, *Children's Literature*, p. 152.

29   Diana Wynne Jones, autobiography from 'The Official Diana Wynne Jones Website', accessed from www.leemac.freeserve.co.uk on 29 July 2010, n.p.

30   Diana Wynne Jones, *Howl's Moving Castle* (London: Collins, 2002), p. 9.

Real Lives: Alcott, Ashley and Wilson

Books for children have offered access to a host of fantasy worlds and magical creatures, but there is also a strong tradition of stories set firmly in the real world. Indeed, as Part Three: 'Alternative Worlds' has shown, many commentators have regarded fantasy with ambivalence at best, arguing that child readers should be provided only with 'truth'. Early children's writers such as James Janeway (1636–74), who reminded his readers that 'children are not too little to go to either heaven or hell',[1] used stories set in the real world as a basis for moral lessons intended to set their readers on the path to heaven. The educational element of realist narratives has continued to the present day: the second half of the twentieth century saw the emergence of so-called 'issues' books aimed at helping children deal with social problems such as racism, bullying or drugs. However, while realism has often been identified as more serious and utilitarian than fantasy, it has also been the site of considerable experimentation and creativity, and even the moral and religious tales of the seventeenth and eighteenth centuries had something to offer to the child readers of their day.

'Realism' includes a wide array of genres: school stories, family stories, historical novels and even adventure books all commonly set their narrative in a recognisable real world and commonly employ realist narrative strategies. In one sense, then, a discussion of realism in children's literature is almost impossibly broad. Historically speaking, however, the question of how much realism should be included in texts for children and how realist strategies should be used has been contentious and it continues to be so today. In a genre which is concerned in various ways with constructing real and imagined childhoods, the way in which writers have attempted to reflect the lives of real children and to provide them with guidance on negotiating their own lives is an important area of study.

Everyday Lives

One of the earliest surviving texts for children, the sixteenth-century poem 'The Schoole of Vertue' (1557), offers the following advice to schoolboys:

> Downe from thy chamber when thou shalte go,
> Thy parentes salute thou, and the family also;
> Thy handes se thou washe, and thy head keame [comb],
> And of thy raiment se torne be no seame.[2]

From a modern perspective, the appeal of these lines might seem limited, but they demonstrate some key realist tactics which have recurred in texts for children up until the present day. The poem recounts everyday experiences such as washing, dressing and combing one's hair, discusses relationships with parents and (in later sections) teachers and schoolmates, and even provides a list of the items which should appear in every good schoolboy's satchel. Such pleasure in the minutiae of daily life is a key feature of books for very small children, such as Jan Ormerod's wordless picture book *Sunshine* (1981), which portrays a small girl's morning routine as she washes, eats breakfast and gets ready for school. In Janet and Allan Ahlberg's *The Baby's Catalogue* (1982) the entire effect of the text rests on the pleasures of recognition: each page displays a set of everyday items or characters such as prams, potties and mums and dads, and small children are able to draw comparisons between the objects on display and those familiar to them in their own lives. Books for older children have also included a focus on the mundane elements of life: much of the appeal of Laura Ingalls Wilder's *Little House on the Prairie* (1935) and the other books in her 'Little House' series (1932–43) about her life as a pioneer derives from the detailed accounts of household chores and daily routines.* School stories in particular tend to provide detailed descriptions of clothes, daily routines and – above all – meals. From the didactic texts of the seventeenth century to the present, children's books have continued to be produced under the assumption that children both need and want books about their day-to-day experiences.

Creating a World: Realism and Ideology

As the title of 'The Schoole of Vertue' implies, the descriptions of daily life in the poem are directed towards guiding children on the right ways in which to behave. Indeed, the poem is not so much a recreation of daily routines as a prescriptive list of just what those routines should be. Catherine Belsey, whose *Critical Practice* (1980) was one of the last major studies to focus on realism in literature for adults, identifies realism as a particularly effective means of encouraging readers to accept and absorb the ideology of a text. Belsey argues that the narrative strategies used in what she terms 'classic realist texts' – which seek to draw the reader into the world of the book and to accept the fictional world as real – work to create a hierarchy of voices within the text in which some versions of events and values are privileged above others, as in Maria Edgeworth's 'The Purple Jar' (discussed below). These strategies are embedded in what

---

* Wilder was writing about her own childhood, so at the time of first publication her books were already documenting a life which was some decades removed from those of her child readers, and today they are firmly in the category of historical fiction. However, while they do not directly reflect the lives of their readers, in every other respect they use the modes and strategies of realist fiction and must be considered as realism.

Belsey terms 'illusionism': the act of creating a version of our world through words. 'Classic' realist texts like the nineteenth-century novels on which Belsey's study is based use strategies such as the description of setting and character to create this illusion of reality, drawing the reader into the text. Belsey further argues that realist texts depend upon the creation of a sense of closure, drawing together a number of threads in the narrative to create a satisfying resolution. This strategy works to discourage the reader from unpicking or challenging what they have read, so that they are likely to accept both the conclusion of the narrative and the underlying ideology and values. John Stephens in the early 1990s criticised the effects of this kind of realist fiction, arguing that, by drawing the child reader into the text, the author heightens his or her tendency to unconsciously absorb the ideological message, leaving children open to 'gross forms of intellectual manipulation'.[3] As discussed below, some realist writers for children have consciously worked to disrupt prevailing ideologies through their texts; however, it is certainly true that realism has been closely associated with the education and socialisation of young readers. One of the earliest texts marketed directly at children, James Janeway's *A Token for Children* (1671–2), uses basic realist strategies to deliver a strong religious message. The religious motive is uppermost in Janeway's stories, which strongly resemble sermons, but the inclusion of specific details, such as dates and place names, and the use of reported speech encourage the reader to believe in Janeway's accounts of preternaturally pious children and their early deaths (invariably eased by their profound certainty in a heavenly afterlife). Similarly, John Aikin and Anna Laetitia Barbauld used stories set in everyday contexts to convey moral and religious messages to their young readers in *Evenings at Home* (1792–6), in which many of the stories take the format of a dialogue between a child and a parent or teacher.

Parents' Assistants: Edgeworth and Alcott

More sophisticated realist strategies appeared in the nineteenth century, when the kind of classic realist texts on which Belsey's study is based began to emerge. Longer, less overtly didactic stories appeared, featuring more natural child characters. Whereas writers such as Janeway had tended to separate saints and sinners in their stories, characters such as Louisa May Alcott's lively March sisters in *Little Women* (1868), rebellious Katy in Susan Coolidge's *What Katy Did* (1872) and the well-meaning but hapless Bastable family in E. Nesbit's *The Story of the Treasure Seekers* (1899) and its sequels are all endowed with faults as well as virtues, and are more recognisably child-like to a modern reader than their predecessors.

Maria Edgeworth's collection of short stories in *The Parent's Assistant* (1796) combines the moral and educational emphasis which characterised earlier realism for children by writers such as James Janeway and Aikin and Barbauld with a greater attempt to create believable child characters. In her preface to *The Parent's Assistant*, Edgeworth emphasises the importance of realism in capturing the attention of child readers, commenting:

> such situations only are described as children can easily imagine, and which may consequently interest their feelings. Such examples of virtue are painted as are not above their conception of excellence, or their powers of sympathy and emulation.[4]

Whereas James Janeway's saintly children might well be described as being above most young readers' 'conception of excellence', Edgeworth's characters have recognisably human virtues and flaws. In the most famous of the stories, 'The Purple Jar' (first published in the second, expanded edition of *The Parent's Assistant* in 1801), the protagonist Rosamund chooses to buy a pretty purple jar rather than the new shoes she really needs. Although her mother advises her to consider carefully before choosing the jar over the shoes, she allows

65

Rosamund to make up her own mind, telling her 'I want you to think for yourself.'[5] Rosamund duly decides to take the purple jar in preference to the shoes, only to be bitterly disappointed by the discovery that the purple colour of the jar is due entirely to the nasty-smelling liquid it contains, and the effects of the moral lesson are hammered home when her father refuses to take her out to visit a glasshouse because she has not got a good enough pair of shoes. Rosamund's reasoning that her shoes are 'not so very, very bad! I think I might wear them a little longer, and the month will soon be over' (p. 179) has an authentic ring, while many child readers must have sympathised with her uncertain assertion that she has learnt her lesson: 'I am sure, no, not quite sure, but I hope I shall be wiser another time' (p. 180).

The moral lessons Maria Edgeworth delivers in her stories are predicated on the idea that, like Rosamund, child readers should be taught to 'think for themselves'. This strategy is at odds with that of most of Edgeworth's predecessors, who typically took care to explicitly state the moral of their stories. 'The Purple Jar', however, is an excellent example of the kind of ideological enforcement Catherine Belsey identifies in realist novels. Rosamund's attraction to pretty but useless things is repeatedly contrasted with her mother's more prudent attitude to money: when Rosamund admires the pretty baubles in the jeweller's shop, ingenuously stating 'I am sure you could find some use or other for them if you would only buy them first', her mother replies repressively 'I would rather find out the use first' (p. 177). The child reader (and this adult one!) is likely to sympathise most with Rosamund's point of view, but the outcome of the story enforces the values of her mother. Rosamund's own expressed wish to be 'wiser in future' inescapably aligns both her and the child reader with the ideology of the text.

The strategy Rosamund's mother uses in order to teach her to be more prudent with her money reflects the child-rearing philosophies of Edgeworth's period, which owed much to the influence of Locke and Rousseau (discussed in Part Two: 'A Cultural Overview'), emphasising the need to develop the child's reason and fit lessons to the child's level of knowledge and experience. The same philosophy is very evident in other nineteenth-century texts such as those by Louisa May Alcott, best known for *Little Women*, a family story which follows the development of four sisters from late childhood into their maturity as 'little women'. Alcott's stories are in fact composed of episodes which apply exactly the same model of 'learning through experience' which is evident in 'The Purple Jar'. In *Little Women*, Marmee's decision to allow the March girls a day of 'all play and no work' results not only in burnt dinner and a dirty house, but also in the death of their pet canary (left without food or water), while Jo's failure to comply with her mother's maxim 'never let the sun go down on your anger' almost results in the death of her sister Amy.

The moral message is slightly less apparent in Alcott's stories than in those of Edgeworth, largely because the novel offered more opportunities for plot and character development than the compact short-story form with which Edgeworth was working. The adventures and mistakes of Meg, Jo, Amy and Beth in *Little Women* are lively and enjoyable in their own right, and the struggle of Alcott's characters to live up to the kind of moral precepts modelled by Edgeworth and her ilk may well live longer in the imagination than the morals themselves. In *Eight Cousins* (1875), the story of an orphaned girl adopted by her uncle and newly exposed to her large extended family, Alcott even allows her heroine to complain about the uncompromising morality exhibited in Edgeworth: on being reminded of 'The Purple Jar', Rose exclaims 'I always thought it very unfair in her mother not to warn the poor thing a little bit [...] Ugh! I always want to shake that hateful woman, though she was a moral mamma.'[6] Nevertheless, it is impossible to enjoy and sympathise with Alcott's characters without also entering into the moral framework of the books: after 150 years, Alcott's use of realism to draw readers in and encourage them to share the moral journey of her characters is still effective.

One striking feature of the realist texts of the nineteenth century is the degree to which they serve as moral guides for parents as well as children, a feature suggested by Edgeworth's title *The Parent's*

Assistant. Parents like Rosamund's mother and the eternally patient Marmee of Alcott's *Little Women* model correct modes of child-rearing, enforcing the dominant ideologies of the text. Both writers, however, also portray bad parenting and its consequences. In Edgeworth's 'Lazy Lawrence', the laziness and dishonesty of the eponymous Lawrence is clearly a consequence of poor parenting. His idleness is condoned by his family – he boasts that he has no need to work because he can get money from his father by asking 'just at the right time, when he [has] drunk a glass or two; then I can get anything I want out of him' with the result that he is drawn into theft and ultimately imprisoned.[7] By contrast, the hard-working and honest Jem of the same story is the product of an 'obliging, active and good-humoured' parent (p. 25). The contrast between the two styles of parenting is intended to demonstrate to children that indulgent parents are not the blessing they may appear to be, but it also provides an object lesson to parents about the dangers of overindulgence. In Louisa May Alcott's work, the message to parents is even clearer. *Eight Cousins* is effectively a child-rearing manual: the orphaned Rose Campbell lives for a month with each of her aunts, each of whom practises her own particular theories about the best way to bring up a young woman. At the end of the experiment, Rose is happy to return to her guardian, Uncle Alec, whose 'eccentric' ideas prompted the initial disagreements about Rose's upbringing. The characters of Rose's eight cousins serve to emphasise the flaws in each of her aunts' parenting techniques, most strikingly in the case of overindulged Charlie, who ultimately dies in an accident caused by his drunkenness and dissipation.

Alcott's work exemplifies the way in which realism can be effective as a tool for appealing moral instruction; however, her books also show that realism does not necessarily have to impose a conservative ideology. On the contrary, the conventional moralism of her books is combined with some relatively radical ideas. While her criticisms of idleness and indulgence conform to conventional ideas about female modesty and self-sacrifice, her condemnation of uncomfortable and restrictive fashionable clothing for girls and celebration of female education and autonomy are more challenging. Alcott uses the likeable character of Uncle Alec in *Eight Cousins* to voice opinions such as the idea that women should be clothed 'both healthfully and handsomely', commenting 'I should think women would rejoice at the lightening of their burdens' and rejecting the shocked claims of the aunts that abandoning corsets and long skirts is 'immodest' (p. 216). In *Little Women*, it is Marmee, the moral voice of the text, who articulates the radical notion that it is 'better to be happy old maids than unhappy wives'.[8] In this case, the strategies Alcott uses to draw the reader into the text serve to deliver an ideology which challenges rather than reinforces some dominant ideas of her period (although it is not less coercive for this).

The Realness of Realism

The extent to which a text appears to truthfully represent the world in which we live is a central issue in most studies of realism; it has also been a key question for writers and critics of children's literature, who have struggled with the question of just how 'real' realism for children should be. Early books for children did not shrink from portraying some of the most difficult aspects of contemporary childhoods: *The History of Goody Two-Shoes* (1765) includes the death of the heroine's parents and relates her experience of poverty and hardship before rewarding both heroine and reader with her rise to prosperity. Death and poverty were common themes in children's stories during the eighteenth and nineteenth centuries, and realistic portrayals of the seamier side of life were often used in order to drive home a moral or religious lesson. The failures of parents and authority figures were also well represented in books of this period: while writers such as James Janeway emphasised the importance of filial respect and obedience to 'very religious parents, whose great care was to instruct and catechise'[9] their children, there were also plenty of examples of drunken, abusive or impious parents (who were often dramatically converted by their pious children).

During the nineteenth century, death and disability retained a strong presence in realist fiction for children. The theme of disability was particularly prevalent in stories for girls: Susan Coolidge's *What Katy Did* is a typical example of the genre, in which temporary disability or illness typically serves to teach the child protagonist the virtues of patience and endurance, allowing her to emerge as a calmer, more 'womanly' and self-sacrificing character. The death of a major character was often also employed to 'tame' girl protagonists: rebellious Judy in Ethel Turner's *Seven Little Australians* (1894) dies saving her younger brother from an accident, in the ultimate gesture of redemptive self-sacrifice.

By the end of the nineteenth century, death, disability and poverty were becoming increasingly rare in realist novels for children, which depicted more and more the safe, middle-class childhoods of their presumed audience. Early children's books had typically depicted working-class childhoods for the edification of middle-class readers; by the beginning of the twentieth century working-class children were almost totally invisible in children's books. Joyce Lankester Brisley's 'Milly-Molly-Mandy' stories (1928–67) epitomise the kind of cosy, white, middle-class outlook which dominated in children's books in the first half of the twentieth century: Milly-Molly-Mandy's charming but supremely unadventurous adventures in the 'nice white cottage with the thatched roof' are untouched by the shadows of poverty or disease.[10] Arthur Ransome's 'Swallows and Amazons' series (1930–47), one of the most influential series for children in the first half of the twentieth century, also focuses on the exploits of secure, middle-class children, while in Noel Streatfeild's immensely popular 'career' novels – most notably *Ballet Shoes* (1936) – poverty usually extends only as far as the need to 'save the penny and walk'.[11] Eve Garnett's *The Family from One End Street* (1937) was one of the first twentieth-century novels to depict the lives of ordinary working-class children: the book was later criticised for its sanitised portrayal of working-class life, which John Rowe Townsend characterised as 'too condescending to be altogether commendable',[12] but the fact that it was awarded the Carnegie Medal over J. R. R. Tolkien's widely acclaimed fantasy *The Hobbit* (1937) illustrates how groundbreaking it appeared when it was first published.

The criticisms aimed at *The Family from One End Street* reflect the growing concern from the 1950s onwards for the need to portray more diverse childhoods in children's literature. During the 1960s and 1970s, realism in children's literature became closely associated with a left-wing, socially progressive ethos. In Britain, social, political and economic changes in the postwar years focused greater attention on lives of working-class children, and literature and literacy became central aspects of the strategy to cope with the pace of social change. Social commentators such as Leila Berg argued that books which realistically reflected the lives of 'ordinary' children were essential in order to encourage such children to develop the love of reading and literature which was already enjoyed by their middle-class contemporaries. Berg's reading scheme for young readers, 'Nippers' (1968–76), sought to bridge the gap with stories about fish-and-chip suppers and single-parent families. The stories are simple and charming, but all the same proved too realistic for some readers: one head teacher wrote to complain that it was 'immoral' to offer children books which showed families with leaking roofs and washing hanging over the stairs.[13] Nevertheless, 'Nippers' reflected the general trend in children's literature during the 1960s and 1970s: John Rowe Townsend's *Gumble's Yard* (1961) portrays children who lived in an urban slum, while Robert Westall's *The Machine Gunners* (1975) reflects the Tyneside dialect of its working-class child characters. Westall's child characters, who tell their peers to 'Bugger off or I'll set our Cuthbert on you', were a radical departure from the sanitised and well-behaved characters of the early twentieth century.[14] School stories also became more likely to be set in ordinary day schools rather than the middle-class boarding schools which had previously characterised the genre: E. W. Hildick's 'Jim Starling' stories (1958–63) and Gene Kemp's *The Turbulent Term of Tyke Tiler* (1977) and its sequels are among the books which reflect this trend.

Creating the New Society: Ashley and Kemp

The desire to include a more diverse range of childhoods during the 1960s and 1970s was also manifested in an increasing number of books that reflected the ethnic diversity of contemporary society. Picture books such as Ezra Jack Keats's *The Snowy Day* (1962), Leila Berg's 'Nippers' series and Rosemary Stones et al.'s *Mother Goose Comes to Cable Street* (1977) tackled the issue simply by introducing characters of colour into racially 'neutral' stories: *The Snowy Day* portrays a small African-American boy enjoying the snow, without an overt comment on his race. In books for older children, the issue of racism tended to be explicitly acknowledged: Bernard Ashley's *The Trouble with Donovan Croft* (1974) and Jan Needle's *My Mate Shofiq* (1978) both explore the effects of racism on their eponymous characters, while Julius Lester's *To Be a Slave* (1969) and Mildred D. Taylor's powerful *Roll of Thunder, Hear My Cry* (1976) tackle the issues of slavery and African-American civil rights from a historical perspective. While these realist texts are (at least marginally) more subtle than their Puritan predecessors, they are no less motivated by the desire to inculcate a set of social and moral values in their child readers.

Bernard Ashley's *The Trouble with Donovan Croft* exemplifies the new didacticism of 1960s and 1970s realism. The book deals with the experiences of the Chapman family, who foster a young boy from a Jamaican background – the eponymous Donovan – when his mother's return to Jamaica to nurse her ill father leaves his family temporarily unable to care for him. This scenario, which introduces Donovan into a white family and community, highlights some of the racial conflicts which were particularly acute in Britain during this period, when high levels of immigration and a deepening recession made anxiety about immigrant communities especially intense. Ashley portrays some overtly racist attitudes, as in the scene when Mrs Chapman tells her neighbour Mrs Parsons about Donovan's family situation:

'Oh, I see,' said Mrs Parsons. 'Very nice for them too, I suppose. Just up and leave the children and we have to pay out to have them looked after.' She made it sound as if Mrs Chapman were making a gigantic profit out of some personal welfare service provided by Mr and Mrs Parsons.

'It's not quite as bad as it seems,' Mrs Chapman put in quickly. 'His father's paying for his keep. But even if he wasn't, they've lived here for twelve years, and Donovan was born here. So really he's as British as you and I.'[15]

This scene effectively demonstrates how the realist strategies identified by Belsey and Stephens work to impose an ideology on the reader. The narratorial voice clearly frames Mrs Parsons's opinion as prejudiced and flawed, with the comment that she 'made it sound' as if Mrs Chapman were making a profit clearly indicating that her view is both incorrect and offensive. By contrast, Mrs Chapman's assertion that black Britons like the Donovan family are 'as British as you and I' is presented as calm and reasonable, and the narrator subsequently reinforces her position by stating that 'she was not the sort of person to be put off a thing by someone's stupid attitude' (p. 9). An anti-racist ideology is similarly enforced elsewhere in the text: Mr Chapman explicitly condemns racists as 'small-minded bigots' (p. 89), and a racist teacher is portrayed as a contemptible figure who is both feared and despised by his students. The ideology presented here is perhaps more palatable than the message of obedience and self-sacrifice which was a feature of nineteenth-century books for children, but it is just as strongly imposed on the child reader.

The relatively heavy-handed way in which *The Trouble with Donovan Croft* seeks to develop socially progressive ideologies in its child readers is characteristic of many realist titles published during the 1960s and 1970s, when bodies such as the Children's Rights Workshop published guidelines on combating racist, sexist and classist attitudes in children's books. However, realist writers also sought to make child readers challenge dominant ideologies for themselves. A subtle and engaging example is Gene Kemp's *The Turbulent Term of Tyke Tiler*. Like *The Trouble with Donovan Croft*, *Tyke Tiler* reflects many of the concerns current in British society at large during the period it was published. Set in an urban primary school, its portrayal of working-class characters reflects the move away from the middle-class dominance of books for children and towards a more representative children's literature. In other respects, the book reproduces many conventions of the traditional school story, with Tyke's well-meaning but often ill-fated exploits providing the narrative. The tale culminates with Tyke climbing the school tower: a typically daring but foolhardy enterprise in the tradition of naughty schoolboys such as those in Thomas Hughes's *Tom Brown's Schooldays* (1857). The end of the story, however, provides a twist as Tyke's full name is revealed: not Theodore, but Theodora. Even today, the revelation of Tyke's gender comes as a surprise to the unsuspecting reader: by withholding this information until the end of the book Kemp forces readers to examine their own preconceptions. The technique is so effective because of the highly recognisable setting and events of Kemp's text, which enable the child reader to recognise their own lived experience, heightening the sense of disconnection when the world within the text is revealed to be not quite the one the reader was expecting.

The work of both Bernard Ashley and Gene Kemp illustrates the degree to which the boundaries of 'acceptable' content in realism for children had expanded by the 1970s. Whereas in the first half of the century books for children had offered a desirable image of childhood rather than a realistic one, by the 1970s realism in children's literature was predominantly focused on offering children help and advice in negotiating an often difficult modern world. *The Turbulent Term of Tyke Tiler* and Kemp's other books set in Cricklepit Combined School are gentle in tone, but her characters cope with dyslexia, bullying and the other vicissitudes of primary-school life. *The Trouble with Donovan Croft* deals not only with the issue of racism, but also with the difficulties involved in adoption and fostering: the story is told from the point of view of the Chapman family, not of Donovan, and focuses on their son Keith's experience of coming to terms with Donovan's presence in his family. Bernard Ashley's other work has similarly dealt with difficult social issues; *A Kind of Wild Justice* (1979) focuses on gang violence, while his more recent work has dealt with issues further afield: *Down to the Wire* (2006) includes children's experiences of civil war, and *Little Soldier* (1999) brings the plight of child soldiers closer to home by examining the experiences of one East African boy struggling to adapt to the conflicts of a London comprehensive school after escaping war in his own country. The inclusion of such challenging social and political issues has become a key theme in contemporary realism for children.

Unpleasant Traits and Crueller Realities

The move to reflect in titles a broader range of childhood experiences which began in the 1960s extended not only to a more diverse range of child characters, but also to themes and topics which had previously been excluded from children's literature. Gillian Avery, writing in 1965, complained:

> [Children's writers] omit (instinctively, not consciously, one feels) all unpleasant traits in a child's personality; all crudity and coarseness. Their children hardly seem to have a physical nature, beyond a good appetite. Family relationships are smooth, mother is always right, father never irks his sons. [...] Truly, we are a mealy-mouthed lot.[16]

However, by 1965 books for children were already beginning to include some of the conflict that Avery complained was lacking. In Louise Fitzhugh's *Harriet the Spy* (1964) Harriet's observations about her classmates – and their reactions when these observations are discovered – reveal children's capacity for unpleasantness, although the overall tone of the text is light-hearted. Much darker in tone is Robert Cormier's *The Chocolate War* (1974), in which the protagonist Jerry unsuccessfully attempts to fight back against the bullies who control his school; the book ends with the badly beaten Jerry concluding that it is better to conform than to try to 'disturb the universe'.[17] In *The Chocolate War* adults as well as children are shown enforcing the corrupt and abusive regime of the school, reflecting the re-emergence of the flawed and unreliable adult characters who had featured in early children's books. In John Rowe Townsend's *Gumble's Yard* (1961) a group of children are abandoned by their feckless guardians, while in Jan Mark's *Thunder and Lightnings* (1976) the family of child character Victor are portrayed as bordering on abusive. From the 1970s onwards a number of books directly tackled the issue of child abuse: Bette Green's *Summer of My German Soldier* (1973) and Rosa Guy's *The Friends* (1973) both portray parental violence, Cynthia Voigt's *When She Hollers* (1994) addresses sexual abuse, and Robert Swindell's *Abomination* (1993) deals with the neglect and abuse of a disabled child. The theme of unreliable or absent parents is particularly important to the work of Jacqueline Wilson, discussed below.

The inclusion of topics such as sexual abuse in children's books has led many critics to question whether realism can be 'too real'. Nicholas Tucker, writing in 1976, asserted:

> books should be about desirable experience rather than realistic experience. It is asking too much of a child to expect him to see life in the raw as it actually is.[18]

The idea that children should be offered a 'desirable' image of life was reflected in the kind of realist narratives offered to children in the first half of the twentieth century: the predominance of middle-class narratives in this period partly reflects the belief that less privileged children needed something to aspire to rather than a reflection of their existing situation. Nevertheless, since the 1970s an increasing number of more hard-hitting topics have emerged in fiction for children. Death has re-emerged as a popular theme in books including Katherine Paterson's *A Bridge to Terabithia* (1977), David Hill's *See Ya, Simon* (1992) and Jandy Nelson's *The Sky Is Everywhere* (2010); whereas early children's books tended to draw a moral message from character deaths, these modern novels are designed to help children work through the experience of grief and loss. A similar focus on coming to terms with difficult life experiences has been present in books about illness and disability such as those by Jacqueline Wilson, whose novels on contemporary social issues have covered mental illness and physical disability. Increasingly, books on disability have sought to demonstrate that disability is a normal part of life rather than a shocking social 'issue': in Jane Stemp's *Secret Songs* (1997) the deafness of her main protagonist Ceri is an essential part of her character without being a source of narrative conflict, while in the picture book *Susan Laughs* (1999) by Jeanne Willis and Tony Ross, Susan is shown laughing, dancing and engaging in other typical childhood activities before the final page of the book reveals that she is a wheelchair user.

Realism has been closely associated with books which reflect the day-to-day lives of their child readers, but some of the most hard-hitting realist novels have dealt with issues at one remove from most of their presumed readers. In the late twentieth and twenty-first centuries, an increasing number of writers for children have dealt with conflict and political unrest in realistic formats. Ian Serraillier's *The Silver Sword* (1956) was one of the first books for children to address the Second World War: the story of a group of children left parentless in occupied Poland conveys some of the danger and hardship of war-torn Europe. Although not strictly children's literature, *The Diary of Anne Frank*, published in English in 1952, has often been read by children: the honesty and directness of this autobiographical text helped to pave the way for fiction which addressed the events of the Holocaust. As the historical distance from these events has increased, writers have addressed them more explicitly: Morris Gleitzman's *Once* (2006) is one of a number of texts to deal directly with the genocide which took place during the

Holocaust, and portrays the death of several of its characters at the hands of Nazi soldiers. Books like this reflect the belief that, by educating children about real abuses, it is possible to prevent such events recurring in the future.* A similar motivation has been present in books about contemporary conflicts: Robert Westall's *Gulf* (1992), written during the First Gulf War, conveys some of the horrors of that conflict through the device of a 'psychic' character who begins to dream about a counterpart in Iraq. More recently, Anna Perera has sought to inform young readers about human-rights abuses by the United States and its allies in *Guantanamo Boy* (2009), which deals with the wrongful imprisonment and political abuse of its fifteen-year-old protagonist Khalid after he is mistakenly identified as a terrorist and Al-Qaeda sympathiser. The details of coercion and torture in the book, which include scenes of humiliating strip-searches and the waterboarding of its protagonist, might certainly lead some readers to question whether it is 'suitable' for child readers; the observation in the author's notes that 'It remains a fact that children have been abducted and abused and held without charge in the name of justice in Guantanamo Bay' highlights the fact that the inclusion of such details is intended to move readers to action against injustice.[19]

The True Stories of Jacqueline Wilson

Jacqueline Wilson is one of the most popular and widely read modern British authors for children: in the first decade of the new millennium she was the most borrowed author in public libraries, and young fans flock to her public appearances.[20] Wilson's books,

* United Nations Secretary General Ban-Ki Moon expressed this belief in a speech given on the International Day in Memory of the Victims of the Holocaust, 2007, when he stated: 'We must also go beyond remembrance, and make sure that new generations know this history. We must apply the lessons of the Holocaust to today's world.' Ban-Ki Moon, 'Secretary-General, in Message for Holocaust Victims Memorial Day, Stresses Importance of Reasserting Commitment to Human Rights', 19 January 2007, accessed from www.un.org on 4 July 2010, n.p.

which cater to readers aged between eight and fourteen, epitomise many of the developments in realism for children in the second half of the twentieth century. Her stories typically focus on working-class protagonists, often in 'alternative' families of some sort, and deal with social issues such as bullying, disability and adoption. Her simple, accessible style and her ability to tap into issues which interest and concern young readers have given her a level of popularity only surpassed by high-profile writers such as J. K. Rowling.

Wilson's books reveal many of the features of 'classic' realism. Although she often deals with situations which affect relatively few child readers – for example the mental illness of a parent in *The Illustrated Mum* (1999) – her books are set in the familiar surroundings of home and school. In *Dustbin Baby* (2001), about a child who has been adopted after her birth mother abandoned her in a dustbin, the unfamiliarity of the situation is offset by a focus on the kind of everyday minutiae that concern most early teens. The book opens with the birthday of the protagonist, April, but, while Wilson is quick to establish that birthdays are particularly difficult times for April because they commemorate her abandonment, April's conflicted feelings are expressed through her disappointment at her foster mother's refusal to buy her a mobile phone:

> 'I just want to be like my friends. Cathy's got a mobile. Hannah's got a mobile. Why can't *I* have a mobile?'

> 'I've just *told* you why.'

> 'Yes, well, I'm sick of you telling me this and telling me that. Who are *you* to tell me all this stuff? It's not like you're my *mother*.'[21]

The immediate source of the conflict – the desire to own a mobile phone – will be familiar to most young readers, but this familiar argument leads into the real source of April's discontent. This short section illustrates the clever way in which the kind of realist strategies identified by Catherine Belsey are used by Wilson in order to draw her child readers into the text and lead them to identify with her child characters.

The sense of realism in Jacqueline Wilson's books is heightened by her use of first-person narrative. The use of first-person narration has been common in children's books since the 1970s; as Part Three: 'Young Adult Fiction' will show, it is a key feature of literature for teenagers. In Wilson's books, the use of child narrators is an important strategy for encouraging the reader to identify with the main character and heightening the illusion that the book is 'real'. In *The Story of Tracy Beaker* (1991), Jacqueline Wilson's most successful novel, the narrative is presented as part of a book being written by Tracy herself and is laid out as if it is written in the kind of 'autobiography' books often marketed to pre-teens, with 'handwritten' information filling in the 'pre-printed' forms:

> **My name is** Tracy Beaker.
>
> **I am 10 years 2 months old.**
>
> **My birthday is on** May 8. It's not fair, because that dopey Peter Ingham has his birthday then too, so we just got the one cake between us. And we had to hold the knife to cut the cake together. Which meant we had only half a wish each. Wishing is for babies anyway. Wishes don't come true.[22]

At first glance this may appear to be nothing more than a rather simplistic gimmick. In fact, however, this opening section displays some sophisticated realist techniques. The diary format heightens the sense of realism, giving readers the sense that they are reading a real diary written by a real child. Wilson employs the same strategy in other books: *The Worry Website* (2002) is written as a collection of posts to a school 'problem page' forum, while in *Midnight* (2003) the main narrative is interspersed with letters from the protagonist to her favourite author. In these books, as in *Tracy Beaker*, the use of a first-person child narrator creates a sense of intimacy which draws the reader into the text. The first-person narration also allows Wilson to use simple, vernacular language, another strategy that reduces the perceived barrier between the reader and the text. Furthermore, the immediate introduction of some universal concerns such as birthdays encourages the child reader to identify with Tracy, despite the fact that details such as the shared birthday cake indicate that Tracy's home life is *not* typical. All these strategies both make Wilson's books appealing and satisfying to readers, and work to encourage them to accept the messages in the text.

The situations and settings in Jacqueline Wilson's books reflect the move towards depicting a more diverse range of childhoods which began in the 1960s. Gillian Avery's complaint about the smooth family life which was still prevalent in books for children at the beginning of the 1960s could certainly not be levelled at Wilson, who has written about looked-after children in *The Story of Tracy Beaker* and *Dustbin Baby*, about family break-ups in *The Suitcase Kid* (1992) and *Candyfloss* (2006) and about domestic violence in *Lola Rose* (2003). Many of her books depict children who take on a parental role for siblings or parents, as in *The Illustrated Mum* (discussed below). These stories reflect the belief that children need to see difficult situations reflected in the literature they read in order to negotiate similar conflicts in their own lives: Wilson has stated that she believes the way she addresses issues such as death is 'helpful to children because it's very difficult if you cannot talk about it'.[23] Whereas in earlier such texts for children, stories about difficult family situations often finished with the difficult situation resolved, Wilson's books typically make it clear that there is no easy resolution, focusing instead on coming to terms with the way things are. A typical example is *The Diamond Girls* (2004), which portrays a modern 'dysfunctional' lone-parent family in which each child has a different father. The story makes no attempt to hide the difficulties posed by this situation: the mother relies heavily on her children for practical and emotional support, and in the course of the book the oldest daughter – aged only sixteen – falls pregnant, continuing the pattern established by her mother. While the situation of the protagonist, Dixie, is far from perfect, however, the narrative contrasts her life with that of her friend Mary, whose apparently perfect middle-class household is in fact controlling and abusive due to her mother's mental illness. At the end of the story, the Diamond family is in much the same position as at the start, but Dixie's mother asserts positively 'we'll all be Diamond girls together',[24] emphasising the importance of love and family bonds.* It is characteristic of Wilson's fiction that she stresses the importance and legitimacy of children's love for their families, even in cases where the parents are clearly inadequate. In *Lola Rose*, the family flee from domestic abuse, but five-year-old Kendall is still shown to love and miss his father, while Tracy Beaker repeatedly makes excuses for her mother's failure to visit or reclaim her from foster care. Texts like these work to legitimise children's feelings, while helping readers who are not in similar situations to understand and sympathise with them. In her own way, Wilson is just as concerned with teaching children appropriate social and moral values as her Victorian predecessors: while the stories she tells are clearly a product of late twentieth-century British society, the messages of tolerance and care for others are not dissimilar from those which appeared in nineteenth-century texts.

In dealing with topics such as domestic violence and child abuse, Jacqueline Wilson pushes the boundaries of what is considered to be 'suitable' reading for children. While most of the topics she addresses appeared in earlier books for young adults, Wilson is typically read by both a younger and a larger audience than her predecessors, factors which might be expected to leave her open to criticism. In fact, however, Wilson has succeeded in dealing with difficult issues with a lightness of touch which has helped her avoid censure. The use of the first person is an important element in insulating the child reader from some of the more shocking elements of the text. In *The Diamond Girls*, the abuse suffered by Mary is largely revealed to the

---

* This closing statement also resolves the key conflict in the book as Dixie's mother admits that her new baby is a girl, not (as she has pretended) the boy she hoped for. Thus her closing statement emphasises not only family bonds, but also female ones.

reader through Dixie, who neither knows everything that has taken place nor fully understands it, while in *The Story of Tracy Beaker* Tracy's own determinedly optimistic personality brings humour and lightness to the text. Nevertheless, the realism of some of Wilson's texts is certainly what Nicholas Tucker referred to as 'life in the raw'. In *Lola Rose*, Jayni's attempt to protect her mother from her father results in him turning his violence on them both: 'He punched her and then when she was on the ground beside me he kicked her. Then he spat on both of us and walked out.'[25] In common with many earlier realist writers for children, Wilson has implicitly justified the inclusion of such controversial material by giving it a clear purpose. While books like *Lola Rose* undoubtedly appeal to young readers partly because of the relatively shocking content – the pre-teen equivalent of the 'misery memoir' – they function to reassure children about difficult situations and to provide advice and support in dealing with them.

Extended Commentary: Wilson, *The Illustrated Mum* (1999)

The Illustrated Mum, published in 1999, is a typical example of the way in which Jacqueline Wilson explores difficult situations without providing easy answers for her child readers. The book centres around eleven-year-old Dolphin, who narrates the story. From the opening lines it is clear that this family is not entirely ordinary, as Dolphin announces: 'Marigold started going weird again on her birthday. Star remembered that birthdays were often bad times so we'd tried really hard.'[26] When she goes on to reveal that 'it was Marigold's thirty-third birthday' it becomes apparent that Marigold is not a sibling or a friend, but Dolphin's mother. Marigold is the 'illustrated mum' of the title: her many tattoos signify her vivid and exciting personality but also mark out her difference from 'ordinary' mothers and her mental instability (her decision to get yet another tattoo marks the beginning of a manic episode). The caring role of Dolphin's sister Star – already suggested by the fact that it is her responsibility to remember that birthdays are 'bad times' – becomes increasingly apparent as the text progresses. It is Star who is responsible for ensuring that food is on the table, social-security money is not spent on frivolities, and they are all clothed and fed. By contrast, Marigold is practically and emotionally childlike: she complains that they have not bought her a birthday cake and, when reminded that she had asked them not to, complains: 'I always have a special birthday cake. You know how much it means to me because I never had my own special birthday cake when I was a kid' (p. 8). This image is a radical reversal of the responsible and reliable parents who appeared in children's literature in the early part of the twentieth century, but with almost 20,000 child carers in contemporary Britain, it reflects many children's lived experience.[27] Wilson frequently depicts families in which the balance of responsibility between parent and child is disrupted in some way, reflecting the move towards the depiction of a more diverse range of childhood experiences which has been a feature of modern children's literature.

Like the majority of Jacqueline Wilson's other novels, *The Illustrated Mum* is narrated in the first person by its child protagonist. This direct address helps to heighten the sense of realism, allowing Wilson to employ an apparently more authentic child voice. The text also includes illustrations by Nick Sharratt, who has collaborated with Wilson since the publication of *The Story of Tracy Beaker* in 1991. Sharratt's illustrations are interspersed with the text and designed to appear as if they have been created by Dolphin, who is portrayed as a gifted artist. Sharratt also pens notes written by Dolphin, creating the impression that the book contains real documents. All these strategies work to draw child readers into the text, encouraging them to believe in and sympathise with Dolphin's story. By using a child narrator, Wilson is also able to portray difficult and frightening situations within safe limits. In the course of the story, it becomes increasingly apparent that Marigold is mentally ill, but Dolphin herself is too young to fully appreciate the implications of this, and is shielded by her older sister. While Dolphin is ultimately exposed to some of Marigold's most frightening behaviour, culminating when Marigold paints herself white in an attempt to hide the tattoos which mark her out as 'not normal', her lack of awareness about exactly how dangerous the situation could become cushions the child reader from the full impact of such episodes.

One reason for the great success of Wilson's novels is her ability to balance the serious nature of her themes with humour and light-heartedness. In *The Illustrated Mum*, this technique enables her to show Dolphin and Star's conflicted feelings about their mother. The manic depression which makes her unstable also makes her fun and impulsive: when Star criticises her mother for spending all their money on ingredients and equipment to bake cakes and cookies, instead of normal food, Dolphin responds: 'Who wants normal formal food? This is much more fun' (p. 39). The idea of a mother who is prepared to serve nothing but cake or ice cream for dinner will certainly appeal to many children, but, as Star reminds Dolphin: 'We lived on stale bread and carrots all the rest of that week because she'd spent all the Giro' (p. 39). Like the depictions of unreliable parents in nineteenth-century novels, scenes like this partly serve to demonstrate to children with 'normal' parents that having a 'boring' parent is better than the alternative. However, there is also genuine love and warmth in Wilson's parent–child relationships: when Dolphin observes 'It was so special, being Marigold and me' (p. 12), Wilson reinforces the idea that children feel affection even for the most unreliable parents.

One important feature of Jacqueline Wilson's books about social issues is her emphasis on the support services which exist for children in difficult circumstances. Many of her characters express a fear of being taken into care: in *The Illustrated Mum* Dolphin pictures a foster mother as 'tall and thin with a frowny forehead and a tight mouth. She had hard hands for smacking and she smelt of disinfectant' (p. 198). Dolphin and Star's attempts to hide their mother's illness are largely motivated by the belief that they will be removed from her care and placed in foster homes, but when

Dolphin finally does enter the foster system she finds that the foster mother has 'bright blue eyes [...] and a big smile' (p. 199), and the burden on both Dolphin and Star is eased when they are put into a situation which allows them to be children rather than carers. An important function of the text is to reassure children in difficult family situations that seeking help from teachers or social workers will not result in negative consequences. By acknowledging and conveying Dolphin's fears and allowing the child to experience them along with her, Wilson encourages readers to accept the positive conclusion, effectively conveying her intended message. Thus her text uses the mode of realism to educate children and inculcate appropriate attitudes in a similar way to those of her nineteenth-century predecessors.

The frightening impact of the negative situations portrayed in *The Illustrated Mum* is offset by the ultimately positive and reassuring message. By the end of the story, Dolphin and Star are both in a secure foster home, and Dolphin's father – whom she meets in the course of the story – is keen to be involved with both their lives, while Marigold is receiving treatment for her manic depression. Dolphin reflects:

> I looked at her, my illustrated mum. I knew she really did love me and Star. We had a father each and maybe they'd be around for us and maybe they wouldn't – but we'd always have our mum, Marigold. It didn't matter if she was mad or bad. She belonged to us and we belonged to her. (pp. 222–3)

This cosy and comforting conclusion is in many ways an unrealistic one: in particular, the introduction of Dolphin's absent father into the narrative is rather too neat. Yet it is important to note that Wilson does not completely resolve the conflicts in the narrative. Dolphin's closing words make it clear that the presence of her father in her life is by no means a certainty, and the possibility that Marigold will continue to be 'mad or bad' in the future is clearly indicated. Ultimately, the closure offered within the text is undercut by a more realistic uncertainty about the way in which the narrative will play out in the long term. Jacqueline Wilson offers her readers the certainty that parents really love their children, while acknowledging that this is not necessarily connected to good parenting skills.

The uncertainty inherent in the conclusion of *The Illustrated Mum* reflects a more conflicted and complex mode in realism for children at the beginning of the twenty-first century. While Jacqueline Wilson's work clearly contains many of the educative and socialising elements present in earlier realist texts for children, the moral certainties present in James Janeway or Maria Edgeworth are largely absent. In acknowledging that failures in society do exist – and in particular that many parents are unable or unwilling to provide their children with appropriate parenting – Wilson moves away from the more optimistic mode of realism of the 1960s and 1970s, which was focused towards producing changes in wider society. The more personal and ambiguous narratives Wilson provides reflect some of the uncertainty of modern life; however, the widespread popularity of her work indicates that children continue to enjoy literature in which they can see themselves, and to welcome the kind of moral and social guidance which realism can provide.

Notes

1   James Janeway, *A Token for Children (the Only Complete Edition Ever Published), in Two Parts* (New York: Whiting and Watson, 1811), pp. 4–5, accessed from http://books.google.co.uk on 20 January 2011, n.p.

2   Francis Seagar, 'The Schoole of Vertue and Booke of Good Nurture', in Patricia Demers (ed.), *From Instruction to Delight: An Anthology of Children's Literature to 1850*, 2nd edn (Oxford: Oxford University Press, 2004), p. 15, ll. 1–4.

3   John Stephens, *Language and Ideology in Children's Fiction* (Harlow: Pearson, 1992), p. 4.

4   Maria Edgeworth, 'Preface' to *The Parent's Assistant* (1796), p. 9, accessed from www.gutenberg.org on 14 July 2010, n.p.

5   Maria Edgeworth, 'The Purple Jar', in Demers (ed.), *From Instruction to Delight*, pp. 176–80, p. 179.
6   Louisa May Alcott, *Eight Cousins* (London: Puffin, 1995), p. 190.
7   Maria Edgeworth, 'Lazy Lawrence', in *The Parent's Assistant*, p. 32, accessed from www.gutenberg.org on 14 July 2010.
8   Louisa May Alcott, *Little Women* (Oxford: Oxford University Press, 2008), p. 95.
9   Janeway, *A Token for Children*, p. 94.
10 Joyce Lankester Brisley, *Milly-Molly-Mandy Stories* (London: Puffin, 2007), p. 7.
11 Noel Streatfeild, *Ballet Shoes* (London: Puffin, 1949), p. 7.
12 John Rowe Townsend, *Written for Children: An Outline of English-Language Children's Literature*, 2nd edn (Harmondsworth: Kestrel, 1983), p. 187.
13 Leila Berg, *Reading and Loving* (London: Routledge, 1977), p. 90.
14 Robert Westall, *The Machine Gunners* (London: Macmillan, 2001), p. 5.
15 Bernard Ashley, *The Trouble with Donovan Croft* (Oxford: Oxford University Press, 2002), p. 8.
16 Gillian Avery, *Nineteenth Century Children: Heroes and Heroines in English Children's Stories 1980–1900* (London: Hodder & Stoughton, 1965), p. 227.
17 Robert Cormier, *The Chocolate War* (London: Puffin, 2001), p. 205.
18 Nicholas Tucker, 'How Children Respond to Fiction', in Geoff Fox et al. (eds), *Writers, Critics and Children: Articles from Children's Literature in Education* (London: Heinemann Educational Books, 1976), pp. 177–89, pp. 184–5.
19 Anna Perera, 'Author's Note' to *Guantanamo Boy* (London: Puffin, 2009).
20 Public Lending Right, 'The Borrowing Habits of the Nation: A Decade of Data 1999–2009', accessed from www.plr.uk.com on 17 July 2010, n.p.
21 Jacqueline Wilson, *Dustbin Baby* (London: Corgi, 2002), pp. 15–16.
22 Jacqueline Wilson, *The Story of Tracy Beaker* (New York: Dell Yearling, 2001), p. 1.
23 Partnership for Children, 'Interview with Jacqueline Wilson', accessed from www.partnershipforchildren.org.uk on 1 January 2011, n.p.
24 Jacqueline Wilson, *The Diamond Girls* (London: Corgi, 2004), p. 230.
25 Jacqueline Wilson, *Lola Rose* (London: Corgi, 2004), p. 30.

26   Jacqueline Wilson, *The Illustrated Mum* (London: Corgi, 2000), p. 5.
27   Katherine Sellgren, 'Child Carers "without a Voice"', accessed from
     http://news.bbc.co.uk on 20 July 2010, n.p.

Adventure Stories: Wyss, Ransome and Muchamore

Spanning a wide range of settings and stories – from voyages on the high seas to forays into the heart of corrupt governments, perilous quests in search of treasure to daring feats of detective work – adventure stories have played an important role in children's literature. The diverse range of books grouped under the 'adventure' heading significantly blurs the boundaries of the genre: as Matthew Grenby points out, 'Few texts can be regarded as *only* adventure.'[1] On the contrary, adventure is usually a component of stories that might just as easily be categorised as fantasy, historical fiction, family stories, or school stories. Zizou Corder's *Lion Boy* (2003), for example, centres around a protagonist travelling to new lands in order to rescue his parents, who have been kidnapped by a sinister organisation: all features which recognisably belong to the adventure genre. However, the fact that the book's hero, Charlie, can speak to cats, and the futuristic setting – air travel has been supplanted by sea travel, and the world is controlled by a single superpower – give the book links with fantasy and science fiction. Similarly, in Janet Lunn's time-slip novel *The Root Cellar* (1982), Rose's journey across Civil War-era America in search of a lost friend has elements of the adventure story, but the Civil War setting ties it closely to the genre of historical fiction, while the time-slip device has a fantasy element. Despite the diversity of the texts which can be classed as adventure stories, however, the genre does have a distinctive identity, and it is possible to trace a clear line of influence from eighteenth-century texts such as Daniel Defoe's *Robinson Crusoe* (1719) to twentieth-century narratives like Arthur Ransome's *Swallows and Amazons* (1930) and Gary Paulsen's *Hatchet* (1987).

If the boundaries of the adventure genre are blurred, so too is the distinction between adventure stories for adults and those for children. The history of adventure stories provides a particularly clear illustration of the permeable boundaries of children's fiction: Daniel Defoe's *Robinson Crusoe* (1719), Jonathan Swift's *Gulliver's Travels* (1726) and James Fenimore Cooper's *Last of the Mohicans* (1896) all made their first appearances as books for adults, but were quickly adopted by and adapted for children. Non-fiction books on explorations and voyages have made an equally strong contribution to the genre: during the nineteenth century, accounts of explorers such as James Cook were widely read and frequently adapted for and marketed to children. More recently, Ian Fleming's 'James Bond' novels (1953–66) have gained popularity with adolescent readers, inspiring the juvenile espionage of Anthony Horowitz's 'Alex Rider' (2000–9), Charlie Higson's 'Young Bond' (2005–8) and Robert Muchamore's 'CHERUB' (2004–10) series, discussed below.

The Adventurer Alone

Spy stories thus offer readers the fantasy of unusual independence and competence. This is central to the appeal of adventure stories for children, which frequently depict their young protagonists surviving with little or no adult supervision or outwitting adult enemies. In Captain Frederick Marryat's *The Children of the New Forest* (1847), set during the English Civil War, four Cavalier children learn to survive in the New Forest after the death of their father and destruction of their home by Roundheads; the detailed descriptions of hunting and household arrangements allow readers to engage in a fantasy that they could become equally proficient in the same circumstances. Enid Blyton's popular 'Famous Five' series (1942–63) allows children to imagine themselves as more competent than adults: Julian, Dick, George, Anne and Timmy the dog invariably evince more intelligence and daring than either the police or the gangs of criminals whose plans they foil. The difficulty of engineering situations in which children can believably be given this kind of autonomy and independence is perhaps one reason for the blurring of the boundaries between adventure and other genres. Modern Western childhoods do not typically afford the opportunity for independence or the degree of risk which are integral to the adventure genre, but a fantasy setting can allow ordinary children to embark on a long sea voyage, as in C. S. Lewis's *The Voyage of the Dawn Treader* (1952), or to form part of a polar expedition, as in Philip Pullman's *Northern Lights* (1995). Historical fiction allows the same scope for independent adventure: stories such as Rosemary Sutcliff's *The Eagle of the Ninth* (1954), set in Roman Britain, and Geraldine McCaughrean's *Tamburlaine's Elephants* (2007), about a boy travelling with the armies of Tamburlaine the Great in fourteenth-century India, are able to portray child and adolescent characters as warriors, explorers and leaders in a believable historical context.

Adventure and Education

Many of the key elements of the adventure genre as it exists today were established by Daniel Defoe's *Robinson Crusoe*, which recounts the adventures of the eponymous Robinson first as a sailor, then as a castaway on a desert island. In the course of the story, Crusoe is captured by pirates and enslaved, shipwrecked, and drawn into battle with native cannibals, situations which require him to demonstrate bravery, physical prowess and self-sufficiency. Although originally intended for adults, the book was quickly adopted by children, and it has appeared in many abridgements and adaptations. In *Émile* (1762), his influential text on education, Jean-Jacques Rousseau cited *Robinson Crusoe* as the only book suitable for the young Émile: Crusoe's adventures exemplified the independence and experience-based learning which Rousseau advocated as an ideal method of child-rearing. Partly because of the influence of Rousseau,* *Robinson Crusoe* inspired a whole body of texts, usually termed 'Robinsonades': Captain Frederick Marryat's *Masterman Ready* (1841), Robert Ballantyne's *The Coral Island* (1858) and Johann Sebastian Wyss's *Swiss Family Robinson* (1812–13) all belong to this genre.

Rousseau's advocacy of *Robinson Crusoe* as part of the education of his fictional child reflects the didactic nature of the text. The appeal of the book to child readers undoubtedly derives from the adventure narrative, but there is a strong religious theme to the story, which is essentially a parable intended to demonstrate the importance of obedience, piety and individual endeavour. Crusoe defies his father's desire for him to work on the family business, instead setting out to sea, where a series of misadventures indicate divine displeasure at his lack of filial obedience. When he is cast away on a desert island, his misfortune helps to turn him towards piety and repentance and forces him to master the skills which will enable him to live independently in a natural setting. Once he has proved both his Christian virtue and his initiative and self-reliance, the narrative rewards him with rescue and a return to civilised society, where he is able to achieve worldly as well as spiritual success. The practical details of Crusoe's life on the island instruct the reader in natural history and survival skills, while the overall narrative provides a religious and moral education. A strong didactic element is similarly present in other adventure stories for children, particularly in the eighteenth and nineteenth centuries: Marryat's *The Children of the New Forest* provides readers with a history lesson about the Civil War, while Johann Sebastian Wyss's *Swiss Family Robinson* (discussed below) functions as a natural-history textbook. Adventure themes such as exploration, battle and feats of daring provide spice to such didactic texts while maintaining the illusion of realism: thus

---

* See Part Two: 'A Cultural Overview' for more on Rousseau and his influence on children's literature.

adventure stories partially reconcile the tension between utility and pleasure which has existed in the discourse about realism and fantasy in books for children (see Part Three: 'Alternative Worlds' and Part Three: 'Real Lives').

Shipwreck and Survival: Wyss

The influence of *Robinson Crusoe* is immediately evident in the title of Johann Wyss's novel *The Swiss Family Robinson*, first published in 1812–13 as *Der Schweizerische Robinson*, and translated into English in 1814 by the philosopher William Godwin.* Wyss, a Swiss pastor who composed the novel for the amusement and instruction of his sons, consciously took *Robinson Crusoe* as his model. The book tells the story of a family of Swiss émigrés, comprising a father, mother and four boys aged between six and fifteen (modelled on Wyss's own family), stranded on an unnamed peninsula after a storm wrecks their ship. The family frequently refer to Crusoe's adventures and compare their own situation with his: the father notes that they 'never failed to feel lively gratitude towards God who had rescued us all together, and not permitted one only of us to be cast a solitary being on the island'.[2] However, as Wyss noted in his preface to *The Swiss Family Robinson*, the book had 'in many respects a different object from that of the original work', and it substantially diverges from the model established by Defoe, most notably in the fact that it deals with an entire family rather than a single individual.[3] The book is also consciously directed at child readers: while the father narrates the story, most of the focus is on the four boys, and both the didactic and the entertaining elements of the book are clearly aimed at children. In adapting the elements of *Robinson Crusoe* for a novel specifically to appeal to young readers, Wyss arguably shaped the 'Robinsonade' in children's literature even more decisively than the original text.

---

* *The Swiss Family Robinson* has had a complex publication history, with major additions made to the text by translators and other authors, multiple translations, and abridgements. The edition discussed here is an 1816 English version: some later editions differed quite substantially.

The fact that Wyss's fictional family are marooned together brings an additional realism to the survival of the children, who benefit from the protection and advice of their parents; it also substantially shapes the character of the text, which emphasises the value of cooperation and community. The four boys are presented as having differing temperaments and skills: Fritz, the eldest, is 'full of intelligence and vivacity', ten-year-old Jack is 'light-hearted, enterprising, audacious [and] generous', twelve-year-old Ernest is 'of a rational reflecting temper, well informed, but somewhat disposed to indolence and the pleasures of the senses', while the character of the youngest son, Francis, is 'not yet pronounced' (p. 23). The boys' characters are modelled after those of Wyss's own children, but he 'strengthened or made more prominent whatever of excellence or of frailty he found in them', enabling him to highlight different virtues and flaws and to show how people of different temperaments can contribute to a community.[4] In one episode, Fritz and Jack climb some palm trees to obtain coconuts, while their brother Ernest remains on the ground. They tease him first for his laziness and then for climbing a palm with no coconuts, but it transpires that he has recognised the tree as a cabbage palm, which provides the family with another food source. Their father reproves them:

> if, instead of envying each other, you were to unite your
> various endowments, what happiness and what success
> might be the result? Ernest would think for you, you
> would execute for him; thus, all would share in the
> advantages which would result from this spirit of concord,
> so necessary among mankind, but particularly among brothers.
> (p. 315)

The emphasis is on tolerance and cooperation: although the boys frequently tease one another for their various character flaws and peculiarities, everyone's contribution is valued. This is particularly striking in Wyss's treatment of gender relations: although the composition of his own family prevented Wyss from including daughters in the family, he consciously attempted to redress the balance by emphasising the role of the mother, who is intended as 'a model of the power given to the female sex over the happiness of their families'.[5] She plays an important role in their survival on the island, both by utilising female skills such as cooking, sewing and taking care of the domestic animals – presented as equal in value to male skills such as hunting and carpentry – and by taking care of the family's spiritual well-being. When she reveals that her 'enchanted bag' – a bag of small, essential items which she has brought from the wreck – contains a Bible, the father exclaims:

> While, in the midst of confusion and horrors, you thought of so many little things conducive to our comfort, and which we as males disdained to be occupied about, have you then also taken care of the most essential of all, the health of our souls? (p. 166)

While modern readers might balk at Wyss's heavily defined gender roles, and his depiction of the mother as both active and important to the narrative, Wyss helped to create a place for girls in the adventure tradition. Following Wyss, there is a long tradition of family adventure stories in which both boys and girls play an important role: *The Children of the New Forest* follows Wyss in basing the adventure around the attempts of a family to survive in the wilderness and placing value on domestic as well as physical contributions; in *Swallows and Amazons* boys and girls are allowed to contribute equally (although they still fall roughly into traditional gender roles); and in C. S. Lewis's 'Narnia' books (1950–6) the contribution of all four Pevensie children is equally important. In more recent adventure stories, gender roles are less circumscribed and girls are able to play an even more active role in the narrative: Tamora Pierce's fantasy adventure series 'Song of the Lioness' (1983–8) centres around a female knight, and in Robert Muchamore's 'CHERUB' series girls and boys work on an equal basis as spies.

The spirit of community and collaboration which is present in the interactions of the family also informs their relationship with the island itself. Although they hunt and kill the animals they encounter, they also seek to domesticate them. Furthermore, both the parents emphasise that animals should be killed only when necessary, emphasising the value of living in harmony with their fellow creatures. When Fritz shoots at a bird which they discover making his courtship display, his father rebukes him:

> Why, said I, must we be always applying the means of
> death and annihilation to the creatures that fall in our way?
> Is not nature a thousand times more exhilarating in her
> animated movements, which express life and enjoyment,
> then in the selfish scheme of destruction you seem so fond of?
> (p. 286)

This is in sharp contrast to many other adventure narratives – both fictional and non-fictional – produced during the eighteenth and nineteenth centuries, which were often bloodstained and brutal. In fact, one of the most enjoyable aspects of the novel is the variety of things they encounter: the flora and fauna of the island include sharks, penguins, kangaroos, duck-billed platypuses, cotton plants, rubber trees and sago plants. The family's encounters with these fulfil Wyss's stated aim of instructing 'young readers in various sciences, particularly that of natural history':[6] the process of identifying each creature provides the reader with a fairly accurate natural-history lesson. Shortly after the family's arrival on the island, Ernest finds an animal they at first believe is a pig:

> After a long silence, he said with importance, I cannot be sure
> that this animal, as you all believe, is a sucking pig; his hair and
> his snout pretty much resemble, it is true, those of a pig: but
> pray observe his teeth; he has but four incisores [sic] in front
> similar to the genus Voracious animals: in general he has a
> greater resemblance to the rabbit than to the hare. I have seen

an engraving of him in our book of natural history; if I am not mistaken he is named the *agouti*. (p. 33)

The process of identifying the agouti demonstrates zoological methodology while providing readers with a description detailed enough to allow them to identify the animal for themselves. The descriptions are interesting in themselves, particularly for readers imagining their own chances of survival in a similar situation. The sheer variety of species on the island is also entertaining, particularly for a modern reader, who might entertain some doubts about the likelihood of finding kangaroos, agouti and monkeys all living wild on the same island (or indeed the same hemisphere).

The strategies used to teach natural history in the book are consciously based on the system of education proposed by Rousseau in *Émile*. Rousseau argued that children should be allowed to learn by practical experience, with a mentor to guide and develop their learning without directly instructing them.* Just such practical reasoning is exemplified in *The Swiss Family Robinson*, with the father playing the role of mentor: when Fritz discovers some sugar canes his father makes him use his 'reflection [and] imagination' (p. 56) to reason for himself the best way of extracting the sweet juice from the cane. The exchange is a fairly dry scientific exposition, but the detailed explanation is appealing because it offers readers the sense that they too could effectively suck sugar from a sugar cane if they were fortunate enough to find themselves in the same situation. Almost two centuries later, the same technique was still alive and well in adventure stories for children: in Gary Paulsen's *Hatchet*, about an urban American boy who is stranded in the wilderness after a plane crash, the main character independently reasons out the effect of light refraction in water in order to successfully spear fish to eat. By presenting the process of experimentation and reasoning as a key survival skill, writers of adventure stories aim to inspire readers with the desire to develop such skills themselves.

* This philosophy is also modelled in the books of Maria Edgeworth and Louisa May Alcott, discussed in Part Three: 'Real Lives'.

The adventure narratives of the eighteenth and nineteenth centuries were closely connected to imperial and colonial ideologies. *Robinson Crusoe* has a strong empire-building theme: Crusoe subjugates both the desert island on which he is stranded and (later) the local native people, creating his own kingdom over which he enjoys absolute rule. In nineteenth-century texts the imperial narrative was even more prominent: Joseph Bristowe argues that:

> the adventure story [...] would take the boy into areas of
> history and geography that placed him at the top of the racial
> ladder and at the helm of all the world.[7]

The Swiss Family Robinson is certainly a colonial text: the family are en route to establish themselves in a new colony when they are shipwrecked, and by the end of the book they have founded a colony of their own, complete with thriving farm and even a church. However, many of the more egregious aspects of imperial discourse are absent in Wyss's narrative: although they carve out a homeland for themselves on the island, the emphasis is on the wonders which God has provided for their survival rather than on the need to subjugate the wilderness. The emphasis on European racial superiority which Bristowe identifies as integral to nineteenth-century adventure stories is also absent: it is notable that, although the family never encounter any native people, the father frequently draws on his knowledge of survival skills among 'savages' and reveals a respect for their knowledge, noting 'A European without instruments must always find himself excelled in such attempts [as seeking to hand carve cutlery] by the superior adroitness and patience of savages' (p. 49).* In some respects, then, *The Swiss Family Robinson* resists the cultural superiority and imperialism which informs both earlier texts such as *Robinson Crusoe* and the adventure tradition which succeeded it.

---

* Later translations and retellings of the story added encounters with native peoples, which borrowed heavily from *Robinson Crusoe* and transmitted the same racist ideologies, but these are not features of Wyss's text or the 1816 edition.

Adventure and Empire

The adventure-story tradition of the nineteenth century was closely connected with Britain's imperial ambitions. Joseph Bristowe argues that the status of adventure narratives moved from popular to respectable as Britain sought ways of bringing working-class boys into line with imperial ideologies, providing an appealing way of teaching them the history, geography, and – most importantly – values required to enable them to serve the British Empire. Writers such as R. M. Ballantyne produced narratives which celebrated the resourcefulness, courage and worth of British boys in stories about expeditions to foreign lands. In Ballantyne's *The Coral Island*, a trio of boys triumphs over shipwreck, attack by pirates and encounters with 'savages', demonstrating the inherent superiority of the British character.* Towards the end of the nineteenth century, however, attitudes towards empire became more ambivalent, a fact which is reflected in many adventure narratives. R. L. Stevenson's *Treasure Island* (1883), one of the best-loved adventure stories of the period, contains many of the elements which had characterised the imperialistic and colonial narratives which had preceded it. The book tells the story of Jim Hawkins, who discovers a map showing the location of buried pirate treasure and sets out on a voyage to recover it. His voyage is disrupted when the crew of his ship mutiny, led by the one-legged Long John Silver – one of the most memorable villains of children's literature – and Jim and his fellows are forced into a battle on the island. Although they do triumph over the pirates and return home with the treasure, the book is more ambiguous then many of its predecessors: Jim's status as an emblem of British virtue and courage is problematised by his attraction to the pirates – he is fascinated by Long John Silver and several times temporarily allies himself with the pirates – and by the portrayal of the island not as a

---

* William Golding's *Lord of the Flies* (1957) is a savage parody of *The Coral Island*: Golding depicts the honour and civility of the British character as a thin veneer which falls away to reveal his stranded schoolboys as savages.

space which Jim has successfully mastered and colonised, but as an 'accursed island' which haunts his worst nightmares. These ambiguities throw the imperial narrative into question and give the book greater moral complexity; this is perhaps one reason for the book's enduring success. *Treasure Island* established many components which later recurred in children's adventure narratives such as *Swallows and Amazons*: the one-legged pirate, the pirate's parrot and the 'Black Spot' (given as a warning to the pirate Billy Bones) are all derived from Stevenson's book.

By the beginning of the twentieth century, the exploration and voyage genre of adventure fiction was beginning to wane. The decline of the British Empire and the coming of war diminished the appeal of the 'blood and thunder' narrative; the omission of Peter Pan's famous line 'To die will be an awfully great adventure' in performances of the play during the First World War is indicative of Britain's changing sensibilities. Nevertheless, the adventure genre as a whole was far from dead: the coming of war and the technological advances of the twentieth century simply altered the character of adventure narratives, producing books such as W. E. Johns's series about the airman 'Biggles' (1930–68), which brought the values of heroism and patriotism to a new context.

Imaginary and Real Adventures: Ransome

One of the influential and popular children's adventure stories of the early twentieth century is Arthur Ransome's 'Swallows and Amazons' series (1930–47). Ransome was the first recipient of the Carnegie Medal for children's literature, which was awarded to the sixth title in the series, *Pigeon Post* (1936), and the books have remained in print since their first publication. Unlike most of the adventure stories which had preceded them, the 'Swallows and Amazons' books dealt with the kind of adventures which ordinary middle-class children might really have. The books are for the most part set not in exotic locations, but in rural Britain, reflecting a growing national interest in the countryside which gave rise to a whole genre of 'camping and tramping' fiction. The adventures too are entirely plausible, albeit specific to the place, period and class of the children: the first book, *Swallows and Amazons* (1930), centres around a sailing and camping expedition undertaken by John, Susan, Titty and Roger Walker – the crew of the sailing boat *Swallow* – in the Lake District.

While Ransome brought a new realism to the children's adventure story, his books are firmly situated in the literary tradition of the genre. From the beginning of *Swallows and Amazons* the expedition is framed as 'a sailing voyage of discovery',[8] and while anticipating their adventure Titty thinks 'of the island itself, of coral, treasure and footprints in the sand' (p. 8), elements drawn from her reading of *The Coral Island*, *Treasure Island* and *Robinson Crusoe*.* The children model their adventures on the adventure stories they have read: they draw up Ship's Articles for their crew, refer to their corned beef as 'pemmican' (a form of preserved meat which was frequently used to provision expeditions), identify the adults who populate the local area as 'natives' and 'savages', and name the unfriendly owner of the houseboat on the lake Captain Flint (after the original owner of the treasure in *Treasure Island*). Many elements of *Swallows and Amazons* are borrowed from *Treasure Island*: the Swallows play the role of British explorers while their counterparts Nancy and Peggy Blackett – crew of the *Amazon* – are cast as pirates, and the two groups of children wage a mock war for the island. The book ends with their discovery of a 'real' treasure island, after Titty and Roger find 'Captain Flint's' stolen typewriter hidden on a rocky outcrop near their own island. *Winter Holiday* (1933) borrows from the tradition of adventure narratives about polar exploration: when a hard frost freezes the river, the Swallows and Amazons – along with a third set of children, Dick and Dorothea – mount a sledging expedition to the North Pole. By interweaving the children's 'real-life' adventures with intertextual references to older adventure

---

* Robinson Crusoe famously first discovers the presence of Man Friday on the island when he finds a single footprint in the sand of the beach.

stories, Ransome appeals to the reader's recognition of traditional tropes and brings an extra element of excitement to the stories without cutting them loose from the possible. The combination is particularly successful because the real exploits of the children are inherently adventurous in their own right; indeed, the imaginative portions of the stories sometimes provide a comforting framework to adventures which are potentially frightening, such as when Titty is left alone on the island at night (discussed in more detail in the extended commentary below).

The interweaving of real adventures and imagination in the 'Swallows and Amazons' books reflects the increasingly protected and circumscribed nature of children's lives in the twentieth century. Whereas eighteenth- and nineteenth-century portrayals of adolescent ships' boys and crew members reflected the possibilities open to teenage boys in real life, Ransome's adolescent character John Walker is still at school, anticipating a future career in the navy.* *Swallows and Amazons* opens with a letter from the children's father giving permission for their expedition and, as Fred Inglis notes, their adventures are 'bounded by the absolute justice of the parental writ'.[9] The independence the children enjoy in the books is therefore appealing in its own right: crewing a sailing boat without adult supervision or camping alone on an island are adventures in themselves. Ransome also dramatises the conflict between the children's desire for autonomy and the expectations of adults: in *The Picts and the Martyrs* (1943) Dick and Dorothea spend the summer camping secretly in a hut in the woods after an unexpected visit from the Amazons' Great Aunt Maria spoils plans for them to stay with the Amazons. By positioning adults as 'natives' in relation to the children's 'explorers', Ransome allows child readers to enjoy the fantasy of freedom from adult rules without ultimately overturning the power dynamic between adults and children.

---

* R. L. Stevenson set *Treasure Island* in the eighteenth century rather than in his own nineteenth, perhaps partly because the autonomy enjoyed by Jim Hawkins was already improbable by contemporary standards.

Like *The Swiss Family Robinson*, *Swallows and Amazons* deals with a group rather than the adventures of an individual; Matthew Grenby has suggested that the book is 'a fairly traditional family story'.[10] However, as the series progresses it might better be described as a 'gang' narrative: many of the stories are motivated by the need to work out interactions between different groups of children. In *Swallows and Amazons* the two sets of children must find a way of sharing 'their' island with one another, and the introduction of Dick and Dorothea in *Winter Holiday* requires the adventurous and athletic Swallows and Amazons to find a way to interact with the much more intellectually inclined 'Ds'. In *Coot Club* (1934), set in the Norfolk Broads, Dick and Dorothea are initially faced with hostility from the local children (the Coot Club), who first assume they are destructive interlopers like the rowdy 'Hullabaloos' whose inconsiderate tourism threatens an important nesting site. Peter Hunt has suggested that some themes in the books offer a response to the political situation at the time they were written: whereas earlier adventure narratives had emphasised physical courage and conquest in keeping with the aims of the empire, Ransome's promotion of harmony between different groups reflects a new desire for peace in the conflict-torn Europe of the early twentieth century. One aspect which is notably lacking from the books, however, is the issue of sexual conflict: John Rowe Townsend observes that Ransome's older characters 'maintain a sexless comradeship which does not quite accord with the facts of adolescence'.[11]

The debt of the 'Swallows and Amazons' series to its nineteenth-century predecessors in the adventure genre is evident; however, Ransome also crosses into other subgenres of adventure. *The Big Six* (1940), another of the stories featuring Dick and Dorothea and the Coot Club, is essentially a detective story: the story is driven by the need to exonerate the Coots of accusations of vandalism by discovering who is really responsible for unmooring boats in the Broads. The unravelling of the mystery and the laying of a carefully planned trap for the real culprits owe much to the popular tradition of detective stories for children which was emerging in the 1920s and

1930s with series such as the American 'Nancy Drew Mystery Stories' (1930–2003) and 'Hardy Boys Mystery Stories' (1927–2005). *Coot Club* contains elements of the fugitive story with the 'enemy' Hullaballoos pursuing the children across the Broads. The success of Ransome's series lies partly in his ability to traverse aspects of the genre in this fashion while mooring the interactions of the children and their actual adventures firmly in reality.

Detection and Flight

The detective elements of Ransome's novels link the books to a newer and highly successful adventure genre: detective fiction. The American 'Nancy Drew' and 'Hardy Boys' series found popularity in the UK as well as in their home country, while Ransome's near-contemporary Enid Blyton dominated the popular children's market in Britain with her young teams of detectives in the 'Famous Five' and 'Secret Seven' (1949–63). Like Ransome, Blyton wrote about ordinary middle-class children camping, sailing and rambling, but her adventure stories were somewhat more fantastical in nature. Villains were more dastardly – prepared to kidnap children and threaten them with death – but improbably lacking in resolve; the children are frequently able to save the day because their criminal opponents succumb to the temptation to brag about their plans. These adventure stories offer the fantasy of competence and daring; although they are improbable, the contemporary settings and very ordinary characters of the children allow readers the fantasy that they might find themselves in a similar situation – in which they would, of course, excel.

Adventure stories in historical settings also became an important part of the genre during the mid-twentieth century. Geoffrey Trease's *Bows against the Barons* (1934), a retelling of the Robin Hood story (another popular theme for adventure stories), brought a left-wing slant to the adventure narrative by depicting Robin Hood as a working-class hero fighting against the feudal system. Rosemary

Sutcliff's historical novels, such as *The Eagle of the Ninth* (1954), also included many adventure elements.

As writers in the 1950s and 1960s began to respond to the political circumstances they had lived through, war stories became an increasingly important part of the adventure genre. Such stories enabled writers to convey some of the danger and turmoil of the war years without straying too completely into a fully realistic portrayal of war. Ian Serraillier's *The Silver Sword* (1956), an account of a group of Polish children forced to escape from Warsaw after their parents are seized by the Nazis, uses many conventional adventure tropes: the details of how the children survive by forming their own community in the 'wilderness' of war-torn Warsaw certainly owes something to the survival tradition set in place by *Robinson Crusoe* and *The Swiss Family Robinson*, as does the final episode, in which the children are shipwrecked as they cross the lake from Germany to Switzerland. The degree to which the narrative conforms to the adventure genre offers the reader a comforting framework for events which are much more real and terrifying (the book was based on a true story). Anne Holm's *I Am David* (1963), in which a refugee boy's travels across Europe alone after escaping from a prison camp, and Beverley Naidoo's *The Other Side of Truth* (2000), about Nigerian political refugees, similarly use adventure to address hard-hitting political issues such as political oppression and displacement.

Spies, School and Sexuality: Muchamore

Since the beginning of the twenty-first century, the dominant adventure genre in children's literature has been the spy story. Beginning with *Stormbreaker* (2000), the first book in Anthony Horowitz's 'Alex Rider' series, children's publishing has seen a whole host of stories about child spies, including Charlie Higson's 'Young Bond' books, which provide a back story for Ian Fleming's famous fictional spy, and A. J. Butcher's 'Spy High' series (2003–5), which features a school for espionage in a futuristic sci-fi setting. Robert

Muchamore's 'CHERUB' series and its spin-off 'Henderson's Boys' (2009–10) are a notable example of this genre, combining traditional elements of the spy novel with a more realistic setting.* Like Horowitz's 'Alex Rider' stories, the books offer child readers the fantasy of entering into the exciting and dangerous world of international espionage; however, CHERUB breaks away from the pure wish fulfilment of the James Bond tradition to engage with real-life concerns, both personal and political.

The 'CHERUB' books follow the story of James Adams, introduced at the age of twelve in *The Recruit* (2004) as a member of CHERUB, a top-secret school for young spies run by the British government. Robert Muchamore addresses the problem of believably portraying children in potentially dangerous situations by making their youth an integral aspect of their mission. When James is invited to join the mission, he is told: 'Children can do things that adults cannot. [...] People are always less suspicious of youngsters.'[12] The members of CHERUB are despatched on missions that cannot be completed by adult agents: in *Mad Dogs* (2007) the members of CHERUB are asked to investigate drug-dealing gangs who habitually use teenagers to deliver drugs and messages, and in *Maximum Security* (2005) James and his friends help to break an inmate out of a juvenile prison. Muchamore thus explicitly utilises the idea of children as harmless and helpless, suggesting it is a cultural construct rather than a reality. The image of his child spies as smarter and tougher than their adult opponents has obvious appeal; the fact that they exist under cover as 'ordinary' children enables the reader to share in the fantasy that they too might be able to subvert the power relations between child and adult.

As in the 'Swallows and Amazons' series, Muchamore includes both boys and girls in his adventures. Although James is the main protagonist in the early books, part of his training involves accepting that the girls with whom he is working are not only equal, but in

---

* In *Secret Army*, the third book in the CHERUB spin-off series 'Henderson's Boys', Muchamore reveals that the acronym stands for 'Charles Henderson's Espionage Unit B'. See *Secret Army* (London: Hodder Children's Books, 2010), p. 354.

many cases superior to him. When he demands of his training partner Kerry, 'Who made you boss?', she retorts:

> I've been here at CHERUB since I was six [...] I did sixty-four days of this course last year before I broke my kneecap and got chucked off. You've been here what? Two weeks? (*The Recruit*, p. 141)

James's success in basic training and in his subsequent missions depends on his ability to work with a team regardless of their gender or age. As the series progresses, his sister Lauren also becomes increasingly important to the stories, further establishing the equality of the genders.*

Muchamore's characters are far more diverse than in earlier adventure stories: whereas Ransome's characters were uniformly white and middle class, diversity is presented as important to the success of CHERUB, which requires agents from different social and ethnic backgrounds in order to fit different missions. James is an ordinary child from a council estate: his overweight mother makes a living by coordinating a shop-lifting network, he attends an ordinary secondary school, and faces problems with bullies and his mother's violent ex-partner, who periodically visits in order to steal from the family. His background is instantly recognisable to contemporary child readers, and his subsequent adventures function as an appealing fantasy of empowerment. At the beginning of the book James is powerless to defend himself against the bullies who slash his school clothes and beat him up; by the end he is able to overpower an attacker and dunk his face in the beans served for school dinner. Readers from deprived social backgrounds are offered a particularly compelling fantasy: children's homes form an important venue for CHERUB recruitment because of the need to find children with

---

* It is important to note that the gender portrayals in Muchamore's books are not necessarily unproblematic: although he firmly establishes the equality of his female and male characters, he also enforces some troubling gender stereotypes.

few family ties (James's mother dies of a heart attack near the start of the story).

The wealth of detail offered in books like *The Swiss Family Robinson* and *Swallows and Amazons* (see the extended commentary below) sought to educate readers and offered them the fantasy of being able to cope in similar circumstances. The CHERUB stories are less didactic, but the realism of the stories extends to the training of the young spies as well as to their backgrounds. Whereas Anthony Horowitz's Alex Rider receives most of the training he needs to be an expert spy 'off-screen', Muchamore takes readers through James's training in detail, addressing his weaknesses as well as his strengths. When James needs to learn to swim before he is able to pass basic training, this involves weeks of lessons and a final test in which his fellow agents force him to swim the 50 metres required. Similarly, although James receives lessons in Russian, he finds it believably difficult: when he is given a copy of his mission briefing in Russian he is forced to guess his way through much of it, commenting 'If I'd known my life would depend on it I probably would have paid more attention in class' (p. 173). The relative realism of CHERUB agents' training reinforces the impression that it could be achieved by the child reader.

One of the most striking aspects of the CHERUB stories is the realism of the characters as well as the settings. James is a highly trained spy, but he is also a teenage boy, and throughout the series he builds friendships and relationships in a believable way. Unlike Ransome's characters, who never show any interest in sex or relationships, James has a series of girlfriends over the course of the books. In portraying James's interest in girls, Muchamore engages with some of the generic conventions of adventure stories for adults: James's romance with a girl on his first mission overtly recalls the James Bond stereotype of the spy as charming ladies' man. However, Muchamore questions and undermines this trope: the experience makes James feel he is 'way in over his head' (p. 263) and when he leaves he takes a photo of the tree where they shared their first kiss, revealing a degree of emotional attachment which does not fit well with the devil-may-care Bond image. In later books, James under-goes more typical teenage experiences, negotiating relationships with his fellow team members, cheating on his girlfriend, and struggling to decide which girl he is really in love with. Muchamore's adventure narrative is exciting, but also extremely accessible.

Throughout the 'CHERUB' series, there is a conflict between enjoyment of some of the more visceral aspects of the adventure genre as it appears in books such as Ian Fleming's Bond series and an awareness of the moral dimensions of these elements. The enjoyment of violence, the value of enduring pain – and the virtue of lovingly describing such episodes – and the morality of casual sex are all questioned at various points in the books. For example, James's ability to outwit the sadistic trainer Mr Large helps to establish him as a hero in the first book, but he questions the philosophy of using pain and humiliation to train agents. When he is responsible for inflicting punishment on younger agents in *Mad Dogs* (2007) he complains, 'I know why CHERUB does it, I know they have to, but I'm not cut out for it. Pushing little kids around is depressing' (p. 66). Muchamore is not always successful at negotiating the boundaries between questioning problematic tropes and simply reproducing them – when James loses his virginity to an older girl he meets on a mission, the book wavers between presenting it as a Bond-like encounter with a *femme fatale* and acknowledging the more problematic issue of James's lack of consent – but the reader is never allowed to take the adventure elements completely at face value.

Muchamore also questions larger social and political questions through his presentation of CHERUB agents' missions. In *The Recruit*, James is left wondering whether his role in preventing an anthrax attack on a petro-chemicals conference really makes him a hero:

> James totted everyone up: Fire, World and Bungle [the
> terrorists] were obviously bad guys for trying to kill everyone
> with anthrax. The oil company people were also bad for

trashing the environment and abusing people in poor countries. The police were bad guys: they had a tricky job to do, but they seemed to enjoy throwing their weight around more than they should. The only good guys were the Fort Harmony residents and they'd all got chucked out of their homes. (p. 308)

In later books the moral grey areas of the CHERUB missions are further explored through disagreements between CHERUB agents. In *Man vs Beast* (2006), James and his sister Lauren are sent to infiltrate an animal-rights group, but while the group's violent tactics are clearly condemned and James is happy to abandon the vegetarian diet he has observed during the mission, Lauren comes out of the mission in support of some of their beliefs, committing to remaining a vegetarian and swearing she will 'download all those leaflets about factory farming off the Internet, make photocopies and try persuading all my mates to go veggie as well'.[13] In other books, Muchamore addresses the death penalty, human trafficking and gang violence: by placing these topics within the fantastical premise of a teenage spy agency, he is able to expose some of their more shocking or frightening elements while maintaining the agency and safety of his young characters, who are not as powerless as their real-life counterparts.

The shift in the power dynamic between adults and children which takes place in Robert Muchamore's teenage-spy setting is a fundamental aspect of the adventure genre in children's literature. While the nature of the adventure can vary dramatically, it is the idea that the child protagonist can survive independently and prevail against older, stronger opponents which gives the genre both its identity and its appeal.

Extended Commentary: Ransome, *Swallows and Amazons* (1930)

Swallows and Amazons, the first book in Ransome's popular series, is a complex example of the adventure story for children, interweaving the nineteenth-century adventure tradition with a more realistic and child-focused narrative. The beginning of the book situates the story firmly within a literary tradition. The Walker children have named a local promontory 'Darien', the narrator tells us, because Titty (the younger of the two girls) 'had heard the sonnet read aloud at school, and forgotten everything in it except the picture of the explorers looking at the Pacific Ocean for the first time' (pp. 3–4). The sonnet in question is John Keats's 'On First Looking into Chapman's Homer', and it is notable that the poem is not about exploration, but about the experience of reading: Keats compares his first encounter with George Chapman's translation of Homer with that of 'stout Cortez when with eagle eyes / He stared at the Pacific'.* Thus Ransome immediately connects his text to two forms of adventure: real exploration, represented by the Spanish conquistador Cortez, and imaginative exploration. This combination remains an important theme throughout the book, as the children conduct their real adventures sailing on the lake and engage in a more elaborate set of imaginative adventures in which they are cast as explorers and pirates. Throughout the text, the children slip seamlessly between the two. When her brothers and sisters set off to wage war against the Amazons, leaving Titty alone on the island to operate the harbour lights, she moves through different imaginative roles as her circumstances change: '[t]he able-seaman watched them with the telescope until the brown sail disappeared behind the Peak of Darien. She then became Robinson Crusoe, and went down into the camp to

---

* John Keats, 'On First Looking into Chapman's Homer', ll. 11–12, in *John Keats: The Complete Poems*, ed. by John Barnard (London: Penguin, 1988), p. 72.

take command of her island' (p. 212). Crucially, the children are in control of their imaginative experiences. Titty's ability to imagine herself as a Crusoe figure ameliorates the loneliness of being left behind, but when real danger or alarm threatens then they are able to move beyond imagination. When the Walkers get their boat stuck among the water lilies in the dark, for example, the prosaic truth proves more reassuring than the fantasy:

> 'Perhaps they are octopuses,' said Roger. 'Titty read to me about how they put their arms out long, and grab people even out of a boat.'
>
> In Roger's voice there were clear signs of panic in the forecastle. Captain John took command at once.
>
> 'Rubbish, Roger,' he said. 'They aren't octopuses. They're only flowers.' (p. 251)

Later, when John Walker realises how dangerous their night-time sailing trip really is, imaginary adventures are abandoned altogether and the entire focus of the narrative is on John's attempts to sail in the dark. Ransome takes the children's imaginative play as seriously as the real events of the story, but makes it clear that they recognise and are ultimately in control of the boundaries between fantasy and reality. Ransome's respect for his child readers and characters is one of the most notable aspects of the series; as Peter Hunt notes, 'He treated his readers as peers, respecting their capacities.'[14]

The respect for children's capabilities which underpins *Swallows and Amazons* is announced in the opening chapter of the book, when the Walkers' father gives permission for their independent sailing trip with a telegram saying simply 'BETTER DROWNED THAN DUFFERS IF NOT DUFFERS, WON'T DROWN' (p. 2). The assumption that the children can be expected to use common sense and to negotiate demanding situations independently (even though Roger, the youngest, has only just learnt to swim) reflects a belief in learning by experience which owes much to the kind of education by experience advocated by Rousseau and exemplified in *The Swiss Family Robinson*. The startling amount of independence the Walkers are allowed – it is difficult to imagine any modern parents taking such a cavalier attitude towards the possibility of their pre-pubescent children drowning – also constitutes a compelling fantasy for the child reader. This 'fantasy of competence' is heightened by the detailed descriptions of practical activities such as sailing, pitching a tent, and lighting a campfire: Nicholas Tucker suggests that the exhaustive detail Ransome provides 'convey[s] a powerful image of self-reliance more meaningful to a child than to most adults', who no longer need to fantasise about the ability to complete small technical tasks.[15] Whereas *The Swiss Family Robinson* is overtly didactic in its detailed descriptions, however, Ransome's narratorial voice assumes a level of parity with the child reader. The detailed descriptions of boats and sailing are only half explained for the reader:

> Susan had got the sail ready. On the yard there was a strop (which is really a loop) that hooked on a hook on one side of an iron ring called the traveller, because it moved up and down the mast. The halyard ran from the traveller up to the top of the mast, through a sheave (which is a hole with a little wheel in it), and then down again. (p. 18)

Ransome's respect for his child readers is conveyed in his assumption that they will possess the knowledge and intelligence to comprehend such passages; the glosses on some of the more unfamiliar terms only serve to deepen the impression that Ransome expects his readers to comprehend the technical terms. The effect could be to exclude the uninformed reader, but by limiting them to a few passages Ransome shows that he values his readers' capabilities without overwhelming them.

Like *The Swiss Family Robinson*, *Swallows and Amazons* is not only an adventure story but also a family story. Each child has a distinctive and different character, illustrated at the beginning of the book by their different ideas about camping on the island:

> John was thinking of the sailing, wondering whether he really remembered all that he had learnt last year. Susan was thinking of the stores and the cooking. Titty was thinking of the island itself, of coral, reassure, and footprints in the sand. Roger was thinking of the fact that he was not to be left behind. He saw for the first time that it was a good thing no longer to be the baby of the family. (p. 8)

The characteristics established in this introductory section define the children's roles within the family and their particular characteristics. The theme of cooperation and collaboration are important aspects of the text: John's seamanship, Susan's practicality, Titty's imaginative approach and even Roger's determination 'no longer to be the baby of the family' all contribute to the success of their ventures. While their family dynamics are heavily gendered – particularly with respect to Susan's role as housekeeper and nurturer of the group – it is important to note that Ransome by no means relegates his female characters to an insignificant role in the story. On the contrary, it is Titty who ultimately enables them to win their 'battle' against the Amazons by stealing their boat after they capture the island. As their name suggests, the Amazons themselves provide a certain correction to the patriarchal dynamic established by the Swallows. On their first encounter, John accepts them as equals, recognising their skill as sailors: 'as John could not admit that there might be easier boats to steer than *Swallow*, he had to give all the credit for that straight line to the sailors of the Amazon' (p. 93). Thus the fantasy of competence provided by Ransome's adventure story is one available to both male and female readers.

The adventures experienced by the Swallows and Amazons would have been beyond the reach of many children at the time the books were written – they depend on a high level of affluence – and certainly seem remote from the circumscribed Western childhoods of today. Nevertheless, Ransome succeeds in creating believable and sympathetic child characters. The family interactions of the Walkers ring true, as in the passage above in which Roger rationalises his disgruntlement at being displaced as the 'baby' by his younger sister, and the everyday setting of the books brings the adventures within reach of the reader. Ransome's intertextual references root him firmly in a tradition of adventure narratives, but in basing his adventure story in an ordinary setting and peopling it with ordinary children, he established a new genre in children's literature.

Notes

1   Matthew Grenby, *Children's Literature* (Edinburgh: Edinburgh University Press, 2008), p. 172.
2   Johann Wyss, *The Swiss Family Robinson* (London: Penguin, 2007), p. 382.
3   Johann Wyss, 'Preface' to *The Swiss Family Robinson*, pp. 1–5, p. 5.
4   Wyss, 'Preface', p. 2.
5   Wyss, 'Preface', p. 3.
6   Wyss, 'Preface', p. 5.
7   Joseph Bristowe, 'Empire Boys', in Janet Maybin and Nicola J. Watson (eds), *Children's Literature: Approaches and Territories* (Basingstoke: Palgrave Macmillan/Open University, 2009), pp. 130–42, p. 137.
8   Arthur Ransome, *Swallows and Amazons* (London: Red Fox, 1993), p. 7.
9   Fred Inglis, *The Promise of Happiness: Value and meaning in Children's Fiction* (Cambridge: Cambridge University Press, 1981), p. 66.
10 Grenby, *Children's Literature*, p. 172.
11 John Rowe Townsend, *Written for Children: An Outline of English-Language Children's Literature*, 2nd edn (Harmondsworth: Kestrel, 1983), p. 186.
12 Robert Muchamore, *The Recruit* (London: Hodder Children's Books, 2004), p. 67.
13 Robert Muchamore, *Man vs Beast* (London: Hodder Children's Books, 2006), p. 281.
14 Peter Hunt, *Children's Literature* (Oxford: Blackwell Publishing, 2001), p. 116.

15	Nicholas Tucker, 'Arthur Ransome and Problems of Literary Assessment', in Heather Montgomery and Nicola J. Watson (eds), *Children's Literature: Classic Texts and Contemporary Trends* (Basingstoke: Palgrave Macmillan/Open University, 2009), pp. 188–92, p. 188.

Rhymes and Rhythms: Stevenson, Seuss and Zephaniah

Poetry is one of the literary forms most immediately associated with childhood: we share lullabies, nursery rhymes and counting games with children from their earliest years, and many books for small children are in rhyme form. Poetry also played an important role in early children's literature, which included many verse works, notably publisher John Newbery's *A Little Pretty Pocket-Book* (1744), often identified as the first text written especially for children's amusement. There are many contemporary poets writing for children today – Michael Rosen, Grace Nichols, Benjamin Zephaniah and Jackie Kay all write solely or predominantly for children – and verse forms have also found their way into novels for children such as Malorie Blackman's *Cloud Busting* (2004) and Sharon Creech's *Love That Dog* (2001). Despite the enduring importance of poetry in children's literature, however, it has received relatively little critical attention, and contemporary children's poets typically receive less popular attention than their prose counterparts. While anthologies of children's verse continue to be produced on a regular basis – Puffin Books has several in print, including a new collection, *Michael Rosen's A–Z* (2009) – single-author works of poetry are less common, and a small handful of names dominate the market.

Whereas the majority of 'children's literature' is created by adults for children, there is a sizeable tradition of poetry created by children for other children. Adults teach their children nursery rhymes and counting songs, and these often appear in published editions, but children themselves retain a particularly strong oral tradition. Skipping rhymes, 'counting-out' rhymes such as 'Eeny, meeny, miney, mo', clapping games, and humorous rhymes and riddles are all forms of poetry invented by and circulated among children themselves. The folklorists Iona and Peter Opie collected many examples of this type of children's poetry during the second half of the twentieth century, noting that variations of the same rhymes could be found across the whole British Isles, and that in some cases poems remained in circulation for over a century.[1] These texts reveal much about children's culture and interests; for example, the Opies note the speed with which topical events can make it into playground rhymes, citing a rhyme about the abdication of King Edward VIII which took less than a month to gain currency among children.[2] Conversely, rhymes can remain current long after the events they refer to have receded into history: the Opies recorded a rhyme referring to the Munich Pact fourteen years after its first appearance, and rhymes featuring Hitler and Mussolini were still circulating during my own childhood in the 1980s.[3] The persistence of rhymes across generations suggests the importance of this vernacular poetry in children's day-to-day lives. While there is a common perception that these traditions are dying out among today's children, there is little evidence to support this: a recent study of children's musical games across the world by Kathryn Marsh indicates that there is a living body of games involving rhyme, rhythm and movement 'owned, spontaneously performed and orally transmitted by children'.[4]

Children's vernacular poetry typically has strong rhyme and rhythm, characteristics which are a necessary component of oral transmission. Nonsense words and phrases too are a frequent characteristic of children's verse, as in 'Eeny, meeny, miney, mo', illustrating the pleasure children find in word and sound play. Children's rhymes are often frequently scurrilous or subversive, with a strong focus on bodily functions, as in this version of 'Mary had a little lamb' collected by the Opies:

Mary had a little lamb,
She fed it castor oil,
And everywhere the lamb would go,
It fertilised the soil.[5]

This rather elegant reference to defecation is one of the more refined instances of a common preoccupation in children's rhymes! Other versions of 'Mary had a little lamb' show children's preoccupation with other taboo subjects such as death – Mary is sometimes portrayed enjoying her lamb 'between two slices of bread' – and sex (the rhymes shared among children are startlingly explicit). Parodies of traditional nursery rhymes, popular songs and hymns reverse the power dynamic entailed in the creation of literature for children by adults: by creating new and often subversive versions, children assert their own power and agency.

In addition to the poetry created and circulated by children, there is a strong tradition of poetry written for children by adults. Until the eighteenth century, children would primarily have shared in literature created for adults, much of which was in verse form: John Bunyan's epic religious allegory *The Pilgrim's Progress* (1678) is one title which was enjoyed by both children and adults, remaining in circulation for several centuries after its first appearance: in Louisa May Alcott's *Little Women* (1868), the four March girls receive the book as their Christmas gift. Verse has often been used to make instructional texts more memorable and enjoyable for child readers: Francis Seagar's poem 'The Schoole of Vertue', discussed in Part Three: 'Real Lives', is one such example, while the 1824 illustrated book *Punctuation Personified*, by 'Mr Stops', uses poetry to remind children that 'The paragraph, which here you view / Always announces something new', along with other rules of English punctuation.[6] The eighteenth and nineteenth centuries saw a growing tradition of poetry designed to give children pleasure. Morag Styles notes that there was an especially strong tradition of poetry written by women, many of whom have been undeservedly forgotten: one notable example is 'Twinkle, twinkle, little star', written by Jane Taylor in 1806, but by the next century already being reproduced without attribution and accepted as a 'traditional' nursery rhyme. Styles suggests that 'Twinkle, twinkle' was a 'landmark in poetry for children',[7] both because of its flawless verse and because of its child-centred perspective. The attempt to represent the child's voice and perspective was even more evident in Robert Louis Stevenson's influential collection *A Child's Garden of Verses*, which had a significant and enduring impact on poetry for children.

While there is a strong tradition of poetry written especially for children, the boundaries between adult and children's literature are particularly thin with respect to verse. Poems originally written for adults have become staple features of poetry anthologies for children, which often include excerpts from Shakespeare, notably Ariel's song from *The Tempest* and the witches' speech from *Macbeth*, Long-fellow's *Hiawatha*, and Alfred Noyes's *The Highwayman*, among many other poems primarily intended for an adult audience. Morag Styles suggests that the canon which has been built up by anthologies seeking to offer 'the best' in verse for children tends to marginalise material written expressly for young readers:

> [The anthologists] believe in a canon of great or 'genuine' poetry which children must read, sooner or later. They believe that what is written with children in mind is inferior to what is written by 'great' poets for adults. They want to please young readers, but that does not necessitate being interested in what they actually choose to read.[8]

The relative accessibility of poetry – as compared to, for example, novels aimed at an adult audience – perhaps makes this approach particularly tempting, positioning poetry as a transition point between juvenile and adult literature. As Styles points out, however, the assumption that poetry written specifically for children should 'talk down or be dull and fey' is a faulty one: Robert Louis Stevenson, Dr Seuss and Benjamin Zephaniah have all produced high-quality poetry which successfully speaks to children as equals.

The work of modern poets who have written for both children and adults illustrates that a change in audience does not entail a lowering of quality: the poetry for children produced by Ted Hughes and Jackie Kay is as complex and serious as their work for adults. At the same time, however, discussions of children's poetry which focus on the texts produced by 'poets' who define themselves as such and publish collections of verse which resemble those produced for adults (usually including more than one poem, with no or minimal illustrations) serve to obscure the wider picture of children's poetry as it is consumed by contemporary children. If we focus on poets such as Jackie Kay, it is easy to conclude that children's poetry in the twenty-first century is largely a minority interest and that relatively few children seek it out beyond the context of school.* If we take a wider view of the genre, however, it is evident that children enjoy not only as much poetry as adults, but arguably more. Many books for small children are written in verse form: popular titles such as Julia Donaldson and Axel Scheffer's *The Gruffalo* (1999) – winner of the Nestlé Award in 1999 and voted the nation's favourite children's book in 2010[9] – Lyney Dodd's 'Hairy Maclary' series (1983–2009) and the books of Dr Seuss are more commonly classed as picture books but owe much of their effect to the use of verse as well as illustrations. Allan Ahlberg has written some of the most popular and successful children's verse in *Please Mrs Butler* (1983) and *Heard It in the Playground* (1991), but his picture-book collaborations with Janet Ahlberg, such as *Cops and Robbers* (1978) and *Each, Peach, Pear, Plum* (1989), are even more widely known and successful.†

---

* It is difficult to ascertain how far this is true even for poets such as Kay or Hughes – particularly since their work is accessible to children both online and via many libraries. However, based on sales of their works we can certainly argue that they do not enjoy the kind of widespread popularity of many of their prose counterparts.

† Janet Ahlberg also illustrated Allan's two poetry collections, but *Please Mrs Butler* and *Heard It in the Playground* are firmly poetry with illustrations, whereas in their collaborative works pictures and text are both integral parts of the work.

Entering the Child's World: Stevenson

Robert Louis Stevenson's *A Child's Garden of Verses* (1885) is one of the most well-known and long-lasting collections of children's poetry; Morag Styles describes it as a 'pivotal collection which changed for ever the way children could be written about in poetry'.[10] While earlier poets had included the playful and the fantastic in poetry for children, Stevenson's work is notable for the degree to which he succeeds in writing from the point of view of the child. Like his near-contemporary Lewis Carroll, Stevenson effectively conveys the way the rules of the adult world perplex children, as in 'Bed in Summer', in which the youthful narrator complains:

> In winter I get up at night
> And dress by yellow candle-light.
> In summer, quite the other way,
> I have to go to bed by day.[11]

Stevenson's take on the adult world as perceived by children is less threatening than Lewis Carroll's, but equally incomprehensible.

The title of Stevenson's collection, *A Child's Garden of Verses*, epitomises a central aspect of the image of childhood he offers in the collection, which focuses around 'Happy play in grassy places'. The Romantic image of the child as essentially innocent and imaginative, and of childhood as an Edenic state closely connected to nature and beauty, is at the heart of Stevenson's created childhood. Many of the poems focus upon imaginative play, as in 'Historical Associations', which casts an ordinary garden as a scene of magic and adventure:

> Dear Uncle Jim, this garden ground
> That now you smoke your pipe around
> Has seen immortal actions done
> And valiant battles lost and won.

[…] Here is the sea, here is the sand,
Here is simple Shepherd's Land.
Here are the fairy hollyhocks,
And there are Ali Baba's rocks. (pp. 89–91, ll. 1–4, 9–12)

Stevenson's depiction of childhood games emphasises the child's ability to view the ordinary world through the lens of fantasy, so that the child both recognises the reality of the mundane 'garden ground' and asserts the primacy of the 'valiant battles' of fantasy. This blending of fantasy and reality functions as an important rebuttal to the criticisms levelled at fantasy in children's literature by some of Stephenson's contemporaries and predecessors: whereas figures such as Sarah Trimmer (discussed in Part Three: 'Alternative Worlds') had been concerned to ensure that children did not confuse the fantastical with reality, Stevenson portrays the child as fully in control of the boundary between imaginative play and the everyday. Thus in 'The Land of Story-Books' the ordinary setting of a family sitting room at evening and the impression of mysterious forest expanses are equally vividly conveyed as the child ventures away from the domestic scene 'Around the fire where [her] parents sit' to 'follow round the forest track / Away behind the sofa back' (p. 67, l. 2, ll. 7–8; an image which recurs in Maurice Sendak's *Where the Wild Things Are*, discussed in Part Three: 'Picture Books').

Although the image of childhood presented in *A Child's Garden of Verses* is idyllic, Robert Louis Stevenson described his own as 'full of fever, nightmare, insomnia, painful days, and interminable nights', noting that he could 'speak with less authority of gardens than of that other land of counterpanes'.[12] His poem 'The Land of Counterpane' directly portrays the way imagination brings life to this 'land of counterpane' in the mind of a sick child, who envisages himself as 'the giant great and still, / That sits upon the pillow hill' (p. 17, ll. 13–14). Imagination is central to the poems of the collection, many of which reference other texts. 'Historical Associations' invokes Ali Baba, while in 'The Land of Story-Books' the child chooses to 'play at books that I have read' (l. 11). As in Arthur Ransome's *Swallows and Amazons*, discussed in Part Three: 'Adventure Stories', the distinctive and special character of childhood is partly constructed out of the books children read. The idyllic and imaginative childhood which Stevenson presents us with is also very consciously an imagined childhood, a fact made explicit in the final poem of the collection, 'To Any Reader', in which Stevenson invites the reader to look 'Through the windows of this book' (p. 104, l. 4) at 'Another child, far, far away' (l. 5), a child who is inaccessible because 'He has grown up and gone away' (l. 14). In other words, the image of childhood as it is presented to us in Stevenson's poetry is overtly and self-consciously a nostalgic look back at a childhood not as it was – since Stevenson's own childhood was dominated by illness – but as it might have been.

While *A Child's Garden of Verses* is dominated by the idyllic image of the child in the garden, it is not divorced from the tradition of moral and instructive literature. 'Good and Bad Children' offers its child readers a moral message about the importance of good behaviour; the assertion that 'If you would grow great and stately, / You must try to walk sedately' (pp. 30–2, ll. 3–4) owes something to earlier moral homilies for children. However, this poem retains the child's-eye view which makes Stevenson's verse appealing: 'Happy play in grassy places' (l. 10) is the key to growing 'to kings and sages' (l. 12), while the closing verse switches the focus from children to adults:

> Cruel children, crying babies,
> All grow up as geese and gabies,
> Hated, as their age increases,
> By their nephews and their nieces. (ll. 17–20)

This closing warning subverts conventional messages about the importance of good behaviour by placing the focus on children's dislike of unpleasant adults, privileging the child's perspective on the world over adult desires for them to behave well. Similarly, in 'Whole Duty of Children', the final line subverts the moral message:

A child should always say what's true,
And speak when he is spoken to,
And behave mannerly at table:
At least as far as he is able. (p. 5, ll. 1–4)

While the first three lines convey a fairly standard lesson on good behaviour, the final line implies that this behaviour is ultimately conditional on the child's own ability to conform, laying open the possibility that he might not be well-behaved all the time – or even at all. Although the image of the imaginative child presented elsewhere in the poems may be considered idealistic, poems like this one present the reader with a more ambiguous image of childhood: one which allows for mischief and bad behaviour as well as innocence and imagination.

Stevenson's work had a significant and long-lasting effect on children's poetry in English. His influence is evident in the work of A. A. Milne, whose collections *When We Were Very Young* (1924) and *Now We Are Six* (1927) similarly utilise poetry to represent the child's voice and point of view (although Milne arguably slips into a more cloying and sentimental presentation of the child than Stevenson). The imaginative elements of Stevenson's work are even more present in the poetry of Walter de la Mare, one of the most successful children's poets of the early twentieth century with poems such as 'The Listeners' and 'The Song of the Mad Prince'. De la Mare's work is more unambiguously part of the fantasy tradition and shows the influence of poets for adults such as Tennyson, but his serious treatment of the imaginative world in his poetry for children owes a debt to Stevenson. More broadly, the influential nature of Stevenson's poetry helped to legitimise a tradition of children's poetry which was serious without being primarily focused on moral and religious messages.

Nonsense Verse

Stevenson's serious treatment of poetry for children and his attempt to 'enter the child's world' had a lasting effect on poetry for children. A strikingly different but equally influential tradition was set in place by Stevenson's near-contemporary Edward Lear, whose *Book of Nonsense* (1846) and later works remain among the best-known nonsense poetry for children. Whereas Stevenson portrays a largely idyllic image of childhood, Lear's poems portray a carnivalesque world in which both children and adults are unpredictable, rude and often violent:

> There was an Old Man with a gong,
> Who bumped at it all the day long;
> But they called out, 'Oh, law! you're a horrid old bore!'
> So they smashed that Old Man with a gong.[13]

The appeal of Lear's poetry lies not in its accurate reflection of the child's experience, but in its unexpectedness and inversion of reality. In 'The Table and the Chair', Lear begins with a riddle-like premise – that chairs and tables have four legs but cannot walk – and uses it to spin out a fantasy story in which items of furniture do 'come out to take the air'.[14] Similarly, in 'The Owl and the Pussycat', part of the appeal of the poem lies in the child's ability to recognise and find amusement in the unlikelihood of an amorous liaison between a bird and a cat. Lear's poetry revels in linguistic inventiveness, a characteristic also evident in the work of Lewis Carroll, whose use of invented words in poems such as 'The Hunting of the Snark' (1876) – with its portentous closing line 'For the Snark *was* a Boojum, you see' – illustrates the way in which disciplined rhyme and rhythm lend coherence and meaning to nonsense sounds. Linguistic play is a key feature of nonsense poetry, which has retained a strong presence in children's literature in the work of writers such as Spike Milligan and Shel Silverstein. Milligan's poem 'On the Ning Nang

Nong' rests almost entirely on the pleasure of language, with a series of satisfying nonsense sounds.[15] Milligan's technique strongly recalls the kind of nonsense verse produced by children themselves in playground games and counting-out rhymes, in which the pleasure of sound is often a major component and the repetition and transmission of rhymes often gradually erodes the original meaning of the words, if it existed in the first place.

Doc in Socks: Dr Seuss

Both linguistic play and the inversion of ordinary relationships and situations are important elements of the verse of Theodore Seuss Geisel, better known as Dr Seuss. Seuss's distinctive illustrations, which form an integral part of his stories, mean that he is often considered in the context of picture books, but he is an inventive and well-loved poet whose verses have become a part of American popular culture. The appreciation of words and sounds has a consciously pedagogic role in Seuss's work, much of which was produced for publisher William Spaulding's series of books for beginner readers, based on the phonic system of reading.* Spaulding had provided Seuss with a list of 300 words deemed readable by a child in the first year of formal school, challenging him to 'Write me a story that first-graders can't put down!'[16] The resulting book was *The Cat in the Hat* (1957) – discussed in the extended commentary below – which became the first in a series of 'Beginner Books' by Seuss. Although the books are consciously designed with theories of reading in mind, they have been successful because of their genuine enjoyment of language and deftness of touch. In *Dr. Seuss's ABC*

---

* Phonics is a system of teaching reading in which children are taught to recognise the relationship between letters or groups of letters and sounds, and to blend different sounds in order to form a word. Thus a child reading the word 'cat' would be encouraged to sound out the letters individually and blend them together to say 'cat'. Poetry is a particularly effective means of highlighting where different collections of letters have the same sound, as in the title of Seuss's *Fox in Socks*.

(1961), for example, Seuss adds a subtle twist to the standard alphabet format.[17] His use of rhyme and the repetition of the 'o' sound together with the regular metre of the poem create a pleasing rhythmic effect while conveying the essential information about the look and sound of the letter 'o'. At the same time, the verse is amusing because of its nonsensical central image, heightened by the solemn assertion that it is realistic and useful – in reality, of course, children do not usually use the letter 'o' to talk about an activity as strange as oiling orange owls! The incongruity of this image is a subtle comment on more conventional early readers (particularly those available in 1961 when the book was written), which typically provide ostensibly more realistic examples which in practice are almost equally far removed from the everyday lives of their child readers. Thus there is a subversive element to Seuss's verse.

The linguistic play characteristic of much nonsense verse is particularly evident in another of Seuss's books, *Fox in Socks* (1965), in which the eponymous fox contrives ever more elaborate tongue-twisters for his friend Mr Knox to say, beginning with the simple 'Fox, Socks, Box, Knox' and progressing towards increasingly challenging constructions as Knox protests about the difficulty of repeating them. Finally Knox snaps, turning the tongue-twisters back on the fox.[18] The images depict Knox shoving the fox into a tweetle-beetles' bottle, while fox, beetles and poodle all look on in shocked surprise. The verse is enjoyable for the child to read, while the increasing complexity of the tongue-twisters and Knox's increasing frustration also make it particularly entertaining when it is read out loud by an adult. Part of the subversive appeal of the book is the potential for it to confuse or challenge an adult reader.

Many of Seuss's books destabilise the usual norms or challenge the reader to think about broader issues. *The Cat in the Hat* subverts the usual balance of power and responsibility between children and adults. Some of Seuss's work has a more overtly political message, as in one of his most famous titles, *How the Grinch Stole Christmas* (1957), in which the lonely Grinch, envious of the happy inhabitants of Whoville, hatches a plan to 'steal' Christmas by stealing all their presents. But Whoville celebrates Christmas anyway, forcing the Grinch to a revelation that Christmas doesn't in fact come from a shop, and has a deeper meaning.[19] The anti-consumerist message is overt, but the liveliness of Seuss's rhymes and illustrations makes it appealing. Perhaps ironically, the story has become a staple part of a typical North American Christmas: it has been adapted into a television animation and a live-action film and is regularly aired over the Christmas period in the United States.

Seuss's short poem 'The Sneeches' (1961) takes on both consumerism and racism as it catalogues the difference between the 'Star-Belly Sneeches' and the 'Plain-Bellied Sneeches'.[20] The use of the colloquial words to serve the rhyme scheme makes it clear that the Sneeches are faintly ridiculous, so the revelation that star-bellied Sneeches consider themselves superior to their plain-bellied cousins (who are, the illustrations reveal, otherwise identical) is cast in a nonsensical light. A 'Fix-it-Up Chappie' arrives with a solution to the plain-bellied Sneeches' problem – a machine that will print stars on their bellies – and then takes advantage of the 'Star-Belly Sneeches' dismay at losing their special status by offering another machine to remove stars. Seuss's characteristic tongue-twisting rhyme provides an effective medium for illustrating the ridiculous chaos which ensues, as all the Sneeches hurry to change their stars depending on the fashion (p. 21). The fact that this passage is in verse makes it particularly effective. The use of anapaestic tetrameter gives it its regular 'da-da-DUM' rhythm which carries the lines forward quickly, while the slightly unorthodox syntax helps to convey the impression of confusion and chaos. This is heightened in the final lines with the repetition of 'this one' and 'that one', leaving the reader as confused as the Sneeches. The poem is effective at conveying both the ridiculous nature of the Sneeches' attempt to privilege one group over another, and the futility of attempting to fix social problems with consumerism.

The popularity of Dr Seuss illustrates that poetry for children continues to be widely distributed and enjoyed. The clear ideological and pedagogical intent of much of Seuss's work demonstrates that nonsense poetry is not necessarily solely focused on pleasure, but his linguistic playfulness makes these elements both more appealing and more effective.

The Language of the Street: Urchin Verse

One reason that Doctor Seuss's poetry is so effective and accessible is that he uses everyday language and slang rather than a specific poetic diction. The second half of the twentieth century saw children's poets increasingly focus on more 'authentic' representations of childhood and the child's voice. From the 1970s onwards, an increasing number of writers rejected the idyllic image of childhood set in place by Robert Louis Stevenson in favour of poetry which dealt with the everyday lives of modern children. 'If you don't put your shoes on before I count fifteen', by Michael Rosen – often credited with the invention of the genre John Rowe Townsend termed 'urchin verse' – is a typical example:

> If you don't put your shoes on before I count fifteen then we
> won't go to the woods to climb the chestnut
> one
> But I can't find them
> Two
>   I can't
> They're under the sofa three
>   No
>   O yes
> Four five six
>   Stop they've got knots they've got knots.[21]

Rather than formal metre or poetic structure, the poem uses free verse and idiosyncratic punctuation in order to mimic the normal pattern of speech between parent and child. The poem itself deals with a completely ordinary scene, and the child portrayed is believably disorganised, with her shoes discarded under the sofa with the laces still knotted. The image of childhood the poem conveys is still essentially a cosy and safe one – the parent's hints about where the shoes are and willingness to help his child convey love and security – but the child herself is not particularly idealised.

Allan Ahlberg, in his well-known collection *Please Mrs Butler* and the later *Heard It in the Playground* similarly focuses on everyday events and mundane moments. The title poem 'Please Mrs Butler' reproduces the back-and-forth of a typical conversation between child and teacher, as the child repeatedly whines 'Please Mrs Butler, / This boy Derek Drew / Keeps ...' (a range of complaints follows).[22] 'Dog in the Playground' uses free verse to convey a classroom full of children shouting at the unexpected diversion of a dog in the school playground. While some critics have raised concerns about the generally light, humorous and informal nature of urchin verse, suggesting that it fails to prepare children for more formal and 'serious' poetry, Matthew Grenby contends that the best examples are 'colloquial, quotidian and accessible, but [...] also thought-provoking, multi-layered, sensitive and artistic'.[23] Certainly contemporary poets have produced some challenging and thought-provoking material in this genre: while the use of colloquial language and loose verse forms may give the impression of frivolity, these poems often demand much from the reader.

The shift towards more everyday language in children's poetry during the second half of the twentieth century was accompanied by a drive to represent a more diverse range of voices. As poets sought to represent the language and rhythms of real speech through the use of devices such as free verse, non-standard spelling, and the use of the vernacular, more writers began to write in dialects of English. In particular, poets from communities originating from former Commonwealth countries increasingly sought to represent their native dialects of English in verse. In the 1970s, Afro-Guyanese poet John Agard and Guyanese poet Grace Nichols blazed the way in producing poetry which conveyed some of the language and rhythms of Creole. Contemporary poet Jackie Kay often uses her native Scottish dialect in her verse, much of which explores issues of race and identity. The increasing use of non-standard forms of English and non-native traditions of verse enriches the linguistic base of children's poetry and also reflects more of the myriad ways in which contemporary children express themselves.

The work of Jackie Kay is indicative of the seriousness which many contemporary children's poets bring to their work, which frequently explores complex and challenging issues. Kay's work draws heavily on her own childhood experiences as a black Briton growing up in a predominantly white Scottish community as the adoptive child of white parents, raising issues of identity which are both complex and occasionally challenging. Her collection *Red, Cherry Red* (2007) includes a number of poems which address the experiences of the elderly, as in 'The Rowans':

> She dresses slowly – purple cardigan
> for a bitter day – then, suddenly,
> spots the red robin on the rowan tree,
>
> all puffed out with its gloriously red chest.
> She watches the bird, avid.
> She loves the robin more than her husband.[24]

It is certainly possible to question whether there is anything in this poem which makes it particularly suitable for children, but its legitimacy as children's poetry has been recognised by the Centre for Literacy in Primary Education, who awarded the book the CLPE Award for Children's Poetry in 2008. Children's poetry can, by implication, have the same wide scope in terms of language and content as that produced for adults.

Talking Turkeys: Zephaniah

One of the most successful poets writing for children in Britain today is Benjamin Zephaniah, who is notable both for his contributions to 'urchin verse' and for his use of his British Jamaican English in his poetry. Zephaniah has built a successful career as a performance poet, and the strength of his voice comes through in his written verse:

> Dere's an Opera
> In me bladder
> A Ballad's
> In me wrist
> Dere is laughter
> In me shoulder
> In me guzzard's
> A nice twist.[25]

Zephaniah's references to traditional Western art forms such as opera in this poem reflect the consciously political element of his use of British Jamaican in his verse. By focusing the poem around parts of his body, he asserts his claim to this artistic tradition while defending the legitimacy of his more personal and spontaneous art form, an act which combines his British and his Jamaican heritage. Issues of race, identity and nationality are a recurring theme in Zephaniah's work: his collection *Wicked World* (2000) explores empire, conquest and cultural diversity, while *Too Black, Too Strong* (2001) – written for adults – addresses the issue of race in British society. While Zephaniah has not hesitated to speak about the more troubling aspects of racism and imperialism – he refused the OBE in 2003 because he felt it symbolised 'how my foremothers were raped and my forefathers brutalised'[26] – his poetry for children largely emphasises the values of tolerance and diversity. In 'The British' he provides a 'recipe' which highlights Britain's history of immigration, beginning with Picts, Celts and Silures who are overrun by Roman conquerors, replaced in their turn by successive waves of immigrants. For a successful outcome, the recipe advises:

Leave the ingredients to simmer.

As they mix and blend allow their languages to flourish
Binding them together with English.

Allow time to be cool.

Add some unity, understanding and respect for the future.[27]

This is far from a subtle poem, but it articulates directly what Zephaniah applies elsewhere in his work by reflecting his own dual heritage.

Benjamin Zephaniah not only employs the language of his own British Jamaican heritage, he also reflects the artistic and colloquial expression of urban Britain. His performance poetry is closely allied to music such as reggae and rap, a connection he makes explicit in poems such as 'Rap Connected'.[28] For many contemporary children and young adults, musical traditions such as rap are their most immediate and personal experience of poetry. Zephaniah's use of rap in his poetry brings together the folk tradition and the literary one, asserting the relevance of both in the same way as his use of British Jamaican asserts the legitimacy of his dual linguistic heritage.

The use of British Jamaican and rap in Benjamin Zephaniah's poetry lends itself to linguistic play and oral delivery, but many of his poems are highly textual in nature. Zephaniah's personal relationship with text is coloured by his experience of dyslexia, and many of his poems assert control over the physical text through the use of different typography, non-standard spelling and punctuation, and illustration. In 'According to My Mood' he writes:

I have poetic licence, I WriTe thE way I want.
I drop my full stops where I like …
MY CAPITAL LeterRs go where I like
(I do my spelling write).[29]

The facing page shows an illustration of the joker from a pack of playing cards. The poem itself is an elaborate joke which simultaneously subverts and upholds conventions of language and writing. By using apparently random spelling and typography, Zephaniah appears to put his assertion that he writes the way he wants into practice. A closer look, however, reveals that this unorthodox writing is far from random: on the contrary, each line is provided with an example of the liberty he is claiming for himself, so that the line about full stops is peppered with several and he opts to use 'write' not 'right' in his line about spelling. In other words, this is a highly structured poem which requires a good understanding of the conventions of writing on the part of the reader: it is impossible to fully appreciate the joke unless you understand how the writing should appear. Once again, Zephaniah can be seen to be playing with ideas about legitimacy and correctness, simultaneously embracing and rejecting the framework within which he is supposed to work.

Benjamin Zephaniah's work is a good example of the way in which contemporary poetry for children can be, as Matthew Grenby suggests, 'thought-provoking, multi-layered, sensitive and artistic'. Although on the surface it appears to be simple, light-hearted and playful, it addresses deeper issues of identity, art and language both overtly and implicitly. By drawing in contemporary art forms such as rap, Zephaniah also reminds us that poetry for children is far from extinct: on the contrary, it has evolved into new forms.

Extended Commentary: Seuss, *The Cat in the Hat* (1957)

One of the most popular and best-known works of children's poetry produced in the twentieth century is Dr Seuss's *The Cat in the Hat*. The book has remained in print continuously since its first publication and has been translated into more than a dozen languages. It has been adapted into multiple formats, including an animated series, a live-action film, a computer game, and an iPad application, not to mention the dizzying array of merchandise featuring Seuss's distinctive illustrations of the cat in his tall, red-and-white striped top hat. *The Cat in the Hat* has even been cited in the US Senate: in 2007, majority leader Harry Reid quoted some lines from the book during a debate on immigration.[30] In this case at least, children's poetry has proven both enduring and culturally significant.

The Cat in the Hat was the first book in Seuss's 'Beginner Readers' series and was written in response to his publisher's challenge to produce an engaging book for children using only a limited vocabulary. After a year and a half of work, Seuss succeeded in producing a book using a vocabulary of only 236 words, selected from a list judged to include the words children would be learning at school. The genesis of the book, then, places it firmly in two traditions of children's literature. As a book designed to teach children how to read, it has a consciously didactic purpose. The desire for it to become a book 'first-graders can't put down', however, indicates that it also focuses on delighting and amusing young readers. In contrast to the painfully dull reading primers to which Seuss was responding, both the story and the pictures of the book are lively and imaginative. It tells the story of two children left alone at home on a wet day, whose boredom is relieved by the arrival of a tall cat in a hat and bow tie, who promises them fun and games.[31] The cat embarks on a series of games which progressively wreck the house and horrify the children, until at the last moment – just before mother returns home – he tidies everything up and departs. Throughout the book, the children's pet fish functions as the voice of conscience, warning the children not to go along with the cat's games. The children within the text are appalled as much as pleased, but the cat certainly provides the reader with fun that is also funny, despite the clear educational function of the book.

The limited vocabulary of the book is primarily functional – designed to aid young readers in developing their reading skills – but it also serves to shape the verse. Just as the sonnet form imposes restrictions which are an inherent part of the artistic effect, the use of a limited vocabulary in *The Cat in the Hat* places more demands on the form of the language (see p. 14). Reading primers such as the well-known 'Dick and Jane' series or their British counterpart 'Peter and Jane' typically showcased simple everyday nouns like 'ball' and 'cup' in stolidly realistic phrases. By contrast, Seuss uses rhyme and rhythm to present a decidedly unusual scenario. The ordinary nouns are literally jumbled as the cat balances his series of items, so that the child has to pay close attention in order to keep track of what he is doing (aided by the picture on the facing page). The verse form keeps each line short – no more than six syllables – but, since the cat's dialogue is continued across several lines and held together by the rhyme scheme, it has none of the stiltedness to which reading primers often fell prey. On the contrary, the rhyme and rhythm create the sense of motion even though the poem might be read slowly, line by line, by a child. The rhyme also helps to convey another key educational element of the text; Seuss believed in the phonics method of teaching reading, which relies on teaching collections of sounds rather than whole words. The repetitive rhyming scheme of *The Cat in the Hat* helps to convey sets of phonemes, so that the child is able to recognise the long 'a' sound in 'fall' and 'ball' and the similar 'u' sound in 'book' and 'cup'. Part of the pleasure of the book is derived from the repetition of sounds, as in this passage when the cat releases 'Thing One and Thing Two' to run riot through the house, bumping and thumping their way around. The satisfying onomatopoeia of the repeated thumps and bumps is enjoyable in a fashion similar to that found in children's playground rhymes, which frequently feature such sound play, as well as helping to reinforce the child's recognition of the phonemes. The poetic features of the text are intrinsic to its success, both as an instructive tool and as a work of art.

In the tradition of nonsense verse, *The Cat in the Hat* is carnivalesque, inverting the usual order both comically and subversively. The pictures make it clear that the cat is an adult figure: in comparison with the children he is the same size as an adult man, and his hat, bow tie and carefully furled umbrella convey the impression of a well-to-do businessman (although the gaudiness of his red-and-white top hat hints at his unconventionality). The text similarly positions him as an adult authority figure: when he arrives he promises to show the children some tricks, assuring them that their mother will have no objections (p. 8). The cat's tricks, however, are decidedly irresponsible: he creates towers of household items, releases his 'pets' 'Thing One and Thing Two' into the house, flies kites indoors and even threatens mother's new dress! Although the fish provides a voice of reason throughout the book (see p. 11), his inability to act against the cat positions him as a particularly conscientious child rather than as an adult (what could be more powerless against a cat than a fish in a bowl?). Indeed, the fish's child-status is tellingly underlined later in the text, when he elides himself with the children, telling the cat that he should not be there when 'our' mother is not (p. 25).* Thus the story inverts the normal order – in which adults enforce responsible behaviour – and requires the children to restore good behaviour. At the end of the book the child narrator delivers a stern admonition to the cat, telling him to pack his bags (p. 52). The inversion of normal roles is both enjoyable and very slightly unsettling.

---

* The fish is also a descendant of another 'voice of reason': its role in the story closely resembles that of the cats in another famous children's poem: Heinrich Hoffmann's *Struwwelpeter*. In 'The Dreadful Story of Pauline and the Matches', the two cats repeatedly warn Pauline against playing with matches, to no avail. Whereas the dire predictions of the fish in *The Cat in the Hat* never fully come to pass (since the cat cleans up after himself), the cats' prediction that Pauline will be burnt to death is fulfilled.

It is possible to read the story as ultimately conservative: the cat's subversive behaviour demonstrates the importance of good behaviour, implying that children would not enjoy the freedom to run wild if they had it. It is important to note, however, that it is not the cat's actions in themselves which horrify the children, but the potential consequences of their mother finding out about the chaos they have participated in. The fish repeatedly reminds them that she would not sanction the cat's behaviour, and when it sees her returning home it exclaims anxiously on the threat of being found out (p. 47). The text therefore leaves open the possibility that, if they could reliably escape the consequences, the children might revel in the cat's disorder as much as the reader. Indeed, the closing words of the book subtly imply the allure of misbehaving in secret. When their mother asks them if they had fun all day, the children hesitate, wondering whether they should tell her, and turn the question back on the reader, asking what they would do in the same situation (p. 61). This neat rhyming couplet presents the child reader with a difficult and interesting problem. While the text itself is simple, what it asks the child to reflect on is actually very complex. It raises the question of whether mother might be happier to remain in ignorance, or whether the children will be happier if she does not find out about the cat. The reader might speculate on whether mother will be angry if they tell her the truth, or whether she might disbelieve them. By posing the question directly to the reader, the book both raises the enticing possibility that the cat might visit in real life, and implies that the child reader might already have their own 'cat antics' which have taken place out of view of adults. In 236 words, Seuss manages not only to tell a complete and lively story, but also to pose a philosophical dilemma appealing to children.

Both the inventiveness of *The Cat in the Hat* and its simple, catchy rhyme and rhythm have worked to make it an iconic text in American and anglophone culture. The book is not successful only as a work of poetry: the simple, eye-catching illustrations, while they have been discussed only briefly here, are integral to the text. Nevertheless, the use of verse in Seuss's text is far from incidental. He succeeded in his aim of creating a simple book which children could enjoy by exploiting the pleasures of rhyme, rhythm and assonance to create a complete artistic work. The limited vocabulary and brevity of the text might have made a prose version stilted; by contrast, in verse Seuss is able to make a virtue of the constraints associated with poetry. While it is rarely considered as a work of poetry, *The Cat in the Hat* in fact demonstrates that children's poetry can be both sophisticated and enjoyable. Its enduring popularity among both children and adults illustrates that, while poetry has received less attention than other literary forms, it is a central and thriving part of children's literature.

Notes

1   Iona and Peter Opie, *The Lore and Language of Schoolchildren* (New York: New York Review of Books, 2001), p. 3.
2   I. and P. Opie, *The Lore and Language of Schoolchildren*, p. 101.
3   I. and P. Opie, *The Lore and Language of Schoolchildren*, p. 6.
4   Steve Roud, 'The State of Play', the *Guardian*, 30 October 2010, accessed from www.guardian.co.uk on 13 January 2011, n.p.; Kathryn Marsh, *The Musical Playground: Global Tradition and Changes in Children's Songs and Games* (Oxford: Oxford University Press, 2008), p. 4.
5   I. and P. Opie, *The Lore and Language of Schoolchildren*, p. 90.
6   'Mr Stops', in *Punctuation Personified* (London: J. Harris, 1824), p. 13.
7   Morag Styles, *From the Garden to the Street: Three Hundred Years of Poetry for Children* (London: Cassell, 1998), p. 93.
8   Styles, *From the Garden to the Street*, p. 187.
9   BBC, 'Gruffalo Tops List of Favourite Children's Books', 19 October 2010, accessed from www.bbc.co.uk on 13 January 2011, n.p.
10   Styles, *From the Garden to the Street*, p. 170.
11   Robert Louis Stevenson, 'Bed in Summer', in *A Child's Garden of Verses* (London: Puffin, 2008), p. 1, ll. 1–4.
12   Robert Louis Stevenson, *The Letters of Robert Louis Stevenson: Volume One* (Charleston, SC: Bibliobazaar, 2009), p. 308.
13   Edward Lear, 'There was an Old Man with a gong', in *A Book of Nonsense* (1894), accessed from www.bencourtney.com on 18 October 2010, n.p.

14   Edward Lear, 'The Table and the Chair', in *Nonsense Songs, Stories, Botany, and Alphabets* (1871), accessed from www.bencourtney.com on 18 October 2010, n.p.

15   Spike Milligan, 'On the Ning Nang Nong', in *The Puffin Book of Nonsense Verse*, selected and illustrated by Quentin Blake (London: Puffin, 1994), p. 107, ll. 10–15.

16   William Spaulding, quoted in Louis Menand, 'Cat People: What Dr. Seuss Really Taught Us', the *New Yorker*, 23 December 2002, accessed from www.newyorker.com on 18 October 2010, n.p.

17   Dr Seuss, *Dr. Seuss's ABC* (London: HarperCollins Children's Books, 1997), p. 34.

18   Dr Seuss, *Fox in Socks* (London: HarperCollins Children's Books, 1993), pp. 58–9.

19   Dr Seuss, *How the Grinch Stole Christmas* (New York: Random House, 1985), p. 48.

20   Dr Seuss, 'The Sneeches', in *The Sneeches and Other Stories* (New York: Random House, 1989), pp. 1–24, p. 1.

21   John Rowe Townsend, *Written for Children: An Outline of English-Language Children's Literature* (Lanham, MD: Scarecrow, 1996), p. 310; Michael Rosen, 'If you don't put your shoes on before I count fifteen', in *100 Best Poems for Children* (London: Puffin, 2002), pp. 94–6, ll. 1–10.

22   Allan Ahlberg, 'Please Mrs Butler', in *Please Mrs Butler* (London: Puffin, 1984), p. 10–11, ll. 1–2.

23   Matthew Grenby, *Children's Literature* (Edinburgh: Edinburgh University Press, 2008), p. 52.

24   Jackie Kay, 'The Rowans', in *Red, Cherry Red* (London: Bloomsbury, 2007), pp. 47–50, ll. 19–24.

25   Benjamin Zephaniah, 'Body Talk', in *Talking Turkeys* (London: Puffin, 1995), pp. 14–15, ll. 25–32.

26   Benjamin Zephaniah, 'Me? I Thought, OBE Me? Up Yours, I Thought', the *Guardian*, 27 November 2003, accessed from www.guardian.co.uk on 28 October 2010, n.p.

27   Benjamin Zephaniah, 'The British', in *Wicked World* (London: Puffin, 2000), pp. 38–9, ll. 20–4.

28   Benjamin Zephaniah, 'Rap Connected', in *Talking Turkeys*, pp. 50–1, ll. 1–4.

29   Benjamin Zephaniah, 'According to My Mood', in *Talking Turkeys*, pp. 24–5, ll. 1–45.

30   Dana Milbank, 'Snubbing the White House, without Snubbing the White House', the *Washington Post*, 8 June 2007, accessed from www.washingtonpost.com on 19 October 2010, n.p.

31   Dr Seuss, *The Cat in the Hat* (London: HarperCollins Children's Books, 1985), p. 7.

Picture Books: Sendak, Browne and Child

Pictures are closely associated with children's literature – so much so that 'a book with pictures' is a definition that springs readily to mind when asked to define literature for children. Although there are many illustrated books aimed at adolescents or adults, novels for children are more likely to include illustrations, and books composed wholly or significantly of illustrations are typically associated with very young children. The apparent simplicity of illustrated texts is one significant factor in the perception that they are particularly suitable for young children, since pictures are assumed to be accessible to the pre-literate child. However, as a number of scholars have shown, 'reading' pictures is actually a complex process: at the most basic level, the child reading a picture book must recognise a two-dimensional arrangement of lines and shapes as a depiction of a three-dimensional face. As this chapter will show, many picture books demand a great deal more of their readers, even when aimed at the very young. Furthermore, while picture books are often associated with small children, they can offer a level of narrative and emotional complexity which challenges and engages much older readers.

There are different types of books with illustrations; as a consequence, various terms have evolved in order to distinguish between them.* An illustrated book is one in which the text stands alone and the pictures are primarily decorative, making the book more appealing without adding anything crucial to the story; examples of illustrated books are Roald Dahl's popular novels, now all distinctively illustrated in their UK edition by Quentin Blake, whose work is now almost synonymous with Dahl's. During the nineteenth and the first half of the twentieth century, illustrations were a common feature of novels published for children aged about ten to fourteen: John Tenniel's illustrations for Lewis Carroll's *Alice's Adventures in Wonderland* contributed to the iconic status of the book, while in the 1950s and 1960s prominent children's illustrators such as Faith Jaques (who illustrated the first UK edition of Dahl's *Charlie and the Chocolate Factory*) and Diana Stanley (illustrator for Mary Norton's 'Borrowers' series) were largely employed in providing pictures for illustrated books. From the 1970s, the use of illustrations in books for older children declined, perhaps as a result of rising production costs and because of the perception that illustrations made a book appear more 'childish'.† Recently, however, prominent author–illustrator collaborations have helped to revive the tradition of including illustrations in books for older children. The text of Neil Gaiman's Carnegie-winning novel *The Graveyard Book* (2008) could effectively stand alone, but it has been published in two heavily illustrated editions, with pictures by Dave McKean and Chris Riddell respectively. Chris Riddell's collaboration with Paul Stewart in the 'Edge Chronicles' (1999–2009) and other works has made a major contribution to the increased profile of illustrations in books for older children: while Paul Stewart's narrative could be enjoyed alone, Riddell's very distinctive line drawings create much of the character and atmosphere of the books, and he is credited equally on

---

* There is some disagreement about the precise use and boundaries of these terms, and they are not consistently used in exactly the same way. However, the overview here provides some generally accepted definitions.

† The decline in the use of illustrations may also reflect changing trends in publishing at large: while books for adults in the nineteenth century were frequently illustrated – George Cruikshank's illustrations of Charles Dickens's work are a notable example – pictures became a less prominent feature of literature for adults during the twentieth century.

the cover. The sophistication of Riddell and McKean's illustrations and the degree to which they interact with the text arguably make them more than simply 'illustrated books'; however, the popularity of these texts has helped to make illustrations a more familiar part of novels for older children.

Illustrated books frequently use only a few images set into large blocks of text, and often use black-and-white images rather than full colour. By contrast, 'picture books' usually include images on almost every page, often in full colour. In a picture book, words and images show essentially the same information, so that reading only the text or only the pictures would convey much the same story. Many books for babies are designed on this principle, so that the word 'apple' is accompanied by a picture of an apple, enabling the child to make a connection between word and picture. Some books for older children, such as the popular 'Topsy and Tim' series by Jean and Gareth Adamson, also retain a close connection between words and image: in *Topsy and Tim's Picnic* (1978), the text tells us: 'Topsy and Tim decided to make their own picnic. They chose their favourite things to eat – tomato sauce, spaghetti-hoops, hundreds and thousands – and made them into sandwiches.'[1] Below the text is an image of Topsy standing at a table, shaking hundreds and thousands onto a slice of bread, with a pile of already made sandwiches and a bottle of tomato ketchup on either side of her. The reader can even infer that these are Topsy's 'favourite things to eat' without recourse to the text, based on the fact that she is smiling and licking her lips. While the pictures definitely *enhance* the text, therefore – the book would be a lot less appealing without them – pictures and text do not really add anything to one another: the story would be essentially the same if one component were removed.

Picture books in which the pictures simply illustrate the text can be both elaborate and appealing. In many cases, however, the illustrations not only enhance the text, but expand upon or even replace it, so that reading the pictures becomes an essential part of understanding and enjoying the book. In John Burningham's *Come Away from the Water, Shirley* (1977), the text and one set of pictures show an ordinary family day at the seaside, as Shirley's parents settle themselves on deckchairs, share a flask of tea, and caution their daughter against various perceived hazards. The illustrations on the facing page show quite a different story, however, as Shirley embarks on a series of adventures, fighting pirates and becoming captain of their ship. The distance between Shirley's experiences as told by the pictures and her parents' perception of events is a satisfying and subtle commentary on childhood imagination: in this instance, the pictures do not simply enhance the text, they are the real narrative. Similarly, in Emily Gravett's *Wolves* (2005), which was awarded the Kate Greenaway Medal for illustration, text and illustrations work together – and sometimes against each other – to form the narrative. Rabbit borrows a book about wolves from the library, but as we read the book with him we realise that he is facing more than a fictional threat. As Rabbit grows increasingly anxious about the wolf within the text, the reader sees the real presence of a wolf looming up behind him. By the time his book warns him that wolves eat 'smaller mammals, such as beavers, voles and …'[2] it is too late: the textual narrative is interrupted by two pages illustrating the cover of Rabbit's book, torn and chewed, with the fateful word 'rabbits' torn out of the book altogether. The nervous child reader can be reassured by the text's assertion that 'Fortunately this wolf was a vegetarian, so they shared a jam sandwich, became the best of friends, and lived happily ever after' (p. 27). However, the illustrations tell a rather more brutal story: the fears raised by the savage destruction of Rabbit's book are confirmed by the end pages, which show a pile of Rabbit's unopened post, topped by an overdue notice from the library. The illustrations and text thus form a dialogue which offers more than one possible interpretation. Many books with pictures utilise illustrations as part of the narrative in this way; in order to distinguish them from books in which the illustrations simply complement the text, they are often referred to by scholars as 'picturebooks', a convention which will be adhered to in this chapter. The same term is used for wordless books in which the entire narrative is conveyed through the pictures, such as Shaun Tan's *The*

Arrival (2006), a highly acclaimed work which demonstrates that it is possible to tell rich and sophisticated stories without text. *The Arrival* tells the story of a migrant worker as he sets out from his home and embarks on a journey to a strange land. The book opens with a series of 'snapshots' of ordinary life – a cracked teapot, a child's drawing, a man's hat – which help to establish a sense of familiarity. The sense of the safe and familiar is disrupted, however, as the man leaves the house with his family in order to set out on his journey: the shadow of a gigantic dragon-like creature looms against the houses behind them, suggesting either a supernatural danger or a more abstract political, economic or personal threat. As the man's journey progresses, more and more fantastical elements appear – strange creatures, weird organic buildings and bizarre modes of transport – vividly conveying the sense of dislocation and strangeness which belongs to the migrant experience. The complex ideas explored by Tan's novel belie the idea that books without text are only for the very young: *The Arrival* is more suitable for teenagers than for toddlers.

Comics and graphic novels (book-length narratives in comic-strip form) are another popular form of illustrated book with their own conventions of illustration and narrative, notably the use of sequential images in a 'strip' of boxes. The popularity and status of graphic novels has increased during recent decades, in part because of the influence of sequential art traditions from outside the Western world such as Japanese manga, which is both respected and popular, and is not considered to be a 'children's' genre. Because comics and graphic novels belong to a distinctive tradition of their own, they will not be discussed in detail in this chapter; however, they have played an important role in children's literature. Comics such as *The Beano* and *The Dandy* were a dominant force in popular British children's literature in the twentieth century: while they have often been (erroneously) criticised as simplistic and insufficiently challenging, this has not inhibited their popularity with children, for whom they have formed a staple of reading. Picturebooks often draw on the same conventions: Raymond Briggs, best known for his wordless book *The Snowman* (1978), typically works with the comic-strip format, although he is usually classed as a picturebook artist. Maurice Sendak and Anthony Browne, discussed later in this chapter, have also made use of comic-strip conventions.

Spaces and Places: Maurice Sendak

Maurice Sendak is one of the most celebrated and well-known children's illustrators of the twentieth century. His seminal title *Where the Wild Things Are* (1963) is instantly recognisable, and has been issued in multiple different media and formats: today's child readers can play with soft plush 'wild things', construct jigsaws depicting scenes from the book, access a greatly expanded vision of the text via Spike Jonze's live-action film adaptation (2009), decorate their rooms with prints from the book, or take on the role of the book's protagonist, Max, in a computer game. *Where the Wild Things Are* has become part of contemporary cultural and commercial discourse. In the world of children's literature, Sendak is regarded as an innovatory and important artist not only for this highly prominent text, but also for his whole body of work, which spans more than six decades. He has been honoured multiple times, notably with the Caldecott Medal for Illustration in 1964 (awarded for *Where the Wild Things Are*), the Hans Christian Andersen Award for children's book illustration in 1970 and the Astrid Lindgren Memorial Award in 2003, and has had an influential effect on picturebooks for children in the twentieth and twenty-first centuries.

The period during which Maurice Sendak began to establish himself as a picturebook author was one of particular significance in the development of picturebooks for children. Improved printing techniques during the 1960s helped to make full colour pictures both cheaper and easier to produce, and many illustrators of the period took advantage of the new possibilities available to them to produce brightly coloured and elaborate illustrations which reflected the vibrancy of the modern art scene. The work of British artist Brian

Wildsmith, for example, who won the Kate Greenaway Medal in 1962 for his *A.B.C.* (1962), is characterised by lush colourscapes, while the American Eric Carle, best known for *The Very Hungry Caterpillar* (1969), utilises bright splotches of colour which stand out against large areas of white space. By contrast, Maurice Sendak's style is characterised by the use of strong lines and careful cross-hatching (parallel strokes in one direction overlaid with parallel strokes at a different angle) which is reminiscent of earlier traditions of children's illustration; while Sendak uses colour to good effect in his work, it is typically less prominent than in the work of many of his contemporaries.

The slightly old-fashioned impression conveyed by Sendak's line illustrations is used to good effect in Meindert DeJong's *The Wheel on the School* (1954), which Sendak illustrated during the early years of his career. The book tells the story of a group of children in a small Dutch village who set out to discover why storks do not nest on the roofs of their houses – though they are common in neighbouring villages – and to bring the storks back to their area. The impression conveyed in the text is of an idyllic society largely untouched by the modern world, and this is reflected in Sendak's illustrations, both through the costume of the characters – women and girls in long, old-fashioned skirts and boys in the sturdy jackets and trousers of an early twentieth-century fishing community – and through the simplicity of the black-and-white drawings. *The Wheel on the School* is very firmly an illustrated book – the illustrations are few in number and they are not integral to the story – but the way in which Sendak reinforces the mood and message of the text makes his pictures more than merely incidental. Chapter 1 is headed with an illustration of a stork, wings outstretched and legs bent as if on the point of landing or taking flight. The sense of motion the image conveys suggests both excitement and possibility, reflecting the importance of the storks as the driving motivation of the plot. This is underscored by the striking contrast of the image: the dark feathers on the stork's wings are almost pure black, making it stand out against the page and emphasising its importance to the story as a whole. A few pages later, the human characters are introduced in an image of the schoolroom. The text has already informed us that the little girl, Lina, has 'raised her hand and asked, "Teacher, may I read a little story about storks?"'[3] Sendak shows Lina standing at the front of the classroom reading the story, while her five classmates and the teacher look on. The illustration is set into the middle of Lina's story, so that it gives the reader a sense of the reactions of the group before they are provided in the text. The faces of all six of Lina's listeners are clearly visible, with smiling faces and alert eyes, and all are turned towards Lina, emphasising their interest in and focus on her story. The teacher is seated at his high desk, looking down on Lina with a smile that conveys his 'proud and pleased' reaction to her reading (p. 4). By positioning the teacher above and behind Lina, Sendak emphasises his power over her, and consequently his indulgence in allowing her to read (she has interrupted their arithmetic lesson). Lina herself is the focal point of the image, the only figure standing and the only one entirely on her own (since the teacher's high desk hems him in). Her standing position also draws attention to the fact that she is the only female figure, since it allows Sendak to show clearly her long skirt and long hair, worn loose around her shoulders. Thus this image conveys some of the key elements of this book: Lina's importance as instigator of the children's attempts to get the storks to nest in the village, the excitement and pleasure brought about by their common project, which helps to build a sense of community, and the centrality of female values of care and nurturing as embodied in the desire to help the nesting storks (a bird traditionally associated with human babies). The richness of this early work by Sendak, then, presages the skill and complexity he was to bring to his later work, and demonstrates the possibilities inherent in children's illustration.

Sendak illustrated a number of novels and picture books by other authors during the early years of his career, and has continued to work with others; however, he is most famous for his work as an author-illustrator. His self-styled trilogy of picturebooks, *Where the Wild Things Are, In the Night Kitchen* (1970) and *Outside Over There*

(1981) demonstrates both the artistic and the conceptual range of the picturebook format. While children's books in general, and books with pictures in particular, are sometimes associated with simplicity, Sendak's work is far from simple; on the contrary, it is highly allusive and pushes boundaries of content and narrative. Sendak is adept at manipulating and exploring space, both literal and figurative. All three books in the 'Wild Things' trilogy deal with journeys out of safe, known space and into fantasy spaces, a pre-occupation which is also evident in much of Sendak's other work. In *Where the Wild Things Are*, the journey from the real to the fantasy space is clearly mirrored in the page layout and structure. The book famously tells the story of Max, who makes 'mischief of one kind and another' and is sent to bed with no supper, whereupon he departs on a journey to where the wild things are.[4] Max establishes himself as the wildest thing of all, ruling over the fantastical wild things until at last he grows weary and returns home to find his supper waiting, 'still hot'. The opening pages, which portray Max at home, employ a great deal of white space. The text 'The night Max wore his wolf suit and made mischief of one kind' is printed in one line on the left-hand page, while the illustration of Max on the facing page is constrained in the centre of the page, so that the white background takes up as much space as the picture, constraining Max within a small space. The sense of claustrophobia is heightened by the dark colour scheme of the picture itself, which is dominated by the heavy cross-hatching making up the walls behind Max, who is positioned on the far right of the picture, foot pressed against the wall and hammer poised to strike as if he is trying to push his way out of the picture altogether. While the word 'mischief' in the text might suggest enjoyment or liberation to the child reader, the look of unhappy defiance on Max's face and the impression of constraint and entrapment in the image effectively convey the sense of an angry and frustrated child who is stifled by his environment. By constraining his first image within such a small space, Sendak is able to use page layout to provide a sense of progression through the story. Each subsequent image takes up more of the page, conveying Max's growing wildness, which is literally represented by the forest which expands to fill the whole right-hand page. When Max breaks out of his home space altogether and embarks on his journey, the illustrations break out too, spilling onto the left-hand page and limiting the text to a smaller and smaller area. Finally the picture takes over altogether: the three double-page spreads following Max's decree 'let the wild rumpus start!' have no text at all, so that the capering forms of Max and the wild things and the lush jungle background take up the entire space. Following the wild rumpus, Max's return home is signified by the way the picture recedes, until in the final double-page spread it is confined to the right-hand page once more. However, it is not the same space he started out in: whereas home at the beginning of the book is a constricting space, by the end it has the same feeling of openness present in the 'wild' spaces. The final image of his room takes up the full page, while Max is positioned facing inwards from the far right of the page, with a wide expanse of pale yellow carpet dominating the foreground in front of him. No longer frustrated or constrained, this Max is much happier and more relaxed, smiling as he pushes the wolf suit – visible symbol of his 'wildness' – back from his head. Following his journey, Max has space for his emotions. Readers too have space for their own interpretations: is Max's journey a 'real' one, or have we simply been privy to the workings of his imagination? It is left to the reader to decide.

In the Night Kitchen depicts the adventures of young Mickey after he falls out of bed (and his nightclothes) and into the 'night kitchen'. Here Sendak similarly uses the ratio between white space and illustration to denote the boundary between the fantastical and the real. At the beginning and end of the book, when Mickey is in the 'real' world represented by his home and bed, the pictures are held within frames with a wide strip of white space at the bottom of each page, a device which makes a safe and cosy space with Mickey usually at its centre. Once he falls out of bed and into the dream world of the night kitchen, the pictures expand, up to the (literal) height of Mickey's adventure, when he flies his plane to the 'top of the Milky

Way'[5] (a gigantic milk bottle). This scene takes up a full double-page spread with no white space and no text: the whole 'cityscape' of the night kitchen, made up of the jars and packages of a typical kitchen, is laid out for the reader to explore for themselves. Sendak's page layout in this book also makes use of conventions of space and framing which originate in the comic-strip format; for example, when Mickey escapes 'from the oven and into the bread dough all ready to rise in the night kitchen', Sendak uses a full-page illustration divided into three frames. Each frame depicts Mickey and the moon in a slightly different position, conveying Mickey's movement, but the three frames also make up a single picture showing the background of the night kitchen, a connection which is made clear by the fact that, in the last frame, the dough surrounding Mickey spills over into the two preceding frames. This device – a common one in comics – conveys action and the passage of time while allowing a large and detailed picture.

Maurice Sendak is a highly allusive and accomplished artist. The sureness of his strong, spare lines and the rounded faces of his characters make his work highly characteristic, but he also draws on a wide range of other artists and artistic traditions. The lush forests of *Where the Wild Things Are* and Sendak's use of line and colour are strongly reminiscent of the work of painter Henri Rousseau, whose sensual depiction of wild spaces in paintings such as *The Dream* (1910) resonates with the narrative of the story. *In the Night Kitchen* uses the conventions of advertising and packaging design to add richness and interest to the narrative: on a box of yeast, the usual slogan 'Up with the Sun' (used on Warner's Safe Yeast) is replaced with one more fitting for the Night Kitchen, 'Up with the Moon'. Artistic allusion is even more overt in *Outside Over There*, which uses a painterly style heavily influenced by the German Romantic tradition. The book begins with two double-page spreads showing characteristic nineteenth-century tableaux, with the text appearing in small frames like the labels on a painting in a gallery. The first depicts Ida and her mother watching as a ship sails away (the text tells us that 'Papa was away at sea'), while the second shows 'Mama in the arbor'.[6] In both pictures, though, the static painting is disrupted by the baby held in Ida's arms, who looks out at the viewer in the first picture (Ida and Mama have their backs to us), and cries and squirms to get down in the second. The sense of danger is heightened by the fact that the bucolic scenes include two figures who assuredly do not belong: hooded and shadowed figures who resemble Death (the goblins who will later steal Ida's baby sister). The richness of Sendak's painting takes advantage of the strategies used by his nineteenth-century models to convey a sense of story within a single image. Later in the book, more allusions appear: the narrative draws on Mozart's *The Magic Flute* (1791), and Mozart himself is visible in the background of one picture; the images of babies seated in eggshells are reminiscent of depictions of *Leda and the Swan*, which show her children hatching from eggs; and the image of Ida floating 'backwards in the rain', swathed in the folds of her mother's rain cloak, is strongly reminiscent of Gian Lorenzo Bernini's sculpture *The Ecstasy of St Theresa* (1652). The variety of Sendak's allusions is beyond the knowledge of most adult readers; the chances that child readers will recognise his sources is extremely slim. Nevertheless, the use of allusion in Sendak's work is profoundly effective, both in its own right and because of the way in which it inducts the reader into a new cultural literacy. Children who read and return to *Outside Over There* are not simply learning to read the story of Ida, who rescues her little sister from goblins and finds her again; they are also learning the codes of a range of different artistic traditions. When they do encounter the artworks to which Sendak alludes, they will understand them more readily and interpret them more effectively. Thus picture books engage a number of different literacies.

Maurice Sendak's work has been controversial for its challenging style and material. The demanding and highly allusive nature of *Outside Over There* poses challenges to the book's status as 'children's literature': while picturebooks are often associated with young children, neither the style of the artwork nor the text lends itself to newly literate readers. The themes of Sendak's books are also challenging: *Outside Over There* deals with sibling jealousy and child abduction, *In the Night Kitchen* explores the fear of being eaten, and *Where the Wild Things Are* represents childhood emotions of anger and rebellion. All three books have attracted controversy, perhaps because the association of picturebooks with very young children means that books which deal with more complex issues or emotions are particularly disruptive to constructions of idealised and protective childhoods.

What's in the Picture? Anthony Browne

The conflicts, dangers and disruptions of childhood are strongly present in the work of Anthony Browne, one of the most highly regarded picturebook authors at work in Britain today. Browne began his career as a picturebook author in 1976, and has received many awards for his work, including the illustrious Hans Christian Andersen Award for services to children's literature in 2000. Working chiefly in watercolour and pencil, he uses his detailed, almost photographic artwork to explore the experience of childhood, in particular the anxieties and conflicts emerging from family dynamics. *Gorilla* (1983), one of Browne's best-known and most celebrated books, is centred around a small girl's feelings of abandonment by her father, who never has time to spend with her. She dreams of a gorilla who plays the role of ideal father, taking her to the zoo and focusing his attention on her. When she wakes in the morning, her father is there, ready to spend the day with her: it is as if the expression of her desires in the dream world has translated into the real world. A similarly reassuring message is present in *Changes* (1990), in which a small boy waits at home while his father collects his mother from the hospital. 'Things were going to change',[7] his father had told him, and things do: as the boy moves around the house the armchair morphs into a giant bear, the kettle grows cat ears and a tail, and the pictures on the walls show his parents with a little piglet. The book is a witty use of illustration which both portrays a common childhood game – seeing exotic shapes in ordinary items –

and conveys the boy's sense of anxiety and fear about his changing life. Only when his parents return home with their new baby – and their expressions of love for their older child – do things regain their rightful shapes, reassuring the child reader that change may not be threatening after all.

Anthropomorphised animal characters with human characteristics and often with clothes are a common feature of children's illustrated books: Beatrix Potter's detailed animal stories such as *The Tale of Peter Rabbit* (1902) are perhaps the best-known example of this device. They are an important part of Anthony Browne's work, which frequently features gorillas, chimps and other primates. In *Gorilla*, the anthropomorphisation is only temporary and is used as a tool to safely explore the little girl's sense of abandonment by her father without making the dream message too explicit. In many of Browne's other works, animal characters completely replace human ones, most notably in his *Willy the Wimp* (1984) and its sequels. Willy the Wimp is a small, shy chimp, who is bullied by the suburban gorillas until he answers a bodybuilding advert and transforms himself into someone big and strong. But, however big he grows, by the end of the book Willy realises he is still someone who 'wouldn't hurt a fly'.[8] Browne has stated that he has a particular affection for gorillas and chimps and enjoys drawing them, but his use of animal characters is also an effective means of emphasising differences in size and build. Next to the bulk of the 'suburban gorilla gang', the smallness and slightness of Willy the chimp is particularly pronounced, emphasising his vulnerability and childlike position. Ellen Handler Spitz has suggested that there are racist overtones to the use of a threatening gorilla gang,[9] but the contrast is really between adulthood and childhood, strength and weakness: Willy's trainer in the boxing ring is also a huge gorilla, whose size and strength provide an amusing counterpoint to the weediness of Willy. Browne's use of animal characters also helps to insulate the child reader from the more fearful aspects of his narratives: Willy is a vulnerable child in the face of the bullies, but the fact that he is not a human child alleviates a little of the threat.

Like Maurice Sendak, Anthony Browne is a highly allusive artist, who includes a host of visual references to other artworks in his books. *The Tunnel* (1989), in which a brother and sister travel through a tunnel to a fairy-tale realm, includes a visual nod to Sendak himself: when the brother crawls into his sister's room to scare her, his wolf mask not only hints at the story of Little Red Riding Hood (further foreshadowed in the painting on the little girl's wall), but also recalls Sendak's Max in his wolf suit, implying the possibility of a similar journey into wildness. In *Willy's Pictures* (2000), these allusions are overt: Willy's paintings resemble well-known works of art, but Willy has painted his own family and friends into the pictures. The book includes fold-out copies of the original pictures and information about the artists: whereas in Maurice Sendak's *Outside Over There*, and in much of Browne's own work, the reader must have existing knowledge to recognise the allusions, *Willy's Pictures* is overtly didactic, providing child readers with a clearly defined introduction to the art world.

Anthony Browne not only employs many artistic allusions, but also creates works which are richly intertextual. Like authors such as Janet and Allan Ahlberg, whose attractive toy book *The Jolly Postman* (1986) shows its eponymous hero delivering letters to a range of nursery-rhyme characters, he makes particularly effective use of fairy tales and nursery rhymes, taking advantage of young readers' familiarity with these texts to echo and rework them in interesting and provocative ways. In *The Tunnel*, the fairy-tale allusions are primarily visual: the image of the boy in his wolf suit and the picture of Red Riding Hood on his sister's wall at the beginning of the book set the story in the reader's mind, so that when the little girl dons a red hooded duffle coat, the reader is primed to expect danger. When the little girl follows her brother through the 'dark, and damp, and slimy, and scary'[10] tunnel and emerges in a wood, the visual references continue to suggest a replaying of the Red Riding Hood story: the woodcutter's axe is leaning against a tree stump, and we can see the shape of a wolf, jaws wide, in the gnarled trunks of the trees. However, Browne subverts our expectations that the little girl will be threatened and rescued: in a feminist twist on Red Riding Hood she is the one who rescues her brother, flinging her arms around his petrified body to bring him back to life. In this version of the story, the woodcutter is not a saviour but a threat: the brother's petrified body stands alone in a field full of tree stumps. The implication is that, without his sister's love, he too might be cut down and lost. The subtlety of Browne's visual allusions is effective because of the familiarity of his source text: since the reader is already expecting a certain version of the story, even a young child will readily identify and interpret the fairy-tale elements in the pictures. Similarly, in *Into the Forest* (2004), Browne uses the reader's expectations about Little Red Riding Hood and their familiarity with other fairy tales to convey a child's feelings of fear and anxiety about parental conflict. At the beginning of the book, a little boy is 'woken up by a terrible sound'.[11] The image of lightning outside his window gives one possible explanation, but when he wakes the next morning to find 'Dad wasn't there', the more astute reader can provide another interpretation of the noise. When the little boy sets out on a journey to give a cake to his grandma, his anxieties about his father's absence are given visible form: he enters a forest which is visually reminiscent of the one featured in *The Tunnel*, where he encounters a range of fairy-tale characters. None are named, but the reader who is familiar with fairy tales cannot fail to notice that all are characters associated with the disruption of home, security and family: his encounter with Hansel and Gretel, who are searching for their parents, is particularly evocative of his fears about his own family. The darkness of the boy's fears is reflected in the colour palette for the pictures: the boy and his home are shown in colour, but the forest and its inhabitants are drawn in black and white. When he dons a red duffle coat (another visual reference to *The Tunnel*) and knocks on Grandma's door, the sense of threat is acute, evoking the boy's growing sense of anxiety. The denouement of the story, in which Dad turns out to be at Grandma's house and returns home with the boy after all, is a profound relief after this dark and disturbing journey: the pictures also return to full colour, emphasising the move from anxious fantasy to a newly secure reality.

Media and Metafiction: Lauren Child

Lauren Child is one of the most recognisable picturebook illustrators working today. She has garnered both critical and popular acclaim: she has won both the Kate Greenaway Medal and the Nestle Smarties Prize, and her 'Charlie and Lola' series for younger children has been adapted into a popular television animation. Lauren Child is one of a new generation of picturebook artists who are able to use both traditional art techniques and the possibilities of digital media. She utilises mixed-media collages to create a distinctive style which is both literally and figuratively multi-layered. Watercolour pictures are combined with fabric and wallpaper scraps, magazine cuttings, scanned and photographed images of physical objects, and diverse typefaces, creating visual appeal and narrative meaning. Child's techniques make full use of the possibilities which have emerged with technological developments in printing and visual art, which allow the reproduction of very complex coloured images. Her retelling of *The Princess and the Pea* (2005), produced in collaboration with photographer Polly Borland, demonstrates Child's ability to merge old and new artistic techniques. The illustrations are made up of a series of high-colour photographs of elaborately constructed doll's-house sets. The intricate sets – complete with real fabrics and even a real lighting chandelier – are peopled with paper dolls drawn by Child and dressed in layers of paper clothes. The combination of verisimilitude created by the photographed sets and the unreal stylised design of the paper dolls creates a curious mixture of fantasy and realism which fits perfectly with the fairy-tale narrative. The book is a rich work of art as well as an engaging version of the familiar fairy tale.

One characteristic aspect of Child's work is the use of very varied typefaces which are superimposed over images or arranged around them. For example, in *I Am Too Absolutely Small for School* (2010), part of Child's popular 'Charlie and Lola' series, Charlie attempts to encourage his small sister Lola to attend school, saying, 'What about learning your letters, Lola? If you know how to write, you can send cards to people you like.'[12] His words are in a wavy line across the page as if handwritten; they are accompanied by a photograph of felt-tip pens, with the black pen at an angle as if it has been used to write them. Lola's response, 'I like to talk on the telephone, it is more friendly and straightaway', is superimposed on a photograph of an orange plastic dial telephone, with the words going round the dial. The telephone has a watercolour picture of Lola in the middle, focusing the reader's attention on her and emphasising that she is asserting her preference (for talking on the telephone) over her brother's justification for attending school. The merging of pictures and words heightens the overall artistic and narrative effects of the book, working to draw the reader in. It also adds a layer of interpretative effort on the part of the reader: in order to enjoy the full effect it is necessary to read the words, 'read' the typographical design and the additional meaning it brings to the story, and recognise and 'read' the picture as a whole. 'Reading' the picture requires the reader to notice the telephone (which despite being a photograph is quite stylised, since it is an old-fashioned dial phone of a design now unfamiliar to most small children) and identify Lola and the importance of her position at the centre of the image. While *I Am Too Absolutely Small for School* is aimed at young children near the beginning of their own school careers, therefore, Lauren Child's picturebook demands considerable interpretative skills on the part of its readers.

Picturebook art demands a suspension of disbelief: although the combination of a circle and a few lines does not really resemble a face, we are able to recognise it as such and are willing to accept the 'reality' of the image for the duration of the book. This means that the picturebooks in a sense ask the reader to accept two fictions: both that the story is real and that the pictures which portray that story are real. Increasingly, however, picturebook artists have used the form as a means of disrupting the illusion of the real, allowing their images to comment on their own constructed nature. In David Wiesner's *The Three Pigs* (2001), for example, the three little pigs of the well-known fairy tale become aware of their own status as characters in a book, breaking the 'fourth wall' which separates characters and reader and climbing out of the page altogether. Lauren Child's very stylised and visibly constructed style of art, with its mixture of drawn and painted images and photography, ideally lends itself to this sort of metafictive experimentation. In *Who's Afraid of the Big Bad Book?* (2002), her protagonist Herb literally falls into his book, so that he must spend the rest of the narrative navigating his way through familiar fairy tales in order to escape the book. The metafictive nature of this narrative is evident from the cover illustration, which features Herb reading a book with the same cover, which of course shows another Herb reading the same book, and so on. The impression that we are reading the same book as Herb is confirmed by the flyleaf, which has 'This book belongs to Herb' scrawled across it in childish handwriting. Further in, we are told that 'Herb read his books everywhere. This is why many of the pages were stickily stuck together, soggy round the edges, and usually had bits of banana, biscuit and the odd pea squashed between the pages.'[13] Sure enough, the page appears to be smeared with squashed pea: Child uses a scanned image of a real pea to heighten the sense that it is 'really' on the page, whereas Herb himself – shown on the facing page – is drawn in pen and watercolour.

The combination of scanned and photographed images of real things and stylised drawings and collages creates a metafictive effect: we can believe that the peas have been smeared on the book by a 'real' Herb, while Herb himself is 'only' in the book. It is not a surprise, then, when a few pages later Herb falls into the book he is reading, waking up in the pages of a book of fairy tales – where Goldilocks is less than pleased to find him invading her story. As he navigates his way through the different tales, seeking to escape, the barriers between the 'real' and the 'fictional' are further disrupted by his encounters with the effects of his own mistreatment of his books. Herb knows how the stories *ought* to go, but everywhere he goes he finds that they are not proceeding according to plan. Cinderella's stepsisters have been cut out of the book and stuck in upside down, leading them to complain 'Now we can't get to the ball and Prince Charming can't fall madly, utterly in love with us. It's so unfair'. Meanwhile Cinderella herself is waiting in vain for Prince Charming – Herb has cut him out to make a birthday card for his mother. Child's use of collaging and mixed media effectively conveys the illusion that the book itself has been cut up, drawn upon and otherwise modified in the ways Herb encounters, while her use of well-known fairy tales plays on the existing knowledge of the child reader. The effects of Herb's modifications are unexpected and amusing precisely because we know how the stories usually go; when Herb escapes at the end of the story and sets things to rights, it is satisfying because the reader shares the sense of everything being returned to its familiar order. Like Anthony Browne, Child is skilled at using fairy tales to explore the nature of fiction and the ways in which narrative is constructed: within an apparently simple and familiar structure she places high demands on her readers.

Extended Commentary: Browne, *Voices in the Park* (1998)

The rich and complex work of Maurice Sendak, Anthony Browne and Lauren Child illustrates the possibilities inherent in the picturebook form. While all three have produced books for young children, even preschool texts like *I Am Too Absolutely Small for School* require their readers to engage with a range of different artistic and narrative devices and to read on more than one level. The complex narrative possibilities inherent in the picturebook format are effectively demonstrated in Browne's *Voices in the Park*, which combines text and art to explore the construction of narrative, raising postmodern questions about reliable narration.

Voices in the Park tells the same story with four different narrators: a well-to-do mother, her small son Charles, an unemployed father, and his daughter Smudge all give their version of a trip to the park with their dogs. Each version sheds a different light on the series of events, as the four characters offer their very different perspectives. Thus the mother sees Smudge's dog Albert as threatening, complaining that 'the horrible thing chased [Victoria, her pedigree dog,] all over the park', but Charles observes wistfully that 'There was a very friendly dog in the park and Victoria was having a great time. I wished I was.'[14] Smudge offers another version, commenting 'Of course the other dog didn't mind, but its owner was really angry, the silly twit.' Meanwhile, Smudge's father is oblivious to the antics of the two dogs, and to the reaction of Charles's mother. The pictures provide a fifth narrative voice: the image which accompanies Charles's mother's complaints about the dogs shows Victoria enthusiastically chasing Smudge's dog, implicitly privileging the children's narratives over the version offered by Charles's mother. The reader must choose which version of the narrative to believe, and must also recognise the possibility that all the narratives could be considered as true, so that ideas about narrative authority are fundamentally destabilised.

The use of the four different narratives forces the reader's attention onto the images, which offer an alternative source of evidence about what 'really' happened. Once the reader begins to look at the images, the book yields more and more. The illustrations for each voice vary in style and colour palette to suit the narrator. The narrative by Charles's mother has a muted colour palette and restrained style which suits what the character might consider to be 'tasteful', whereas Smudge's working-class father begins his narrative with dark, gloomy colours which reflect his state of mind, and ends more cheerfully with the brash, high-contrast colours of a tabloid newspaper. Thus Browne subtly conveys the kind of character he is portraying, their emotions, tastes and experiences, with very little explicit comment from the text.

The variety of narratives offered by the text is paralleled by those offered by the images, which both reinforce and disrupt each voice's narrative. The first image of Charles in the park shows him standing in the shadow of his mother, while the clouds, the trees and the lamp posts in the park are shaped like her very distinctive hat, suggesting the degree to which she controls and constricts Charles. The scene is dull and cloudy, and the branches of the trees are bare. By contrast, Smudge's entry into the park immediately establishes it as a realm of freedom and excitement: the scene is depicted in bright primary colours, the bushes and trees are fruiting and in full leaf, and we can glimpse various tantalising objects in the park, including a gigantic strawberry. Browne even uses the typefaces to provide the reader with clues about his characters: the faint and formal type used for Charles's narrative suggests the constraint and fear which characterise his childhood, whereas friendly, confident Smudge has her narrative printed in a bold, informal typeface. Thus the child reader is able to infer that even if Charles's childhood is more economically privileged, it is not necessarily happier.

The theme of equality is an important one throughout *Voices in the Park*. By giving each character their own narrative, Browne positions them as equally important and equally valid. The theme of equality and mirroring is repeated in subtle ways across the book. While Charles's dog is a pedigree and Smudge's a mongrel, their names – Victoria and Albert – link them together, and the dogs' willingness to play together suggests that they accept one another as equals. The first image of Charles and Smudge together similarly suggests a connection as the two look at one another from opposite ends of the park bench. A lamp post divides the image in half: on Charles's side the park is still dark and wintry, while on Smudge's side it is sunny and a fairy-tale castle can be seen in the background. The two sides are connected by the dogs, cut 'in half' by the lamp post so that they appear to be one single dog, presaging the friendship Smudge and Charles will form. Sure enough, in the next picture Charles and Smudge are together at the centre of the image, and the landscape behind them is all the same.

While the friendship between Charles and Smudge is the most appealing narrative – and the one reinforced by the illustrations – Browne refuses to give any one of the four voices complete authority. Charles's mother is the least appealing character, but the illustrations to her narrative make her realistic and somewhat sympathetic. When she believes Charles has disappeared, the trees behind her are shown with wide-open 'mouths' which mimic the panicked expression she wears on the facing page as she shouts for her son. If Charles's mother is fearsome, she is also fearful: the illustrations help the reader to understand that her perception of Smudge as 'a very rough-looking child' is based on genuine (if erroneous) fears. By refusing to simply dismiss her narrative, Browne maintains a genuine multiplicity of interpretations; he also suggests that the narratives we choose to follow are important. The division between 'us' and 'them' which dominates Charles's mother's internal narrative infects her view of the world as a whole: thus Browne not only gives readers the freedom to construct their own narrative from the text, but also suggests it is legitimate to construct a narrative which is appealing and joyful.

The richness of visual detail in Browne's books is engaging and important in its own right; it is also intimately connected with Browne's narratives, amplifying and sometimes disrupting the story in the text. While the surface narrative of *Voices in the Park* is apparently simple, the book is in fact extremely complex, raising postmodern questions about the nature of narrative and the role of the reader in constructing meaning. Browne's work illustrates the groundbreaking possibilities of picturebooks: while pictures are accessible to very young children, they offer a level of interest and complexity which is certainly not limited to the preliterate reader.

Notes

1   Jean and Gareth Adamson, *Topsy and Tim's Picnic* (Glasgow: Blackie, 1978), p. 12.
2   Emily Gravett, *Wolves* (London: Macmillan Children's Books, 2006), p. 22.
3   Meindert DeJong, *The Wheel on the School*, illustrated by Maurice Sendak (New York: Harper Trophy, 1972), p. 2.

4   Maurice Sendak, *Where the Wild Things Are* (New York: Scholastic, 1973). This text is unpaginated as are all those that follow where no page numbers have been provided.

5   Maurice Sendak, *In the Night Kitchen* (London: Red Fox, 2001).

6   Maurice Sendak, *Outside Over There* (London: Red Fox, 2002).

7   Anthony Browne, *Changes* (London: Walker, 2008).

8   Anthony Browne, *Willy the Wimp* (London: Walker, 2008).

9   Ellen Handler Spitz, *Inside Picture Books* (New Haven, CT: Yale University Press, 1999), p. 192.

10   Anthony Browne, *The Tunnel* (London: Walker, 2008).

11   Anthony Browne, *Into the Forest* (London: Walker, 2004).

12   Lauren Child, *I Am Too Absolutely Small for School* (London: Orchard, 2010).

13   Lauren Child, *Who's Afraid of the Big Bad Book?* (London: Hodder Children's Books, 2003).

14   Anthony Browne, *Voices in the Park* (London: Picture Corgi, 1999).

Young Adult Fiction: Blume, Chambers and Larbalestier

The earlier chapters in this book have discussed literature aimed specifically at or read by children. It may seem surprising, therefore, to include a chapter on books for young adults. This tension has played an important part in the history of young adult literature, which has been characterised by debate about whether it should exist as a specialist category, whether it should be seen as a branch of children's literature, and how old its prospective readers should be. Even its name has been a source of disagreement: should it be called 'young adult literature', 'adolescent literature', 'teenage literature' or simply 'books for older readers'? Despite such debate, however, by the end of the twentieth century books written specially for readers aged roughly twelve to twenty – in other words those in their teenage years – had become established as a thriving branch of 'children's' literature, and young adult literature continues to flourish today.

Young adult literature as a distinctive category is a relatively new branch of children's literature. While several well-known works of children's literature – notably Louisa May Alcott's *Little Women* (1868) and Mark Twain's *Adventures of Huckleberry Finn* (1884) – feature protagonists moving from childhood into the independence and self-awareness of adulthood, it was not until the 1950s that a specialist body of work explicitly defined as being for adolescent readers began to emerge. Economic prosperity and social changes in the postwar era had produced a new generation of adolescents – for the first time dubbed 'teenagers' – with their own money to spend and a distinctive cultural identity: the author Natalie Babbitt has observed ironically that the 'teenager' was created 'partly by parents, partly by manufacturers, and partly by Frank Sinatra'.[1] The idea that teenagers were different from both children and adults also owed much to psychologists: the influence of Jean Piaget's developmental psychology, which portrayed childhood as a series of distinct stages, helped to establish the belief that teenagers might have particular needs and interests.

Both the phenomenon of the 'teenager' and the development of books written especially for this age group emerged first in the United States, where young adult fiction was heavily influenced by J. D. Salinger's *The Catcher in the Rye* (1951), first published for adults but quickly embraced by adolescent readers. The story recounts the experiences of adolescent Holden Caulfield, alone in New York after being expelled from his expensive boarding school and – it is implied – undergoing a nervous breakdown. The colloquial first-person narrative of Salinger's protagonist – which owes a clear debt to Mark Twain's Huckleberry Finn – heralded the birth of a new literature which spoke to and about teenagers.

Holden's direct address to the reader and his use of slang[2] were to leave a lasting mark on young adult literature: first-person narrative has remained a consistent feature of books for adolescents, from S. E. Hinton's *The Outsiders* (1967) – written when the author was herself in her teens – and Paul Zindel's *The Pigman* (1968), through to Virginia Euwer Wolff's *Make Lemonade* (1993) and Melvin Burgess's *Lady: My Life as a Bitch* (2001). The device helps to create the illusion of a direct connection between author and reader, allowing the use of a teenage demotic and offering a more apparently authentic adolescent voice. It also creates the sense of exclusivity and intimacy: Salinger implies that Holden Caulfield is narrating his story to a psychiatrist, while in *The Pigman*, which deals with the friendship of two teenagers with an elderly man and their ultimate betrayal of his trust, the story is presented as a confession written by the protagonists John and Lorraine. A similar device is present in many other books for young adults, which often use the conceit of a diary, letters or blog in order to allow the teenage protagonist to directly narrate events: Louise Rennison's 'Confessions of Georgia Nicolson' series (1999–2009) is one particularly successful recent example.* In *Make Lemonade*, Virginia Euwer Wolff heightens the sense of an authentic teenage voice through the use of blank verse, which reproduces the fragmentary nature of real conversation.[3] Although highly literary in nature, Wolff's blank-verse narrative, addressed directly to the reader, creates the illusion of an authentic teenage voice apparently unfiltered by the more formal constraints of an adult narrating voice. Wolff's narrative style in *Make Lemonade* thus illustrates the innovative possibilities of young adult literature, which has often pushed boundaries of both content and style, as the discussion of Judy Blume and Aidan Chambers in this chapter will illustrate.

An important and influential element of Salinger's *The Catcher in the Rye* is its depiction of an adolescent in crisis and in conflict with the adult world. Holden Caulfield perceives the majority of the adults he meets as 'phonies' and struggles to come to terms with his own place in the world. The themes of conflict with authority and the struggle towards adolescent self-realisation have played an important role in many books for young adults: Ursula Le Guin's fantasy novel *A Wizard of Earthsea* (1968) brilliantly explores the tension between the increasing power and autonomy of its protagonist as he emerges into adulthood and the necessity of tempering adolescent power and agency with an understanding of the rules set in place by adults, while her realist novel *A Very Long Way from Anywhere Else* (1976) explores the pressures on adolescents to view their relationships in sexual terms. A much darker and more nihilistic look at the interaction between adolescents and social

---

* Neither first-person narrative nor epistolary fiction are solely the province of young adult literature; however, these narrative strategies have been particularly popular in books for adolescents.

structures appears in the work of Robert Cormier, notably *The Chocolate War* (1974), which portrays the (futile) attempts of teenage Jerry to fight back against the corrupt power structure which governs his high school. The themes of self-discovery and increasing autonomy are natural choices for a literature aimed at readers who are transitioning from childhood to adulthood; however, the work of writers like Robert Cormier illustrates that this does not confine young adult literature to a straightforward *Bildungsroman* structure in which the protagonist always emerges victorious from his or her process of maturation and discovery. On the contrary, young adult literature can also serve to challenge and disrupt narratives of growth and maturation.

Young adult literature has the potential to raise troubling questions in the minds of its readers, but it also has a strong tradition of books which offer adolescents help and advice intended to guide them through the challenges of growing up. The development of young adult literature as a distinctive category during the 1960s and 1970s was closely associated with a move towards more social realism in children's literature. The rapid pace of social change in Britain and America during this period heightened adult anxieties about the 'new' teenage demographic, and many commentators argued that a specialist literature was needed to help adolescents deal with the increasing complexity of the modern world. The critic and author Aidan Chambers was one of the most vocal proponents of books which addressed the everyday concerns of modern adolescents, arguing that the problem of the so-called 'reluctant' adolescent reader stemmed from the lack of books which focused on their key concerns and interests. Chambers identified friendships and relationships as a central concern for adolescents, along with parents, authority, work, the self – in the sense of strong emotions, opinions and the development of identity – and what Chambers terms 'the standard problems', among which he includes illegitimacy, drugs, illness, death, conflict and race.[4] Social issues like these have consistently been an important component of literature for young adults: teenage pregnancy has been a recurrent theme in books from

Paul Zindel's *My Darling, My Hamburger* (1969) – still unusual for its portrayal of a teen pregnancy which ends in abortion – to Berlie Doherty's *Dear Nobody* (1991), in which seventeen-year-old Helen chronicles her pregnancy through letters to her unborn child, and Malorie Blackman's *Boys Don't Cry* (2010), which addresses the topic from the point of view of the adolescent father. The theme of drug addiction has been tackled in a number of titles, most notably Melvin Burgess's acclaimed novel *Junk* (1996). Burgess's frank exploration of heroin addiction attracted much criticism for portraying his protagonists' initial enjoyment of the drug as well as the devastating consequences of their addiction, but was awarded both the Carnegie Medal and the Guardian Award for children's literature and has been the most commercially successful of Burgess's novels. The controversy surrounding *Junk* illustrates one of the ways in which literature for teenagers often pushes the boundaries of what is considered 'acceptable' for children's literature: while many adolescents encounter issues such as drug addiction in their real lives, it is not always comfortable for adults to recognise the relevance of such apparently 'adult' concerns to teenage readers.

Letters from Aunt Judy: Blume

The real-life issues encountered by ordinary adolescents are at the heart of the work of American writer Judy Blume, one of the most popular and influential writers for young adults in English. Blume made a major contribution to the 'problem' genre with her simply written and appealing books for both children and young adults. She is notable for her ability to deal honestly and sympathetically with the concerns of adolescence, in books which appeal to those in their early teens as well as older readers.

Blume's first young adult novel, *Are You There, God? It's Me, Margaret* (1970), illustrates many of the key elements of young adult literature. The book follows eleven-year-old Margaret's struggles with puberty, chronicling her anxieties about issues such as menstruation and acquiring her first bra, but also exploring her attempts to come to terms with deeper issues of identity as she seeks to reconcile her dual Jewish–Christian heritage. The book follows the tradition set in place by *The Catcher in the Rye* in its use of first-person narrative, interspersing Margaret's direct account to the reader with her conversational prayers: '*Are you there, God? It's me, Margaret. We're moving today. I'm so scared God. I've never lived anywhere but here. Suppose I hate my new school? . . . Please help me God. Don't let New Jersey be too horrible. Thank you.*'[5] The prayers enable Blume to effectively convey the vulnerability and conflict of early adolescence without sacrificing the realism of Margaret's narratorial voice, which addresses the reader like a close friend. The first-person narration helps to create the sense of an equal relationship between author and reader: in the guise of Margaret, Blume is able to reassure her readers that their anxieties and questions are normal, without condescension or lecturing.

Nevertheless, there is a strong didactic element to all Judy Blume's novels, which combine an exploration of the emotional experiences of their protagonists with some clearly outlined advice and guidance. *Deenie* (1973) is a good illustration of the techniques Blume uses to reassure and educate her readers. The main plot of the book centres around the eponymous heroine's discovery that she has scoliosis, a curvature of the spine which necessitates that she wear a back brace, but the story has attracted much notoriety for the frank discussion of masturbation which forms one of its secondary themes. Blume introduces the issue in a low-key and positive way with Deenie's comment: 'I have this special place and when I rub it I get a very nice feeling.'[6] Since Deenie does not consciously identify what she is doing as masturbation, there is no judgement or anxiety attached to her matter-of-fact reference, enabling Blume to convey to the reader that it is both normal and unexceptionable. Later in the book, Blume addresses cultural taboos about masturbation by including a scene in which Deenie and her schoolmates discuss the topic with the school nurse: when a fellow student says that she has heard that 'boys who touch themselves can go blind or […] even grow deformed' (p. 89), Deenie – as well as the reader – is moment-arily faced with the fear that her scoliosis is a direct result of masturba-tion, but the school nurse dispels these anxieties with the reassurance that: 'it's normal and harmless to masturbate' (p. 90). Blume has a clear didactic purpose here, but her didacticism is successful because it is connected to the emotional experience of her characters. The inclusion of advice and information has been a major feature of young adult literature, and one which has often attracted criticism – the author Nina Bawden commented disparagingly that readers in search of a 'young adult' novel were likely to be asked what problem they needed to solve – but Blume's genuine sympathy and engage-ment with her characters allows her to navigate the boundary between didacticism and genuinely meaningful and engaging narrative.

The discussion of masturbation in *Deenie* reflects Judy Blume's willingness to tackle taboo subjects in books for young adults. While Blume's protagonists typically come from secure middle-class families and her books are typically reassuring in tone, she has consistently pushed the boundaries of acceptable content in books for children and young adults. Her frank approach to topics such as masturbation and sex (for example in *Forever*, discussed in the extended commentary below) appears groundbreaking even today, and many of her other titles tackled issues which were largely absent from children's literature at the time they were published. Blume has dealt with racism and anti-Semitism in *Iggie's House* (1970) and *Starring Sally J. Freedman as Herself* (1977) respectively, and with bullying in *Blubber* (1974). *Deenie* explores the impact of illness and disability on Deenie's life and the conflict between parents' aspirations for their children and young people's own agency and desires. *Tiger Eyes* (1981), one of Blume's titles aimed at older adolescents, tackles the impact of a man's murder on his teenage daughter. Her willingness to discuss difficult and taboo topics has consistently earned Judy Blume criticism as well as praise: the American Library Association's lists of banned and challenged books, which document reports of attempts to ban books in schools and libraries in the United States, show that Blume has been one of the most common targets for attempted censorship. The degree to which Blume's books push at the boundaries of what is considered to be 'acceptable' content illustrates the way in which young adult literature frequently comes into conflict both with cultural ideas of what childhood and adolescence 'should' be like and with conservative ideologies: as the commentary on *Forever* will show, Blume's broadly left-wing, liberal approach to the controversial topics she discusses is one of the reasons she has attracted such fierce criticism in some quarters.

Real Life to the Present Day

Blume's success at addressing difficult real-life issues in books for adolescents has had an important impact on young adult literature as a whole. Jacqueline Wilson – discussed in detail in Part Three: 'Real Lives' – has continued the tradition of books which incorporate guidance and advice for their teenage readers into narratives which explore difficult emotional territory. Another notable contemporary 'issues' novelist is American Sarah Dessen, who has become popular in the United States and the UK with books such as *Just Listen* (2005), which centres around the impact of sexual assault on its protagonist Annabel and her gradual progression towards reclaiming her own identity. Challenging social issues are the focus for many contemporary young adult novels: Jacqueline Woodson explores issues of race and sexual identity in books such as *From the Notebooks of Melanin Sun* (1995), which centres around the impact on African-American Melanin Sun of his mother's lesbian relationship with a white woman; Laurie Halse Anderson tackles elective mutism and sexual assault in *Speak* (1999); and Sherman Alexie addresses racism and the struggles of Native American peoples in his moving and hilarious book *The Absolutely True Diary of a Part-Time Indian* (2010).

The critic Roberta Seelinger Trites has argued that young adult novels are fundamentally concerned with power and with the power relations between the self and society – that is, between the adolescent and the adult society he or she must negotiate – and that books which seek to advise and guide adolescents serve to enforce the dominance of adult ideologies.[7] Nevertheless, as Trites points out, young adult literature does not necessarily need to reinforce the unequal power dynamic between adult and adolescent. Increasingly, social realism in young adult literature has moved away from offering the kind of straightforward reassurance and advice which is typically present in Judy Blume's works, towards more ambiguous narratives which only partially resolve the issues they raise. In *After Tupac and D Foster* (2008), which recounts the impact of the real-life imprisonment and murder of rapper Tupac Shakur on a group of friends in New York, Jacqueline Woodson explores the impact of poverty and discrimination on African-American communities and the cultural criminalisation of young black men. The book sends a clear message about the injustice of contemporary American society, but there is no glib resolution to the conflicts it explores. On the contrary, when the narrator reflects at the end of the novel, 'Most days I'm just trying to figure it all out',[8] she speaks for the reader as well as for herself: Woodson is more interested in encouraging her readers to ask questions than in providing all the answers.

Narrative and Form: Pushing the Boundaries

Social realism for young adults frequently pushes the boundaries of 'children's' literature by its discussion of difficult or controversial topics such as sex, drug use or family conflict. Young adult literature has also been characterised by authors who push stylistic and narrative boundaries. Alan Garner, who won the Carnegie Medal for *The Owl Service* (1967) has experimented with narrative forms in many of his books, most notably in *Red Shift* (1973), which comprises three stories following separate sets of characters in different time periods, interconnected by a votive axe which characters in all three periods invest with power and meaning. Each part of the narrative plays out the same themes in different configurations; the oblique connections between the sections and the use of stream-of-consciousness narrative in some sections mean that readers must work hard to reconstruct the different narratives of the book for themselves. *Red Shift* has echoes of the Scottish fairy legend of Tam Lin, which also underpins another narratively complex title for young adults, Diana Wynne Jones's *Fire and Hemlock* (1985). *Fire and Hemlock* begins with its protagonist Polly realising that her memories of her childhood have been somehow tampered with, and the reader shares Polly's reconstruction of what really happened, in a narrative which breaks down the barriers between fantasy and reality. In common with many of Diana Wynne Jones's other titles – discussed in more detail in the chapter on fantasy – it forces the reader to be actively aware of the creation and manipulation of narrative, destabilising the authority of the authorial voice. These challenging narrative techniques often serve to resist the kind of top-down power dynamics which Seelinger Trites identifies as pervasive in young adult fiction, placing increasing responsibility on the reader and crediting them with the intellectual and emotional skills to interpret these demanding texts.

Reading the Adolescent: Chambers

Complex narrative modes and the destabilising of textual authority are a central feature of the work of Aidan Chambers, whose loosely connected series of novels, which he terms the 'Dance Sequence' (1978–2005), employs a variety of different forms and narrative voices to interrogate literary conventions and themes of identity.[9] In his critical work on young adult literature *The Reluctant Reader*, Chambers made the case for books which engaged with the kind of realist themes often associated with the kind of 'problem' novels produced by Judy Blume, but, whereas Blume typically offers her readers clear guidance about how to approach the issues she writes about, Chambers's 'problem' novels are also 'problematic', resisting a single interpretation or a clear didactic message.

The first novel in the 'Dance Sequence', *Breaktime* (1978), directly addresses the question of what literature means to adolescents, a question which plays an important role in the series as a whole. Ditto's friend Morgan accuses literature of being 'a sham, no longer useful, effluent', instigating Ditto's attempt to prove otherwise by embarking on a 'jaunt' which he will use as the raw material for his fiction.[10] Ditto travels to meet a girl, gets involved in a brawl at a political meeting, burgles a house and loses his virginity, before returning home to write about his experiences and present them to Morgan as a refutation of his 'Charges against Literature'. Ditto's story is told in a variety of different forms: lists of information, exchanges of dialogue written as for a play, handwritten notes between characters, excerpts from other texts, stream-of-consciousness accounts of Ditto's experiences, and conventional third-person narrative. These different narrative strategies have a paradoxical effect: the varied and fragmentary nature of the story, and the inclusion of ostensibly 'real' documents such as letters, heightens the sense of realism. Morgan – Ditto's reader within the text – takes the realism at face value, complaining: 'I was talking about fiction! And your little masterwork isn't fiction' (p. 138). At the same time, Chambers's use of such a variety of literary forms serves as a constant reminder to the reader that they are reading a literary construct: the illusionist strategies which John Stephens criticises for imposing an ideology on the reader (see the chapter on realism) are disrupted here by the tangible sense that the text is a text. At the end of the book, Ditto demands, 'How do you know I didn't sit in my room all week making the stuff up?' (p. 138), a question which disrupts the reader's trust in Ditto as a narrator. Having accepted his account of events during the course of the book, we are forced to wonder which parts are 'real'. At the very end of the book Chambers totally destabilises the illusion of reality, as Morgan asks '"Are you saying I'm just a character in a story?"' and Ditto replies laughingly '"Aren't we all?"' (p. 139). This ending forcibly reminds the reader that Ditto is, in fact, just a 'character in a story' and that none of the story he has presented is real in the sense that it has actually occurred. By breaking the illusion of reality in this fashion, Chambers forces the reader to consider the nature of fiction, the degree to which it can be considered 'true', and the reader's own responses to this book or any other. Thus he undermines the authority of all texts by reminding the reader that they are simply constructed realities, encouraging a more thoughtful and self-aware approach to reading. This tactic is not unique to young adult literature – as the chapter on fantasy notes, Diana Wynne Jones's metafictive techniques perform the same function in her books for younger readers as well as those aimed at adolescents – but it is particularly important in the context of a literature which has been fundamentally concerned with issues of power and authority.

Chambers's books also deal with issues of identity and selfhood. In *Breaktime*, Ditto's quest to disprove Morgan's charge that literature is worthless is also deeply connected with his need to assert his own identity and self-belief. Literature forms the focus of the conflict between Ditto – studious and focused on books and literature – and his father, a former joiner who is now incapacitated by illness. Ditto's attempt to prove that literature has an intrinsic worth is therefore also an attempt to prove his own value and to reconcile his identity as a reader with his father's more practical focus. At the end of the story, Ditto achieves this sense of reconciliation – or at least so his narrative would have the reader believe – implying that literature can in itself function as a tool through which to engage with real life. In Chambers's own words, 'certain books are an epiphany, a showing forth, that help us know who we are and what we are and what we can be',[11] a philosophy which is evident throughout the 'Dance Sequence'. The fourth book in the sequence, *The Toll Bridge* (1992), is the most overtly concerned with issues of identity: at the beginning of the novel the protagonist, Jan, says: 'I want to be honest with myself. I don't know how else to begin finding out what I really truly *am*.'[12] Jan's attempts to find out 'what he is and what he can be' intersect with those of his new friends Tess and Adam, and the book is composed of their narrations and renarrations of their lives, until a final revelation about the identity of one of the characters throws the constructed nature of identity into sharp relief. The subjective nature of identity is further exposed through the shared narration: Jan's account is interspersed with Tess's comments, which sometimes challenge and contradict his version of events and his representation of the characters. At the end of the book, it is suggested that identity is simply a matter of finding 'a story which is enough to keep [you] going on [your] own' (p. 195). We are the stories we tell about ourselves, Chambers suggests, and understanding this offers us the ability to take control of our own narratives.[13]

Chambers explores the relationships between narrative and identity and between the reader and the text in each book of the 'Dance Sequence'. His narrative strategies grow more complex as the series progresses, requiring the reader to take an increasingly active role in the creation of meaning. Although *Breaktime* forces the reader to consider the constructed nature of Ditto's story, his narration gives the book a cohesive structure. In the second book in the series, *Dance on My Grave* (1982), the authority of Hal Robinson's narrative about his own life is disrupted by alternative accounts of his actions from a newspaper report and his social worker's file. The later novels in the series successively break down textual authority by introducing more – and often conflicting – narrators who tell different stories or different versions of the same story. Finally, in *This Is All: The Pillow Book of Cordelia Kenn* (2005), Chambers returns to a single narrator – the eponymous Cordelia – but breaks down the authority of her narration by drawing the reader's attention to the book as text.

Nineteen-year-old Cordelia, pregnant with her first child, sets out to write an account of her life from the age of sixteen as a gift to her unborn daughter. Her book, modelled after the pillow book of classical Japanese writer Sei Shonagan, is comprised of a collection of different documents, loosely arranged into five books or boxes. The narrative written by Cordelia at nineteen is interspersed with documents created at the time she is writing about – poems, diary entries, reflective pieces – and the different fragments often interrupt one another or are presented side by side on facing pages, so that the reader is forced to choose the order in which they read. At the end of the novel, another narratorial voice intrudes: Cordelia's husband Will reveals that she has died before completing her book and that he is the one who has ordered the documents into the order presented to the reader. Thus the reader is simultaneously forced to participate in the creation of meaning within the text, and made aware of the subjectivity of *any* narrative, which is necessarily filtered through its tellers and which necessarily represents a version of the truth rather than an absolute truth. Chambers's representation of narrative breaks down structures of power and authority while empowering the reader. On the one hand, as Mary Harris Russell points out, Cordelia's death 'reveals the fictionality of authorship as power and control':[14] Cordelia cedes control over her own narrative to those she has left behind. On the other hand, by highlighting the fact that Cordelia's book – and by extension all texts – are constructed narratives, Chambers offers his adolescent readers the power to deconstruct the narratives they encounter: if the power of the author is a fiction then adolescents are no longer subject to that power.

Authors like Chambers, who push the boundaries of form and narrative in young adult literature, offer an alternative model for constructing adolescence. Chambers's novels are complex, highly literary and allusive – all the books of the 'Dance Sequence' contain heavy intertextual references to other works – and expect much of their readers. Whereas Judy Blume and her successors advise their readers, Chambers offers tools with which to think. While Chambers's particular brand of narrative experimentation is unique, similar strategies are evident in other texts for young adults across multiple genres: social realism remains an important part of young adult literature, but it is certainly not confined to the straightforward 'problem' novel.

Breaking Out of the Real: Fantasy for Young Adults

Although young adult fiction has been closely associated with realism, it crosses multiple genres, and there is a strong tradition of fantasy for adolescent readers. In the past decade, fantasy has been a particularly prominent part of the young adult market, and many new writers in the field are predominantly or partly writers of fantasy or science fiction. The cult television show *Buffy the Vampire Slayer* (1997–2003) demonstrated the possibilities inherent in narratives which blended the supernatural with everyday teenage life. Beginning with the premise 'high school is hell', the show explored how typical adolescent conflicts might play out if this were literally true: Buffy struggles to combine her destined role as a vampire slayer with the ordinary demands of high school, college and early adulthood. Stephenie Meyer utilises similar strategies in her hugely successful 'Twilight' series (2005–8), which gives high-school romance an epic quality by making its heroine Bella Swan fall in love with a vampire. Bella is essentially an ordinary adolescent, and her experiences are set firmly in the everyday (North American) world of gym classes and senior prom, but the drama surrounding decisions about issues such as when to lose her virginity is heightened by the fact that her boyfriend is a vampire. Fantasies like these offer a means of exploring the intensity of adolescent experience in an entertaining fashion, and often provide a means of discussing controversial issues more indirectly, enabling authors to touch on topics which might be considered too controversial for young adult readers.*

Using fantasy to tackle real-world issues can result in more conservative texts which neutralise threatening or problematic tropes; however, there are also subversive possibilities. Meyer's portrayal of sex in the 'Twilight' books has been criticised for its conservatism, both because its use of vampirism as a metaphor for

---

* Fantasy is not necessarily used to avoid addressing real issues, however: in *Buffy the Vampire Slayer* the show used witchcraft as a trope through which to explore lesbian identity, but quickly moved beyond the metaphor by depicting a lesbian relationship directly.

sexual desire seems unduly coy in the twenty-first century, and because of its politically conservative advocation of abstinence. However, by presenting her human heroine as the one who demands both literal physical contact and metaphorical sex – Bella repeatedly presses her vampire boyfriend to turn her into a vampire – Meyer does normalise strong female sexual desire in a way which is relatively unusual in mainstream young adult literature. Melvin Burgess takes the subversive possibilities of fantasy much further in *Lady: My Life as a Bitch*. When teenage Sandra is accidentally turned into a dog, the hedonistic delights of a life devoted to food and sex prove preferable to the pressures of GCSEs and family life. The fantasy elements allow Burgess to show his heroine indulging in literally animal pleasures, and enjoying a complete liberation from her real-life responsibilities; the ambivalence of the text about whether Sandra's decision to remain as a dog is positive or negative raises troubling questions about the high-pressure life of contemporary teenagers.

Magic and Metafiction: Larbalestier

One new author who has played with the genre possibilities of young adult fiction is Justine Larbalestier, whose books mix fantasy and realism. Larbalestier's work frequently challenges the reader, using different narrators and gradually developing plots which continually undermine what readers believe they know. Her 'Magic or Madness' (2005–7) trilogy sets its supernatural elements in the real world, dividing its narrative between Sydney and London. At the beginning of the narrative, her protagonist tells us: 'My name is Reason Cansino. […] My mother believes in all those things: logic, reason, and the rest, and in mathematics, which fortunately wasn't on the list of possible names.'[15] When Reason tells us that she and her mother have spent their lives on the run from her grandmother, who believes she is a witch, the realistic setting of Larbalestier's story – a recognisable twenty-first century Sydney – forces the reader to wonder whether the book will deliver a realist narrative rather than a fantasy. The revelation that Reason's mother has gone mad suggests that her stories about Reason's grandmother are nothing but delusions, an idea which is reinforced when Reason arrives at her grandmother's house to find that it is a completely ordinary suburban house rather than the supernatural headquarters she has been led to expect. The title of the book, however, primes us to assume that Reason's mother is actually deluded in her belief that magic is not real; an assumption which is confirmed with the introduction of a second narrator, Tom, who has received training in magic from Reason's grandmother. Reason's discovery that she herself is a magic user further challenges the idea that magic is dangerous and corrupt, but Larbalestier creates the sense of magic as a birthright which offers Reason access to wonderful places and experiences only to overturn everything once again. The instability of Larbalestier's narrative is increased by her use of three different narrators: Reason and Tom, both from Australia, and Jay-Tee, from New York, each of whom provides a different perspective on the events which take place. As in Aidan Chambers's *The Toll Bridge*, the reader must work to reconstruct the truth from the different sets of information the text provides, a technique which both deepens the sense of mystery in the story and destabilises truth and authority within the text.

Magic has been used as a metaphor for adult powers and responsibility in texts for young adults such as Ursula Le Guin's *A Wizard of Earthsea*; Larbalestier similarly connects it to the possibilities and problems which accompany adulthood. Magic in the 'Magic or Madness' series presents its users with a terrible choice: if Reason chooses to use her magic, she will drain her life force and die an early death – a situation already faced by her grandmother – but if she chooses not to use it at all, she will go mad as her mother has. Although Reason ultimately finds a way to escape magic altogether, the refusal of her friend Tom to take the cure and the final revelation that Reason's own child is magic prevents a complete resolution to the issues it raises. Larbalestier's exploration of magic serves to suggest that some of the problems which adolescents will face as they emerge into adulthood cannot be entirely solved, a distinct break from the tradition of young adult literature which offers guidance and solutions to the problems of adolescence.

The contradictions and uncertainties created by Larbalestier's use of multiple narrators in the 'Magic and Madness' books are even more present in her stand-alone novel *Liar* (2009), which mixes realism, fantasy and plays with notions of truth and authority. At the beginning of *Liar*, we seem to be presented with a traditional realist novel in the tradition of Judy Blume, narrated in the first person by its teenage protagonist. 'I will tell you my story and I will tell it straight', Micah promises readers. 'No lies, no omissions.'[16] But Micah is, by her own admission, a liar, and her promise to tell the truth only highlights the possibility that her story could be a lie. Micah lies about everything, even her gender, allowing other students at her school to believe she is a boy. Micah's status as an unreliable narrator forces the reader to consider troubling possibilities about her story, which purports to tell the truth about the murder of her boyfriend. In each section of the book, she doubles back, retracting previous truths and replacing them with the 'real' story, so that it is impossible for the reader to trust her narrative. The narrative uncertainty created by Micah's lies is intensified by the apparent impossibility of some of Micah's stories. At the beginning of Part 2, entitled 'Telling the True Truth', Micah 'confesses' the truth behind her lies, but her explanation takes the book into the realms of fantasy.* If we believe Micah's story, then we must mentally recategorise the book as fantasy, rather than as the realist account it has appeared to be. Alternatively, we can choose to read against the grain of Micah's narrative by assuming that her 'true truth' is the product of madness – true only in Micah's mind – or a lie designed to cover up her real involvement in the murder of her boyfriend. Like Aidan Chambers, Larbalestier places significant demands on her adolescent readers, forcing them to engage with questions of truth and authority, and to confront their preconceptions about genre.

---

* It is not possible to give details of Micah's story without drastically changing the experience of reading the book; therefore this summary confines itself to the frustratingly vague!

Micah's story in *Liar* is also deeply concerned with difficult issues surrounding identity. Her initial lie about her gender reveals her discomfort with the identity imposed upon her by existing social narratives: '[w]hy not be a boy? . . . A boy who runs, isn't interested in clothes or shows on TV. A boy like that is normal' (p. 8). Micah's ability to co-opt assumptions about gender in order to convince others that she is a boy suggests the subjective nature of gender identity: it is easy for her to pretend to be a boy because she fits male stereotypes better than female ones. Later in the book, Micah's teacher suggests that her unbelievable revelations about herself stem from a confusion about her identity, reassuring her that she doesn't have to pretend to be something she's not: 'You have to stop suppressing the girl parts of yourself. Is that why you keep your hair so short, Micah? Why you never wear skirts or dresses?' (p. 353). On one level, this explanation offers the reader another way to read the text by providing an explanation for her lies. On another, it gives voice to some of the real-life experiences faced by people who do not conform with gendered social norms: by aligning Micah's apparent madness with her desire to 'suppress the girl parts' of herself, Micah's teacher privileges gender conformity. Since Micah's narrative voice is the dominant one, the reader is encouraged to reject this simple correlation: we do not believe that Micah does want to be a boy, and thus we tend to resist her teacher's version of events. Nevertheless, whereas the equivalent speech in a Judy Blume novel would have sent an unequivocal message about how readers 'should' think, the complexities of Larbalestier's narrative make for a more ambiguous message. It is possible to accept her teacher's interpretation of events, or to reject both the teacher's account and Micah's account. It is even possible to read the whole scene as one of Micah's inventions. By disrupting the authority of the narratorial voice in this manner, Larbalestier forces her readers to consider the issues she raises for themselves, without providing a single 'correct' answer.

The blurry boundaries between fantasy and realism and between truth and lies in Larbalestier's novels are emblematic of the way in which young adult literature has developed in the twenty-first century. Straightforward, reassuring narratives like those written by Judy Blume and Jacqueline Wilson still play an important role in literature for adolescents, but increasingly even this tradition has devolved into more complex and ambiguous forms. The narrative experimentation utilised by writers like Justine Larbalestier and Aidan Chambers resists a simple top-down power relationship between author and reader, positioning adolescents as co-creators of meaning, while writers such as Jacqueline Woodson offer social realism which explores real issues without providing any simple answers. Like children's literature as a whole, young adult literature pushes boundaries in content and style. The emergence of new voices such as Justine Larbalestier's in recent years suggests that it will continue to do so well into the twenty-first century.

Extended Commentary: Blume, *Forever* (1975)

'Sybil Davidson has a genius IQ and has been laid by at least six different guys.'[17] The opening line of Judy Blume's *Forever*, one of the most popular and most controversial young adult novels of the twentieth century, illustrates many of the key elements of young adult literature as it emerged in the postwar era. Like *The Catcher in the Rye*, the book is narrated in the first person by its teenage protagonist, eighteen-year-old Katherine. Her opening words establish one of the key concerns of the novel: sex – and the right or wrong circumstances in which to have it. The focus of *Forever* is the developing relationship between Katherine and her first boyfriend, Michael. The couple meet, fall in love and, when they have decided that their love is 'forever', sleep together. Despite Katherine and Michael's commitment to their relationship, Katherine's parents express doubts about whether the relationship will last; their doubts are vindicated when Katherine meets and falls in love with another boy while working as a counsellor in a summer camp (a job that her parents insist she take in order to 'test' her relationship with Michael). In the periphery of the novel are the couple's friends, Erica and Artie – pursuing a doomed relationship of their own – and Sybil Davidson, whose sexual adventures ultimately result in an unplanned pregnancy. In addition to relationships, *Forever* addresses a number of other issues identified by Aidan Chambers as particularly important to teenagers: the heart of the novel is Katherine's growing self-awareness and understanding of adult relationships, but it also deals with Sybil's unplanned pregnancy and decision to have her illegitimate child adopted, the implied homosexuality of Michael's friend Artie and his attempted suicide, Katherine's relationships with her friends, parents, grandparents and younger sister, her university applications, and the changing sociopolitical circumstances of the period. All these themes have continued to play a dominant role in literature for young adults.

Judy Blume takes a frank approach to teenage sexuality in *Forever*, and the book includes several relatively explicit sex scenes. It was particularly groundbreaking in its emphasis on Katherine's sexual agency. She initiates sex, and recounts: 'I came before he did. But I kept moving until he groaned and as he finished I came again, not caring about anything – anything but how good it felt' (p. 149). The inclusion of such 'adult' content is one of the hallmarks of young adult fiction: while young adult novels do not necessarily include sex or other potentially controversial content, the inclusion of such content is often one of the primary reasons for marketing a book as a young adult rather than a children's novel. This is certainly a primary reason for the identification of *Forever* as a young adult novel: in style and difficulty of language it bears close similarities to Blume's other books, some of which have been marketed at much younger audiences, but the publication history of the book illustrates the degree to which concerns about controversial content have influenced children's and young adult literature. Although it is today accepted as a typical young adult novel, it was originally published – against Blume's own wishes – as her 'first adult novel', a decision which reflects the publishers' uneasiness with the explicit nature of the book.[18] Their concern was certainly warranted: the American Library Association lists *Forever* as one of the most frequently challenged books of the first decade of the twenty-first century, more than thirty years after the book's original publication.[19] The levels of explicit content in *Forever* are relatively tame compared to some contemporary young adult literature, although the book still stands out for its depiction of Katherine as the initiating partner. The controversy which is attached to it reflects continuing levels of discomfort about the barriers between children's and young adult literature; Blume's status as a popular writer for younger children perhaps helps to intensify concerns that her young adult books will be read by the 'wrong' audience.

The criticisms which *Forever* has attracted stem partly from her positive presentation of sex; however, there is also a strong didactic element to the book. Prior to *Forever*, the desire to offer books which provided young adults with information about sex and relationships frequently produced overtly didactic novels such as Josephine Kamm's *Young Mother* (1965), which delivered a heavy moral message about the consequences of underage sex, punishing its hapless protagonist with an unwanted pregnancy and social ostracism. Judy Blume has stated that she was consciously responding to such books when she wrote *Forever*, commenting that she wrote it after her own teenage daughter asked for 'a story about two nice kids who have sex without either of them having to die'.[20] True to her word, Katherine and Michael both make it to the end of the book alive and unharmed, but *Forever* retains a strong didactic message. Early in the novel, Katherine summarises an article on sexual relationships sent to her by her grandmother, saying 'A person shouldn't ever feel pushed into sex [...] or that she has to do it to please someone else' (p. 95); a summary which could just as well be applied to *Forever* itself. As Roberta Seelinger Trites points out, Blume takes pains to show that Katherine and Michael are modelling a 'good' sexual relationship; the promiscuous Sybil is punished with an unplanned pregnancy which turns out to be 'more than she bargained for' (p. 157), and when Katherine's friend Erika – who claims to see sex 'as a physical thing' (p. 26) – falls in love, her boyfriend attempts suicide.[21] Furthermore, Katherine and Michael's own assessment of their relationship is ultimately revealed to be false: after sleeping with Michael, Katherine reflects: 'there are so many ways to love a person. This is how it should be – forever' (p. 149), but by the end of the book we are already aware that their relationship was not as permanent as it seemed. If forever is 'how it should be', then Blume suggests that teenagers may not be in a position to judge. While it is legitimately groundbreaking and controversial, therefore, *Forever* stands in a long line of young adult books which are focused on educating and socialising their teenage readers.

Notes

1   Quoted in Michael Cart, *From Romance to Realism: 50 Years of Growth and Change in Young Adult Literature* (New York: HarperCollins, 1996), p. 5.

2   See J. D. Salinger, *The Catcher in the Rye* (London: Penguin, 2010), p. 1.

3   See Virginia Euwer Wolff, *Make Lemonade* (New York: Scholastic, 1993), p. 3.

4   Aidan Chambers, *The Reluctant Reader* (London: Pergamon Press, 1969), p. 75.

5   Judy Blume, *Are You There, God? It's Me, Margaret* (New York: Delacorte Press, 1988), p. 1.

6   Judy Blume, *Deenie* (London: Macmillan Children's Books, 2001), p. 57.

7   Roberta Seelinger Trites, *Disturbing the Universe: Power and Repression in Adolescent Literature* (Iowa City, IA: University of Iowa Press, 2002).

8   Jacqueline Woodson, *After Tupac and D Foster* (London: Puffin, 2008), p. 151.

9   The name derives from the second book, *Dance on My Grave* (1982), and reflects Chambers's sense that they are 'an intricate kind of dance' and sequentially related 'like members of a family'. Aidan Chambers, 'The Dance Sequence', accessed from www.aidanchambers.co.uk on 13 January 2011, n.p.

10 Aidan Chambers, *Breaktime* (London: Red Fox, 2000), p. 10.

11 Aidan Chambers, 'Anne Frank's Pen', in *Reading Talk* (Stroud: Thimble Press, 2001), pp. 9–28, p. 24.

12 Aidan Chambers, *The Toll Bridge* (London: Red Fox, 2000), p. 17.

13 Lissa Paul discusses the relationship between narrative and identity in Chambers's novels in more detail in 'Dancing in the Hall of Mirrors', in Nancy Chambers (ed.), *Reading the Novels of Aidan Chambers* (Stroud: Thimble Press, 2009), pp. 62–72.

14 Mary Harris Russell, 'Interpretation as Power in Aidan Chambers's *Postcards From No-Man's Land* and *This Is All: The Pillow Book of Cordelia Kenn*', in Nancy Chambers (ed.), *Reading the Novels of Aidan Chambers*, pp. 135–56, p. 153.

15 Justine Larbalestier, *Magic or Madness* (New York: Razorbill, 2005), p. 1.

16 Justine Larbalestier, *Liar* (New York: Bloomsbury, 2009), p. 3.

17 Judy Blume, *Forever* (London: Young Picador, 2005), p. 1.

18   Cat Yampbell, 'Judging a Book by Its Cover: Publishing Trends in Young Adult Literature', *The Lion and the Unicorn*, 29:3 (September 2005), pp. 348–72, p. 351.

19   American Library Association, 'Top 100 Banned/Challenged Books: 2000–2009', accessed from www.ala.org on 31 May 2010, n.p.

20   Judy Blume, 'Forever', accessed from www.judyblume.com on 31 May 2010, n.p.

21   Roberta Seelinger Trites, *Disturbing the Universe: Power and Repression in Adolescent Literature* (Iowa City, IA: University of Iowa Press, 2002), pp. 86–96.

Part Four
Critical Theories and Debates

Criticising Children's Literature

Children's books are different from other texts. They are different in what they are, and different in the way in which we, as adult readers and critics, are positioned with regard to them. This means that how, why and what we write about them will be distinctive – to the extent that people bringing different skills, interests, motives and points of view to the criticism of children's books will differ radically in what they think is worth saying about a text.

Basic Issues in Children's Book Criticism

At its simplest, there are two ways of approaching texts: the first, 'intrinsic', looks at each work of literature as separate from the world – as 'a self-contained object of both study and veneration'[1] – and remains at the root of 'conventional' thinking about and talking about books. The second, 'extrinsic', which has dominated critical thinking since the early 1980s, places texts in the context of social, cultural and linguistic forces – and, in the case of children's literature, of the audience.

A book such as Frances Hodgson Burnett's *The Secret Garden* might be looked at, intrinsically, as an interaction between deprived children and the forces of nature, in the symbolic spaces of house, garden and moor, and as an interaction between children and inward-looking and outward-looking adults. The interest lies in how the characters develop within, as it were, the theatre of the book. Extrinsically, we might take a historical view – what is the literary context of the book (it may be derived from *Jane Eyre*), or the political context (Burnett is critical of the corruption of empire and the rigidity of the English class system), or the cultural context (gardens, and mystical approaches to gardens, such as Lilias Trotter's *Parables of the Cross*, 1890, were highly popular at the time)? Or one could apply theories from other disciplines, such as psychology (what is the latent sexual attraction of Mary and Dickon?) or feminism (is Mary marginalised at the end of the story?).

Then we can place *The Secret Garden* in the context of its readers (past and present). What do (or did) children make of the book? Will they enjoy it; will they understand it; will they be influenced by it? This is to leave aside book historians, who are interested in what changes Burnett made to her manuscripts, what differences there are between American and British editions, which illustrations are included, and whether the first American edition was pirated and similar matters.

This is where children's literature criticism begins to distinguish itself from criticism in general. A distinction can be made between 'book people' and 'child people': the 'book people' are those who would study books without reference to their audience, and feel that to consider the audience invalidates any general (and therefore useful) statements we might make about books; 'child people' are those who think that unless we involve real children, then the exercise of criticism is pointless.

The Difference of Children's Literature Criticism

The most extreme reaction to the 'child-people' critics has been Karín Lesnik-Oberstein's assertion, initially in *Children's Literature: Criticism and the Fictional Child*, that adults writing about children's books often create an essentialist concept of the child, a generalised and unverifiable concept against which they then match their judgements.[2] This idea is developed from Jacqueline Rose who argued that there could never be such a thing as children's literature, that is, a literature belonging to children, or truly of childhood, because the concepts of children and childhood were created by adults.[3] Rose also proposed that these concepts and their manipulation are necessarily malign; this was a view springing from a particular historical moment, but it has been reflected in recent governmental child-protection excesses, and it also reflects the discomfort of very many adults with their relationship with childhood (theirs and others').

These views have provoked a great deal of discussion, possibly best summarised in Perry Nodelman's *The Hidden Adult*;[4] clearly, Lesnik-Oberstein is right that a good deal of what is written about children's books is reviewing – matching the book to the child – but that is also true of adult literature: the problem is that the structures of academic and popular criticism are not as highly developed in the children's book world, and so there is a good deal of overlap between practical criticism and theoretical criticism. The vast majority of academic critical writing about children's books, however, actually ignores children (to the annoyance of the 'child people'), while there has been a great deal of effort to approach Lesnik-Oberstein's conundrum directly. As Nodelman puts it, criticism of children's books has evangelical overtones:

> While I can't describe how a 'real child' understands children's
> literature […] I can certainly use my knowledge of reading and
> textual practices to attempt a description of how the literature
> works to affect its implied readers – the child readers
> constructed by its texts. And I believe I have a moral
> responsibility to proceed with the conviction that such a
> project is pointless without a long-range goal of actually
> affecting how real people read and think about what they read
> – including, eventually, children.[5]

There is little point in trying to make reductive generalisations (as many writers have done) about what constitutes children's books – considerations of length, complexity, ideology or content items are meaningless in a form that, worldwide and for several centuries, has involved every genre, every mode and every circumstance of text production. Equally, as we have seen in this book, it is a fallacy to assume that children's texts are simpler than adult texts: all texts are part of a web of ideology, language and culture, and although the emphases of one genre or type might be different, no text can be dismissed as 'simple' – or, as with children's texts over the years – beneath the notice of serious criticism.

This means that every critical device available to adult critics is available to children's book critics. There is no need to compromise our thinking, or 'scale down': we can bring our armoury from whatever our primary field of interest is – from literacy, education, history, folklore, theatre, art and so on – and we *have* to. If we take an apparently simple example – that of Roger Hargreaves's 'Mister Men' and 'Little Miss' books, we might think that the bold colours and limited number of shapes and lines symbolising crude stereotypes such as *Mr Happy* or *Little Miss Splendid* would not bear much discussion. These are, however, highly conventional symbolic shapes and colours; to derive meaning from them we need a great deal of aesthetic and cultural knowledge. The written texts may seem to be derivative and expedient, but we cannot make such a judgement (let alone validate it) without a lot of extratextual knowledge and intratextual skills.

The Difference of the Books

Despite their similarities to adults' texts, texts 'for children' do have one essential, overriding difference: every text for children has, necessarily, built into it some idea of a child or childhood. The complexity of that apparently simple statement can be bewildering: the writers write with a 'child idea' – a specific child, their childhood, their publishers' idea of childhood, their culture's idea of childhood and so on. The fact that, as Rose and Lesnik-Oberstein rightly point out, such constructions are self-invalidating merely complicates matters further.

Add to this the fact that many peoples' relationship to their own childhood is profoundly ambivalent, and the relationship of the reader and writer to the child (or child idea) in a book is likely to be ambivalent as a result. Under the guise of innocent entertainment, which is a guise colluded with by many adult readers, 'children's' texts may well be exorcisms, idealisations or confessions – one only has to look at the work of Lewis Carroll, struggling with his relationship to a young girl, at Enid Blyton coping with the loss of and rejection by her father through her adventure fantasies, or at Roald Dahl's explorations of the dark sides of human nature in his ostensibly humorous and slapstick books. What is going on in a children's book, and how each reader interprets what is going on, is one of the central puzzles for children's book critics.

On top of this, there is the exaggerated power imbalance of children's books: every writer–reader relationship is based on an imbalance of power, but with children's books – because an experienced writer is writing to a less experienced reader – that power imbalance is more exaggerated. Consequently, the way stories are told, the tone, narrative voice, viewpoint, structures and so on are particularly interesting for children's book critics.

Attitudes to power are also behind the way in which certain types of writing have gravitated to children's books. What have folk and fairy tales, for example, with their often graphic violence, murder, cannibalism, nightmare wolves, appeal to primal fears, and preoccupation with sexuality and gender roles, to do with a childhood which, in the twenty-first century in the West, is constructed as a place to be protected? What has the primary theme of most of the Disney Corporation's movies – marriage – to do with its ostensible pre-pubescent audience? As J. R. R. Tolkien observed:

> Actually, the association of children and fairy-stories is an
> accident of our domestic history. Fairy-stories have in the

modern lettered world been relegated to the 'nursery', as shabby or old-fashioned furniture is relegated to the play-room, primarily because adults do not want it, and do not mind if it is misused. It is not the choice of the children which decides this. Children as a class – except in a common lack of experience they are not one – neither like fairy-stories more, nor understand them better than adults do.[6]

The Difference of the Relationship

The process of criticism has traditionally driven personal response to the edges: we are educated to refine out our personal response (I like it/I like it not) and to regard individual response as subservient to general responses. Similarly, most critics are brought up to assume that there is something superior in texts, called 'literature' or 'great art', and that there is an absolute scale of relativity. On such a scale, children's books are, by definition, at the lower end, along with comics, popular daily newspapers and mass-market paperback romances.

These concepts are not appropriate to, or helpful for, children's books. Because many people feel that they have control over the book just as they have control over their children, the whole critical process becomes more democratic: there are no Leavis-like critical high priests telling us what we must like, and what we must value. The Canadian critic Perry Nodelman described his surprise, having worked in a traditional university English department, at encountering guides to children's literature for the first time:

> They all made judgements of excellence in terms of the effects of books on their audience – and that astonished me, for in the ivory tower of literary study I had hitherto inhabited, one certainly did not judge books by how they affected audiences; in fact, one often judged audiences by the extent to which they were affected by books, so that, for instance, anyone who wasn't overwhelmed by Shakespeare was simply assumed to be an intransigent dummy.[7]

Consequently, what we feel about the texts now becomes a legitimate part of the critical matrix. It is quite possible – and in the academic, adult world of the criticism of adult texts, quite normal – to create the illusion that the relationship between text and critic is a purely intellectual one, unproblematic, unstained by the personal reactions that are so essential to non-academic readers; however, this is much less likely to be the case with children's literature. Even the best of academic critics suspect that there may be a blind spot here. J. M. S. Tompkins, in a scholarly examination of Kipling, for example, wrote:

> It is not easy to take a dispassionate view of a book to which we have been much indebted in youth [...] If this study had aimed at a critical evaluation, I think I should not have dared to write this chapter [...] There should be, then, some value in the testimony of a reader who was a child of the generation for which [these stories] were written.[8]

Suddenly the silenced child that was, or the silenced child that is, has a voice in the critical process.

Reading Children's Literature Critically

All of this means that the process of criticising (discussing/thinking about) children's literature is a good deal more complex than the process of discussing adult literature.

When as adults we read a book designed for adults, we read it (usually) in one or two ways, separately or simultaneously. We read it for ourselves, for pleasure, stimulation, information, excitement or whatever we read books for; we may read it, perhaps especially if we are students, so that we can talk about it or write essays on it. There may, of course, be a silent slippage between what we think about a text and what we say about a text – between what we think and what we know we ought to think – or, less sceptically, between our immediate, visceral, emotional or intellectual response, and an analytic, contextualised, theorised reading, designed to be part of a different discourse.

So far, so ordinary. However, when we come, as adults, to read a children's book, life is at least twice as complicated. We read the book (or look at the picture, or watch the film) in the two ways just described, but the first way, reading for ourselves, divides itself almost inevitably into two.

First, we read as our adult selves – some critics think that we cannot do anything else: we do not ignore the 'implied reader' – every book implies the kind of reader or reading it requires – but we do not identify with it. This can often be an uncomfortable reading. Second, we read as children – that is we accept the role of the implied reader, and in doing so to some extent react as our child selves might have done. We adjust both to what is required of us and to what part of us remembers, however residually, it was like to read a book like this. This is, it seems, often a pleasure – and often a guilty pleasure – but it is often (again, some critics think, inevitably) an incomplete, fractured reading. This is quite apart from the problems that emanate, as we have seen, from the unhappy relationship between many adults and their childhood.

The second of our original two reading strategies – reading a book in order to discuss it – suddenly becomes much more complicated when a children's book is involved. Discussing an 'adult's' book with friends or in a literature seminar requires a certain set of analytical skills. When we are discussing a children's book we are likely to be doing it in a much wider and more challenging context. We will need to ask: why are we discussing it? Is this a discussion of education, literacy, aesthetics, politics … or what? Are we 'book people', interested in what we see in the book and its history, background, size and shape, where it fits into national or cultural history and so on, or are we 'child people', interested in how the book affects its readers? Are we parents, teachers or psychologists, trying to find out what happens when specific books and specific children meet?

This brings us to an extra way of reading: very often, we are reading for a child, on behalf of a child. We are the gatekeepers (to use a fashionable term): as adults we have to make decisions about what children will like, or what they should like – what will frighten them and/or entertain them. The decisions that we make here are very particular: with adults' books, the answer to what people like is relatively simply found by asking them or watching their choices. It is not always easy, or possible, for an inexperienced reader to articulate judgements – or even to make judgements in terms that will be accessible to an adult. Those who work closely with children are often frustrated or puzzled by observing a child's reaction to a book, but being unable to identify the stimulus or interpret the response. They may regard David Lewis's dictum that 'those who think that children can tell us nothing of any use about the books they read have simply not been listening' as more idealistic than practical.[9] Reading 'on behalf of the child' immediately raises issues of power and violation, never more so than when it includes deciding what children will not be allowed to read. We will look at censorship in Part Four: 'Children's Literature and Ideology', but a moment's thought should show that to judge the effect of a book requires an understanding of the way in which the intended readers make meaning, and, individually and collectively, that is hardly a simple matter.

A Case Study: Reading *Harry Potter and the Philosopher's Stone*

How does this work in practice? Imagine that you are, as an adult reader, picking up *Harry Potter and the Philosopher's Stone* for the first time, perhaps after the second volume, *Harry Potter and the Chamber of Secrets*, was published, and the 'Harry Potter phenomenon' had started. You are probably typical of many adults, with no specific motive beyond natural curiosity about what is rapidly becoming a phenomenon.

On the first level, you are reading for yourself, making your own emotional and intuitive judgements. You do not have any problem with reading a children's book, nor do you have anything against fantasy (unlike those 12 per cent of readers who preferred the 'adult' version of the cover),[10] and you are prepared to give the book every chance. You may have some doubts about the authenticity of the publicity stories being built up around the book ('starving author writing in coffee shops for warmth'), but many famous books, such as *Alice's Adventures in Wonderland* or *The Wind in the Willows*, have carefully cultivated myths attached to their origins. To begin, you are slightly distracted by the physical layout of the book – the narrow margins, the unusual typeface, the amateurish (or faux-naïf) cover illustrations with a sign-post growing out of Harry's head.

There was a time when such facts would have seemed critically irrelevant, but it would be idle to deny that the experience of a book is, in some part, influenced by them – otherwise, why have different covers for adults and children? Even if, at this level of reading, we are not obliged to share our personal circumstances or preferences with anyone, our experience and knowledge will colour what we read.

To return to *Harry Potter and the Philosopher's Stone*: if you are a reader of a certain age and experience and have certain preferences, you may immediately stumble over language that is different from your expectations: the first few paragraphs are thick with clichés and characters such as Mr Dursley appear more as caricatures.[11] Many critics have seen this as an inauspicious start – an indication, as the subsequent rows over the Whitbread Award demonstrated, that these books were of low quality. You might find it more profitable to change your expectations – not to read this prose comparing it to a more subtle and nuanced fantasist such as Kipling, but rather to see it in a literary context in which subtlety or freshness of language is not an issue. As you read on, you might not be able to avoid being reminded of Jill Murphy's 'Worst Witch' series, and being entertained by the relish with which ancient devices from the school story are employed.

So far, this is a very adult reading: we might assume that a less experienced reader, not having the knowledge of Jill Murphy or school stories, or being entirely used to this kind of language, would be having a very different experience. At which point, you might well begin to read in the way that the kind of child implied by the text might do: the text implies that the reader is someone prepared to accept the simple shorthand of style in return for the rapid succession of image and caricatures, as if doors were endlessly being opened with images that are different and new (to the reader). A box of delights, perhaps, and while your experienced-reader mind may frown over the obviousness of names like Malfoy, Crabbe and Goyle, your surrender-to-the-storyteller mind accepts the events, and your inexperienced/child-reader mind is gradually seduced by the exuberance of the invention: see, for example, the description of Hogwarts on page 98. There is a serious danger here that we might begin to assume this reading is actually the kind of reading that a young person, or persons, might make when encountering the text. We in fact do not know that, for it is unknowable individually, and once we go beyond the individual and begin to characterise childhood, it is only knowable in terms of our own characterisation.

The next kind of simultaneous reading is 'reading to talk to others about it'. This is the most difficult jump to make for the average reader: with children's books, the struggle to move from involvement in the story to analytic judgement is probably more intense than in books being read in a carefully segregated academic context. Consequently, at this stage, if we are going to be critical, we need to draw on the sort of 'external' questions that criticism is now commonly concerned with, and which are commonly codified in critical textbooks: what is going on in terms of gender? Is this predominantly a male book? Is Hermione a caricatured brain – the token girl? Such questions then have to be directed somewhere – are we interested in the social context of the book and, if so, is Rowling out of step with contemporary thinking? Or are we interested in the psychological impact of the book in terms of its effect on its readers? Similarly, with the school setting: can we draw comparisons with a major English genre, and demonstrate how the school is an ideal place for setting children's books, teaching ritual in a safe space? Or are we interested to know why such a quintessentially English institution is popular worldwide? Are all enclosed, rule-bound institutions similar, so that Hogwarts strikes chords everywhere, or is its popularity to do with the world's view of the English? Finding things to say is a matter of focusing on what is important in a given context.

We then come to reading on behalf of the child. You may have strong feelings that children should be allowed to read anything they want: some families operate an 'open-shelf' policy in their homes, on the principle that parental example will be sufficient to allow children to make good decisions. Or you may hold sincere beliefs that cause you to object to the books being about witchcraft, whether or not Rowling could be accused of advocating it. The important point here is that the sort of problems that come with this 'reading for' exercise, the sort of questions that we as children's literature critics find ourselves asking, are not questions that we would have to ask of any other form of literature. Adult readers can look after themselves, and adults have a responsibility to children. Therefore, reading a children's book leads almost inevitably to a kind of practical judgement.

Perhaps the biggest danger to interesting criticism comes at this point – the need to answer the question: why is a book successful? Again, it is a question of not much interest elsewhere. There is a great deal of this kind of discussion surrounding the 'Harry Potter' series:

> What makes Harry Potter so popular is not just the alternative world Rowling brilliantly creates – but the wonderfully drawn interior world of Harry. Readers see an imperfect character come to terms with his fame and notoriety, struggle movingly with the loss of his parents.[12]

or

> The success of the Harry Potter books is due to their popularity with children [...] Adults certainly enjoy them, but it was children who got there first.[13]

Even a distinguished critic such as Jack Zipes can slip into this generalised way of thinking, which really says very little. Zipes points out that:

> there is something wonderfully paradoxical about the phenomena surrounding the phenomenon of the Harry Potter books. For anything to become a phenomenon in Western society it must become *conventional* [...] In the case of the Harry Potter books, their phenomenality detracts from their conventionality, and yet their absolute conformance to popular audience expectations is what makes for their phenomenality.

He then slips into the banal: 'Harry appeals to young readers (and adults) because Rowling has endowed him with supernatural powers of the sort we can see in numerous [...] TV shows and films.'[14] Such extrapolations can be seen as dangerous. However, encountering a book like *Harry Potter and the Philosopher's Stone* through the four ways of reading can provide us with a firm basis for discussion of the book – whatever the context of the discussion.

Conventional Criticism and New Criticisms

As many critics have demonstrated, the well-established methodologies of criticism in general can be remarkably fruitful in discussing children's books: the gap between children's literature and the most arcane philosophical criticism is not large.[15] It is therefore perhaps not surprising that specialist critical approaches to children's literature have been slow to develop.

Although, as we have seen, there is a fracture in children's book criticism between book people (text-based) and child people (response-based), there has been until quite recently a shared liberal humanist faith in the value of the book. At the 'book-people' end of the spectrum we can find enthusiasts such as Francis Spufford, Seth

Lerer and Fred Inglis,[16] whose credos can be summed up by John Goldthwaite, lamenting the modern world:

> With the advent of the comic book, the motion picture, and television, the growth of make-believe as a literature of ideas came to a standstill. A literary audience became a mass market, make-believe became entertainment, and encountering the miracles of story became the passive activity of an audience trained to consume images [...] A literature should not be merchandised as an amusement park, when it is predicated on the quiet surmise that a materialistic reading of the world is insufficient to account for who we are [...] There have always been some authors who have understood that the true role of make-believe is to baptize the imagination.[17]

As with the work of prominent educationalists and literacy experts, such as Margaret Meek, Aidan Chambers and Geoff Fox,[18] children's literature becomes part of a civilising influence, and is criticised in such terms. At the other end of the political spectrum, there have been some examples of Marxist readings, such as those by Bob Dixon and Robert Leeson.[19] Clearly, as we shall see in our discussion in Part Four: 'Children's Literature and Ideology', the children's book critic is entering a political world, and it is good to establish one's own ideological standpoint at the outset.

In this general context, children's books have developed their own specialist modes of criticism. The theorising of picture books, which has burgeoned along with the development of 'new media' and the shift to the visual in children's texts, is considered in Part Four: 'The Future of Children's Literature'; five other relatively distinctive 'schools' or methods of criticism are noted here.

Cross-Writing

At the 'book-people' or textual end of the spectrum, two American critics, the Victorian scholar U. C. Knoepflemacher and the late

Mitzi Myers, developed the idea that within many (if not all) texts for children there are two voices:

> a dialogic mix of older and younger voices occurs in texts too often read as univocal. Authors who write for children inevitably create a colloquy between past and present selves. Yet such conversations are neither unconscious nor necessarily riven by strife.[20]

Examples are Rudyard Kipling's *Just So Stories* and E. Nesbit's 'Bastable' stories.

The opposite view of the same idea is given by Barbara Wall, who suggests that there are three modes of address in children's literature – single, double and dual.[21] She feels that the single address, which is adult to child only, is the purest. Dual address, which is a respectful address to adults and to children simultaneously, is the most practical – and, other critics have suggested, the only possible form. The third, double address, is when the writer is ostensibly talking to children but is actually talking above the children's heads. Identifying these modes is one of the most fascinating critical approaches to children's books. A. A. Milne, notably, uses the third, double address, in the early pages of *Winnie-the-Pooh*, and Wall would argue that the joke about Winnie-the-Pooh living under the name of Sanders illustrated 'literally' by Shepard (Pooh sits beneath a sign which reads 'Sanders') is accessible only to the knowing adult reader, and is thus disrespectful to the implied primary reader. How far this is also true of writers like Roald Dahl can be debated – and the discussion has been complicated (at least in film) by the concept of postmodern childhood. Thus the string of adult-oriented jokes in the 'Shrek' film franchise might have been seen as a cynical betrayal of the child audience, but is now more likely to be interpreted as part of a contract between knowing adults and knowing children (and children may know something that the adults do not). This kind of textual analysis provides an opportunity to reassess many classic texts in the light of changing concepts of childhood.

Childness

The second theory moves the text slightly closer to the child (however conceptualised). Peter Hollindale attempts to identify or define children's texts in terms of both writer and reader: 'childness' is the quality of being a child – it is the

> shared ground, although differently experienced and understood, between child and adult [...] Childness is the distinguishing property of a text in children's literature [...] and it is also the property that a child brings to the reading of a text [...] The childness of the text can change the childness of the child, and vice versa.[22]

This is evangelical thinking, based on Hollindale's view that:

> there is much that modern theory can do to illuminate children's literature, but there is also no question [...] that much contemporary theory is hopelessly incompatible with the very concept of 'children's literature', and with what authors think they are doing when they write it, and what children appear to be doing when they read it.[23]

Writers need, in effect, to engage children with the concept of childness in the face of commodification – and in the face of what is perhaps a growing generation gap. How far writers, particularly of science fiction, which is so notably marked with dystopias, achieve this will be of great interest to future critics.

Childist Criticism

A rather more theoretical approach to what readers make of texts is that of childist criticism, which has been described as both a Romantic concept and an attitude of mind rather than a critical method. It developed from the idea that criticism was primarily an adult preoccupation, and ignored any possible input by children. By analogy with feminist criticism, it proposed that children read distinctively from adults, and that this should be taken into account when interpreting texts. Its two primary tenets – that children's responses are unknowable, and that conventional value judgements made by adults are not applicable to any specific reading – are rooted in undermining or challenging the invisible norm of the adult interpretation.[24] Thus it is very difficult to find a commentary on a picture book, for instance, that does not at some point say, 'this picture shows' – as if this interpretation of the picture were inevitable. Childist criticism does not pretend to read the minds of children, or to guess what individuals are thinking: it merely wishes to question the primacy of unexamined adult judgements: why is what 'we' (the adults) see correct? Of course, such a theory is prey to generalisations and speculations – but any speculation is perhaps more likely to be accurate than generalisations based on adult power. It is a salutary exercise to take any stretch of text, and ask: what meaning might you make if you did not understand the denotations or connotations of certain words; what sense could you make of this text if you did not know its structures and rules?

Child Criticism

The most obvious omission from this theorising is the child, the young reader himself or herself – that is, a real reader, rather than a theoretical one, as in childist criticism. Increasingly, researchers and critics have allowed children's voices to be heard – evidence from what children say (usually in classrooms) is now seen as critically significant. The pioneers of this approach were the psychologists Hugh and Maureen Crago, who studied the reading development and response of one of their daughters over several years, and Aidan Chambers, who proposed both theory and method for eliciting and analysing children's responses. An important contribution to methodology has been in the field of picture books, with Arizpe and Styles's *Children Reading Pictures* (2003).[25]

It has to be said that such a critical strategy goes against a long tradition of adults being in control of reading. The historian, critic and bibliographer Brian Alderson famously observed that consulting children on their books is:

> innocuous if pointless: but when the critic seeks to use child-response to establish or refute a critical position, it can be much more dangerous. At best it forms a type of special pleading foreign to the art of criticism [...] In calling on the views of children [the critic] is almost bound to receive opinions that are immature and often inarticulate.[26]

Times are clearly changing.

Childhood Studies

Finally, children's literature criticism is taking its place within the growing meta-discipline of childhood studies. This relatively new partnering of sociology, psychology, law, medicine, history and literature (among others) focuses on 'childhood as a conceptual category and as a social position for the study of a previously overlooked or marginalised group – children'.[27] The role of children's book criticism in this context has yet to be explored, but its potential for exploiting both intrinsic and extrinsic methods, and relating them to the audience, is very great.

Criticising the Popular – Children's Book Criticism at Work

The criticism of children's literature, then, is possibly at its best when it is eclectic in its use of methods and theories, and frees itself from the value systems of adult writing. The confusion occurs in trying to equate the children's literature 'system' with the adult 'system' – and they are not parallel.

To demonstrate the potential of criticism freed from the problems of 'literature', it is helpful to take a famous, popular, but far from 'canonical' or 'classic' text, and demonstrate its critical potential – as long as we approach it with an open mind. Taking a book more or less at random from a very well-read section of the family bookshelves, we find one of Enid Blyton's novels, *Five Go Down to the Sea* (1953), the twelfth of twenty-one books about 'the Famous Five' – not counting many more written after Blyton's death. Criticism of Blyton tends towards the numerical – her more than 600 titles, the millions of books still sold each year – and towards her iconic status as the epitome of the popular and, in literary terms, the worthless. All of that, however, is not to do justice to the necessary complexity of her books, both intrinsically and extrinsically.

Five Go Down to the Sea, if approached with an open mind – or, perhaps, approached with the degree of respect that we accord an established 'classic' – can be read contextually, first in terms of Blyton's other books. Her work is very English, mid-twentieth century, middle class, largely fantasy, and very often that most potent form of fantasy: fantasy that masquerades as realism. A glance through this book shows recurrent Blytonian motifs – an opposition between the lush country and the threatening (ruined) castle, the symbols of movement and freedom in caravans and nomadic people, an emphasis on food as comfort, renewal and security, a strong sexuality/sensuality as well as sexism, economy of character, and a basic wish fulfilment by the least empowered (the children). Intertextually, within the oeuvre and the series, reference can be made to a complete world, to the irascible parents, to the timidity of one of the characters, the stereotyped female, Anne, and to the ironic inevitability of certain kinds of events: "'I just want a holiday, nothing more. Let's have a jolly good time, and not go on looking for anything strange or mysterious or adventurous.'"[28] In the context of post-Second World War literature, Blyton's books are entirely consistent with the ruralist, pacifist, nostalgic trends exemplified by writers for adults such as John Moore and H. E. Bates; in terms of children's literature, *Five Go Down to the Sea*, with its acknowledgement of the cruel reality of shipwrecks and potential violence, is a precursor of writers such as Philippa Pearce or the early

Alan Garner, where fantastic (and serious) happenings are contextualised in the secure family, or in economically drawn characters. This may be 'lightweight', but the political context and content is inescapable.

And so from the title onwards, in which the key words – *Go Down* – imply a lost, golden, idyllic world, with the image of walking down to the sea, the atmosphere of an Arcadian Cornwall is established. In the opening chapters, when the children (aged, as established in the first book of the series, between ten and twelve) go on an unaccompanied holiday, we have bicycles, a puncture, a steam train, dusty, empty lanes – in which the children are innocently free and empowered. Not only have the period details become potent (and we might ask, for whom?) – the isolated railway halt, the village shop with lemonade kept cool in the cellar – but the emphasis is on food catered as much for the desires of 1953 England as for the symbolic meanings we now perceive.

A great deal has been written about the function of food in children's books[29] as comfort, as desire, as sexuality: what is to be made of Blyton's postwar food orgies? In *Five Go Down to the Sea*, the children are presented with a 'magnificent' high tea, with a 'huge ham', 'a salad fit for a king', 'lashings of hard boiled eggs', plus 'a cherry tart made with our own cherries' and even the promise of 'a snack ready for you when you come in' (pp. 17–18, 25). Just as *The Wind in the Willows*, *Tom's Midnight Garden*, *Swallows and Amazons* or many of Jacqueline Wilson's novels are built around ceremonial food, so *Five Go Down to the Sea* uses food (or its absence) to indicate acceptance or rejection, initiation or outsiderism, security and insecurity – as at the end, when the wild boy, Yan, is only allowed to join the feast if he voluntarily cleanses himself and accepts the basics of civilised behaviour.

This is carried by a prose that can be subtle. Consider a line from the first chapter: 'It was about five o'clock and a lovely evening. They met nobody at all, not even a slow old farm cart' (p. 13). The device of describing an absence, an expectation, moves into an intimate collusion between narrator, character and reader, virtuoso use of free indirect discourse. As Barbara Wall, in her study of narrative voice in children's literature, puts it:

> The pervading tone of the dialogue becomes inescapably blended with the narrative voice. The narrator briefly recounts an action and then slides imperceptibly into the thoughts of the character, so that it appears as though the narrator is commenting on the action in the voice of the child character. This has the effect of causing the narrator to appear to be confiding in the narratee.[30]

Nor is *Five Go Down to the Sea* entirely escapist – fantasy, after all (and this is primarily fantasy, although that might not be obvious to all its readers), is often the opposite of escapist. Blyton even approaches grim historical reality, with the account of wreckers on the Cornish coast.

Then there is Blyton's personal background, and personal details are no longer a taboo element in criticism. Blyton's father left the family when she was thirteen, and was estranged from her mother, which some have seen as a potent explanation for the insistence on the happy family group, the displaced, lost or misjudged father figures, the ambiguous men, and the overcompensating, obsessive mother figures in her books. Blyton was described at one stage as 'the mother of the world's children', and yet seemed to have limited maternal instincts towards her own daughters. Her younger daughter Imogen Smallwood noted:

> Her feeling for her readers and for all children in the abstract was intense and loving; but as one of her two children who should have been closest to her of all, I saw her only as a distant authority, a clever person, a strong and imaginative actress on the little stage of my life, but never, or almost never, as a mother.[31]

From this psychological, social and literary background emerges a complex texture, which balances dark and light, security and violence, power and helplessness, which explores (often with the crudity and directness of a certain construction of childhood) insider and outsider, as well as class, race and sexual distinctions. In *Five Go Down to the Sea* these complexities are seen even in the behaviour of the Cornish dogs, who are wild and working class, in comparison with the middle-class and well-trained Timmy, in the otherness of the masks of the travelling players, of the acceptability of everything from accents to beards. *Five Go Down to the Sea* is a rich text, not only capable of being read in a 'literary' way, but almost certainly given endless such readings by hundreds of thousands of readers. For if the experience of literature means being absorbed, taken over, and having your life changed, then the experience of Blyton's books by millions of children has been a literary one.

Criticising children's literature is a challenge: we have an almost infinitely complex and rich body of texts, designed for an audience less (and differently) experienced and less intellectually developed than the writer. We have many disciplines involved in its study, many audiences for its criticism. Perhaps above all, it forces us to reconsider how and why we are writing about the texts: it takes us back to the first principles of criticism.

Notes

1   Roderick McGillis, 'Criticism Is the Theory of Literature', in David Rudd (ed.), *The Routledge Companion to Children's Literature* (London and New York: Routledge, 2010), p. 19.

2   Karín Lesnik-Oberstein, *Children's Literature: Criticism and the Fictional Child* (Oxford: Clarendon Press, 1994).

3   Jacqueline Rose, *The Case of Peter Pan or the Impossibility of Children's Fiction*, rev. edn (London: Macmillan, 1994).

4   Perry Nodelman, *The Hidden Adult: Defining Children's Literature* (Baltimore, MD: Johns Hopkins University Press, 2008), pp. 86–90.

5   Nodelman, *The Hidden Adult*, p. 7.

6   J. R. R. Tolkien, *Tree and Leaf* (London: Allen and Unwin, 1970), p. 34.

7   Perry Nodelman (ed.), *Touchstones: Reflections on the Best in Children's Literature*, vol. 1 (West Lafayette, IN: Children's Literature Association, 1985), p. 4.

8   J. M. S. Tompkins, *The Art of Rudyard Kipling* (London: Methuen, 1959), p. 39.

9   David Lewis, 'Children's Literature Studies: The State of the Art?', *Children's Literature in Education*, 28:4 (1997), pp. 235–8, p. 235.

10   Claire Squires, *Marketing Literature: The Making of Contemporary Writing in Britain* (Basingstoke: Palgrave Macmillan, 2009), p. 167.

11   J. K. Rowling, *Harry Potter and the Philosopher's Stone* (London: Bloomsbury, 1997), p. 7.

12   Carol King, cited in Julia Eccleshare (ed.), *1001 Children's Books You Must Read Before You Grow Up* (London: Cassell, 2009), p. 662.

13   Lindsey Fraser, cited in Daniel Hahn, Daniel Flynn and Leonie Flynn, with Susan Reuben (eds.), *The Ultimate Book Guide: Over 600 Great Books for 8–12s* (London: A. and C. Black, 2004), p. 106.

14   Jack Zipes, *Sticks and Stones: The Troublesome Success of Children's Literature from Slovenly Peter to Harry Potter* (New York and London: Routledge, 2001), pp. 175–6, p. 180.

15   See, for example, Perry Nodelman and Mavis Reimer, *The Pleasures of Children's Literature*, 3rd edn (Boston: Allyn and Bacon, 2003); Roderick McGillis, *The Nimble Reader: Literary Theory and Children's Literature* (New York: Twayne, 1996).

16   See Francis Spufford, *The Child that Books Built* (London: Faber and Faber, 2002); Seth Lerer, *Children's Literature: A Reader's History from Aesop to Harry Potter* (Chicago, IL: University of Chicago Press, 2008); and Fred Inglis, *The Promise of Happiness: Value and Meaning in Children's Fiction* (Cambridge: Cambridge University Press, 1981.)

17   John Goldthwaite, *The Natural History of Make-Believe* (New York: Oxford University Press, 1996), p. 12.

18   Margaret Meek, *How Texts Teach What Readers Learn* (South Woodchester: Thimble Press, 1988); Aidan Chambers, *Booktalk: Occasional Writing on Literature and Children* (London: Bodley Head, 1985); Geoff Fox (ed.), *Celebrating Children's Literature in Education* (London: Hodder & Stoughton, 1995).

19   Bob Dixon, *Catching Them Young*, vol. 1: *Sex, Race and Class in Children's Fiction*, and vol. 2: *Political Ideas in Children's Fiction* (London: Pluto Press, 1977); Robert Leeson, *Reading and Righting* (London: Collins, 1985).

20   U. C. Knoepflemacher and Mitzi Myers, 'From the Editors', *Children's Literature*, 25 (1997), p. vii.

21   Barbara Wall, *The Narrator's Voice: The Dilemma of Children's Fiction* (London: Macmillan, 1991).

22   Peter Hollindale, *Signs of Childness in Children's Books* (South Woodchester: Thimble Press, 1997), p. 47.

23   Hollindale, *Signs of Childness*, p. 69.

24   Peter Hunt, *Criticism, Theory and Children's Literature* (Oxford: Blackwell, 1991), pp. 189–201.

25   Hugh and Maureen Crago, *Prelude to Literacy: A Pre-School Child's Encounter with Picture and Story* (Carbondale, IL: Southern Illinois University Press, 1983); Aidan Chambers, *Tell Me: Children, Reading and Talk* (South Woodchester: Thimble Press, 1993); Evelyn Arizpe and Morag Styles, *Children Reading Pictures: Interpreting Visual Texts* (London: Routledge Falmer, 2003).

26   Brian Alderson, 'The Irrelevance of Children to the Children's Book Reviewer', *Children's Book News* (January/February 1969), p. 10.

27   Mary Jane Kehily (ed.), *An Introduction to Childhood Studies*, 2nd edn (Maidenhead: McGraw Hill/Open University Press, 2009); and see also Mary Jane Kehily and Joan Swann (eds), *Children's Cultural Worlds* (Chichester: John Wiley, 2003).

28   Enid Blyton, *Five Go Down to the Sea* (London: Hodder Headline, 1991), p. 10.

29   See for example Kara K. Keeling and Scott T. Pollard (eds), *Critical Approaches to Food in Children's Literature* (New York: Routledge, 2008).

30   Wall, *Narrator's Voice*, p. 191.

31   Imogen Smallwood, *A Childhood at Green Hedges* (London: Methuen, 1989), p. 12; and see Barbara Stoney, *Enid Blyton, a Biography* (London: Hodder & Stoughton, 1974).

Gender and Sexuality

The issue of gender is pervasive in children's literature. As one critic has said, 'Is there such a thing as children's literature, in any case? Might it be more accurate to speak of a boys' literature and a girls' literature?'[1] From the beginning of commercial children's literature to the highly developed commodification of the twenty-first century, gender has been fundamental to sales of children's texts, and to reinforcing and reflecting social mores through them. As Nodelman suggests:

> The reinforcement of traditional gender assumptions is one particular and particularly important aspect of the colonizing work of children's literature – so much so that a defining characteristic of children's literature is that it intends to teach what it means for girls to be girls and boys to be boys.[2]

This means, of course, what adults think it means for girls to be girls and boys to be boys, and so there has been a constant tension between childhood as it is and childhood as constructed, as well as between the responses of the real child and those of the ideal child. For over 250 years, publishers have produced genres that teach boys to be boys – desert islands, sea stories, war and empire, public schools, flying adventure and most recently secret agents – and girls to be girls – waif novels, fairy stories, pony books, girl-guide stories, and most recently variations on babysitting, high-school romance, and first-person diaries dealing with social realism (Jacqueline Wilson) or princess fantasies (Meg Cabot's *The Princess Diaries* series, from 2000). 'Shared' genres, from the family holiday story of the 1930s to Stephenie Meyer's 'Twilight' series of vampire novels (2005–8), commonly emphasise the acceptable (or unconsciously accepted) male and female roles in society and the cultural characteristics that go with them. There has always, of course, been a crossover of readership, although girls have always been more inclined to read boys' books than the other way around, and since the early 1980s there have been a good many conscious attempts at social engineering.

Gender – coded social behaviours – and biological sex and sexuality are not the same but, in children's texts, with their complicated adult–child power relationships, they have an uneasy relationship. As Kehily and Montgomery note, 'the privileging of innocence as a central feature of childhood often involves adults in a denial of childhood sexuality.'[3] There has historically been, as a consequence, a distortion of childhood and adolescence: they have been constructed as asexual – sexuality is airbrushed out of the lives of empire-building boys or charitable girls in nineteenth-century fiction, and the very notoriety of books in which it has been acknowledged or explored since the early 1970s, from Judy Blume's *Forever* (1975) to Melvin Burgess's *Doing It* (2003), suggests that the concept of innocent childhood is still important to many adults. As Nodelman points out, in the late twentieth century in children's literature:

> gender is at least theoretically divorced from sexuality, and boys must be boyish and girls girlish for reasons that have nothing to do with the underlying reasons that there are gender categories at all. The focus on gender implies a hidden awareness of children as at least potentially sexual beings and suggests the possibility that sexuality is at least part of the sublimated, hidden adult content of children's literature.[4]

Children's literature protects adults as much as children; the idea that children's literature is an escape for children from the messy problems of adolescence has at least partly been replaced by the idea that fiction can be a handbook for life, and is thus necessarily explicit. As Cadogan and Craig noted in the 1980s:

> the sense of moral obligation, which governs all writing for children, has acquired a new bias. It used to entail keeping your stories as anodyne as possible; now, if anything, the opposite holds true.[5]

Part of Judy Blume's declared motivation for writing *Forever* was to provide her daughter with a story in which sexual transgression did not result in punishment (or damnation) as it had so spectacularly in the nineteenth-century novel. In doing so, she shifted not only the limits of what it was (generally) acceptable to talk about in children's books, but also the gender roles and role models. Whereas Beverley Cleary's bestseller *Fifteen* (1956) begins: 'Today I'm going to meet a boy, Jane Purdy told herself' and ends 'She was Stan's girl. That was all that really mattered', twenty years later, *Forever* begins: 'Sybil Davison has a genius I.Q. and has been laid by at least six different guys', and ends 'I think it's just that I'm not ready for forever.'[6] Twenty years on from that, Babette Cole could address explicit sexual topics in the comic picture book *Mummy Laid an Egg* (1993), while *Buffy the Vampire Slayer* (1997–2003) could provoke arguments as to whether the female hero is sexual, asexual, post-modernist, feminist or post-feminist. In the twenty-first century, there has been something of a backlash – driven both commercially and evangelically – towards more 'traditional' gender roles (both marketable and moral), and a more conservative attitude to the portrayal of sexuality. Clearly, questions of gender and sexuality will remain a problem as long as the idea that adults' involvement with children contains the potential for violation of some kind – and as long as children's books are seen as influential.

All of this needs to be placed in the context of the fact that girls read more than boys, and girls read differently from boys – girls are more ready to see themselves as readers of traditional forms of text, whereas boys, partly through electronic gaming, may be 'staking a claim to the more powerful means of communication by participating more actively in the biggest revolution of literacy practices since the introduction of print'.[7] Then there is the fact that the majority of writers for children since the beginning of children's literature have been women (although whether their books are female-gendered is another question), and most publishers and editors of children's books are women – a fact that was notoriously highlighted by John Goldthwaite:

> There are too many women in children's books, and far too many holding down editorial positions. This imbalance of male and female sensibilities might have been accepted in 1919, when Macmillan put together the world's first juvenile department, and, under the delusion that children's books belonged to the ladies, gave it over to one; but there is no excuse for it today. There is no evidence that women understand more than men what children need and want; and even if there were it would hardly affect the verdict on books given us by several generations of women editors who have proven that, whatever their good intentions, their standards are timid and commercial [...] In this henpecked world, no-one speaks the unspeakable: that, with the exception of Beatrix Potter, every great children's novel was written by a man, and nearly all of them by a man with little or no professional interest in children or their literature.[8]

What difference does this make, if any? Does it imply a confusion between sex and gender – perhaps female publishers feel it necessary to adopt male gender-behavioural characteristics in a ruthless world? There are also incidental interesting questions: how far do modern female heroes, such as Lyra in Philip Pullman's 'His Dark Materials', Hermione in J. K. Rowling's 'Harry Potter' series or Buffy the Vampire Slayer, redress the gender imbalance? How far have the successors to the pioneering gay and lesbian novels for children – notably John Donovan's *I'll Get There: It Better Be Worth the Trip* (1972), Aidan Chambers's *Dance on My Grave* (1982) and Sandra Scoppetone's *Happy Endings Are All Alike* (1978) – succeeded in normalising the gender behaviour portrayed? Why does naughty boy William Brown survive into the twenty-first century, but not his naughty girl equivalent, Evadne Price's Jane? How far can a twenty-first century reader accurately assess the all-male or all-female relationships portrayed in adventure stories or school stories of a hundred years ago – or the non-sexual behaviour of teenagers in novels into the 1970s? And why was Billy Bunter funny, but not Bessie Bunter?

> Her brother had buffooned his way through the *Magnet* for eleven years to the delight of boy and girl readers, but obesity in a girl produced quite a different effect, making her a figure of sympathy rather than contemptuous amusement.[9]

The study of gender in children's books has been extremely fruitful: historically, as in Lynne Vallone's *Disciplines of Virtue: Girls' Culture in the Eighteenth and Nineteenth Centuries*, or in terms of literary theory and *l'écriture féminine* – the theory of the difference of women's writing – as in Christine Wilkie-Stibbs's *The Feminine Subject in Children's Literature*, or in terms of gender theory, as in John Stephens's *Ways of Being Male*, or Kenneth Kidd's 'Boyology in the Twentieth Century'.[10] This chapter explores some of the basic issues.

Gender and Children's Book History

Early Lessons

Gender roles are deeply embedded in folk tales, and are implicit in the earliest books for children, such as Bunyan's *A Book for Boys and Girls* (1686). The first commercial publishers for children recognised the potential of the two markets. John Newbery's *A Little Pretty Pocket-Book* (1744) is a forerunner of the gender marketing in today's bookshops: the original advertisement for the book, in the *London Penny Advertiser*, reads:

> A Little Pretty Pocket-Book, intended for the Instruction and Amusement of Little Master Tommy and pretty Miss Polly, with an agreeable Letter to each from Jack the Giant Killer, as also a Ball and a Pincushion, the use of which will infallibly make Tommy a good Boy, and Polly a good Girl.[11]

The immediate stereotyping of gender roles is clear in books such as Newbery's *The History of Goody Two-Shoes* (1765), in which Margery Meanwell becomes village schoolmistress, and Sarah Fielding's collection of stories about Mrs Teachum's school, *The Governess, or, the Little Female Academy* (1749), which begins with a declaration of intent:

> The design of the following Sheets is to endeavour to cultivate an early inclination to Benevolence, and a Love of Virtue, in the Minds of young Women, by trying to shew them, that their True Interest is concerned in cherishing and improving those amiable Dispositions into Habits; and in keeping down all rough and boisterous Passions; and that from this alone they can propose to themselves to arrive at true Happiness, in any of the Stations of Life allotted to the Female Character.[12]

The family story – attempting to portray (and therefore encourage) the ideal family – developed primarily as a portrayal of the nuclear family, itself a sixteenth-century phenomenon.[13] A gendered hierarchy was established, which can be traced in children's literature through to the mid-twentieth century as an actuality, and into the twenty-first century as a nostalgic ideal. The bestselling *History of the Fairchild Family* (1818 and sequels) by Mrs Sherwood is characteristic: the father is head of the family, standing in place of

God; the mother is subservient, representing the Church, and passing on the male orders to the children. The children are stereotyped: the boy is boisterous and occasionally rebellious, the girls delicate, sensitive and conformist.

Although there was a gradual relaxation in attitudes to the discipline of children, underlying gender markers remained: for example, in Catherine Sinclair's *Holiday House* (1839), when Harry sets fire to the nursery, he hides: 'for Harry always thought it a terrible disgrace to cry, and would have concealed himself anywhere rather than be observed weeping'. When Laura cuts off her hair, her punishment is that 'every looking-glass she sees for six months will make her feel ashamed of herself.'[14] While this kind of gender stereotyping is still with us, the history of children's books over the past two centuries has shown a constant tension between society's ideas and individual subversion – and some profoundly ambiguous attitudes.

Masculinities

It is easy to generalise: boys don't cry – or do they? As Kimberley Reynolds notes,

> attributes of masculinity which were perfectly acceptable in 1858 – such things as crying [not, as with Harry, from pain or fear, but from emotion], hugging, expressing love rather than comradeship – had by the *fin de siècle* been banished to the realm of the feminine.[15]

What is clear is that, through the nineteenth century, the idea of masculinity projected in stories for boys was built on images of manhood of the clearest kind. Consider two of the heroes of R. M. Ballantyne's *The Coral Island* (1858):

> Jack Martin was a tall, strapping, broad-shouldered youth of eighteen, with a handsome, good-humoured, firm face. He

had had a good education, was clever and hearty and lion-like in his actions, but mild and quiet in disposition. Jack was a general favourite [...] My other companion was Peterkin Gay. He was little, quick, funny, decidedly mischievous and about fourteen years old. But Peterkin's mischief was almost always harmless, else he could not have been so much beloved as he was.[16]

These are boys who honoured their parents, loved their mothers and sisters, and were chivalrous on those rare occasions when they encountered any other females. Our hero is honest, loyal to Queen and country, and fights fairly; although he does not shrink from violence, as the century wore on his stereotype even runs to preferring to fight with fists, in the British way, rather than using a weapon. The manliness of boxing might stand as a symbol for all this. In G. A. Henty's *Condemned as a Nihilist* (1893) the hero, Geoffrey, justifies it:

One learns to keep cool and have one's wits about one; for anyone who loses his temper has but a poor chance indeed against another who keeps cool. Moreover a man who can box well will always keep his head in all times of danger and difficulty. It gives him nerve and self-confidence, and enables him at all times to protect the weak against the strong.[17]

The hero's dedication to the Bible is rather more variable across the century, but he is always pious, and ready to die for his cause. This also means, of course, that to many twenty-first-century readers he is also violent, racist and sexist, because masculinity was inextricably related to empire and imperialism. As Jeffrey Richards noted:

evangelism [and] the commercial and cultural imperialism [of the mid-century] [...] gave way in the last decades of the nineteenth century [...] to aggressive militarism [...] as the evangelical impulse itself became secularised and fed into full-blown imperialism, which became in many ways a new religion blended of the Protestant work-ethic and the public school code.[18]

Definitions of masculinity gradually moved from the concept of courage and endurance (plus brutality) as in the adventure stories of, for example, R. M. Ballantyne, towards the 'muscular Christianity' of writers like Thomas Hughes and Charles Kingsley, and the inherently Romantic concept of the chivalric gentleman. The codes of 'proper' behaviour were inculcated in the public schools, and spread through society via boys' fiction and boys' magazines. Even in the 1960s, when the British Empire (and public-school fiction) had largely disappeared, and a more thuggish idea of masculinity emerged, the underlying nineteenth-century masculinities of children's books, it can be argued, remained unchanged: Harry Potter's values are well over a hundred years old.

It is important to note that there is a distinction to be made between adventure stories for boys and adventure stories for men. In the latter:

> to take risks, to travel is to leave the masculinity of the shore or metropolis. Hence transgression [...] is inherent in the processes of masculine formation or experience [...] To be masculine is to be in revolt.[19]

Nineteenth-century British boys (as opposed to their American counterparts) were encouraged to be adventurous, but to respect limits set by the adult culture, often symbolised by restrictive settings. An example of a story set in the outdoors, but still within boundaries, is Richard Jefferies's *Bevis: The Story of a Boy* (1882), a book initially for adults which became a staple of boys' reading. Bevis and his friend Mark spend several weeks fending for themselves on a lake island on Bevis's father's farm. In what now seems to be a stunning display of political incorrectness, they build a gun and slaughter rare animals; they recruit a local girl to act as their servant; and they eventually return home in the manner of the soldiers of empire:

In those days of running, racing, leaping, exploring, swimming, the skin nude to the sun, and wind and water, they built themselves up of steel, steel that would bear the hardest wear of the world. Had they been put in an open boat and thrust forth to sea like the Viking of old, it would not have hurt them.

Throughout their adventures, the boys reference the adventure stories they have read – they work their way through jungles, are attacked by savages and, as Bevis says when they are playing cards, 'The proper thing is to shoot you under the table [...] That's what buccaneers do.'[20] This self-referential fictionality added to the self-confidence of the idea of the masculine, and the idea was reinforced by the school story or, more precisely, the English boys' public-school story.

This important genre was established, with many of its codes of behaviour, its characters and its basic plot lines, with Harriet Martineau's *The Crofton Boys* (1841). The English schoolboys' code involved standing up to the bully, protecting the weak, keeping faith, not crying (or, if one must cry for home, doing it in private):

> a boy is full of action – if he tops the rest at play – holds his tongue, or helps others generously – or shows a manly spirit without being proud of it, the whole school is his friend.[21]

All these ideas were confirmed in Thomas Hughes's *Tom Brown's Schooldays* (1857): Tom's father sends him to school to turn out to be 'a brave, helpful, truth-telling Englishman, and a gentleman, and a Christian'.[22] This tradition was taken to its pious (and sadistic) extreme in Frederick Farrar's *Eric, or Little by Little* (1858), and was popularised by writers like Talbot Baines Reed in the *Boy's Own Paper*.

A considerable dent was made in these ideas of the masculine by Stevenson's *Treasure Island* (1883) and Kipling's *Stalky and Co.* (1899). In *Treasure Island*, Jim Hawkins is everything that the boy hero should not be – self-serving, borderline cowardly and disillusioned with the treasure-seeking enterprise. *Treasure Island* is a radical rewriting of the sea, treasure and empire brand of adventure-story tradition, in which the male characters (females were deliberately excluded) are almost all corrupt or otherwise flawed. The ambiguities inherent in the masculine idea surface in the character who has proved to be most popular – the devious but charming murderer, Long John Silver, a creation not unlike the twentieth-century role model James Bond in terms of morality. The more risible – and smugly nostalgic – trappings of the school-story genre were similarly savaged by Rudyard Kipling in *Stalky and Co.* Although he shows his schoolboys as violent pragmatists, however, he does not break faith with the masculine codes of duty and loyalty to Queen and country.

In the United States, a parallel tradition of masculinity was far more anarchic and individualistic, although the underlying values of decent behaviour were much the same. If the West was to be won, boys must be prepared to break rules; if they were to rise from log cabin to White House (as in William Makepeace Thayer's 1880 biography of James Garfield), or rise from poverty to respectable riches (as in Horatio Alger's 1868 *Ragged Dick*), then they must be freethinkers as well as hard workers. Perhaps the most famous of these books are Mark Twain's *Tom Sawyer* (1876) and *Huckleberry Finn* (1884), although Thomas Bailey Aldrich's semi-auto-biographical *The Story of a Bad Boy* (1870) has some claim to being the founder of the genre: he saw himself not as 'the impossible boy in a story-book' but as 'an amiable, impulsive lad [...] and no hypocrite'. By the 1880s, this good 'bad-boy' character had become a comic caricature, as in G. W. Peck's *Peck's Bad Boy and his Pa* (1883). Peck summed up the tradition:

> The 'Bad Boy' is not 'myth' [...] he shuffles through life until the time comes for him to make a mark on the world, and then he buckles on the harness [...] and becomes successful.[23]

The closest British equivalent was Richmal Crompton's anarchic William Brown, whose long career (1919–70) began in stories directed at adults.

A similar humorous dilution occurred with the school story in Britain, notably with the work of Charles Hamilton (alias Frank Richards, Hilda Richards and many others). In the story papers *The Gem* (1907–39) and *The Magnet* (1908–40), the school story became predominantly light comedy – although the first of Hamilton's stories set at Greyfriars School, 'The Making of Harry Wharton', was firmly traditional.

It has been said that British chivalric codes received a deathblow with the First World War, although, literary inertia being what it is, writers such as Captain Brereton and Percy F. Westerman continued the gung-ho approach to adventure throughout the 1920s and 1930s (with what now seems to be appalling taste). Similarly, as Mark Girouard noted:

> bands of brothers abounded, chivalrously protecting the weak and doing down villains, under the leadership of Bulldog Drummond, Major-General Hannay, Group Captain Bigglesworth and others [...] [But] as a dominant code of conduct it never recovered from the great war [...] Chivalry, along with patriotism, playing the game, and similar concepts became not so much devalued as simply irrelevant.[24]

However, chivalry and its associated attitudes lingered for a long time in children's books. When Geoffrey Trease interviewed Captain W. E. Johns in the 1950s about his hero, 'Biggles', Johns said:

> I teach a boy to be a man, for without that essential qualification, he will never be anything. I teach sportsmanship according to the British idea [...] I teach that decent behaviour wins in the end as a natural order of things. I teach the spirit of team-work, loyalty to the Crown, the Empire, and to rightful authority.

Even in those non-politically correct days, Trease was led to muse, perhaps a little uneasily, that 'several points arise from the foregoing statements' including 'nationalist bias [...] attitude towards foreigners [...] violence [...] and [...] the cult of the hero'.[25]

The ruralist and pacifist turn taken by children's literature after the First World War with A. A. Milne, Hugh Lofting and John Masefield blended the wounded ideal of chivalry with that of a more sensitive masculinity. Some of the most popular and influential books, such as Ransome's 'Swallows and Amazons' series (which influenced the world's bestselling author, Enid Blyton), demonstrate this. In *We Didn't Mean to Go to Sea* (1937), the fourteen-year-old John Walker sails a yacht with his three younger siblings, against the odds, across the North Sea in a storm and at night. He is surrogate head of the family (his sister Susan is the 'mate' and cook), and his mantra is: 'what was it Daddy had said?' Ransome structures his families with the males in control – even the first expedition onto the lake in *Swallows and Amazons* (1930) cannot be authorised by mother alone, but depends on the distant father's telegram – but Ransome's gendering is far more even-handed than that of most writers before him. Even in the world of Middle Earth (first described in *The Hobbit* in 1937), controlled as it is by codes of male behaviour, Bilbo and Frodo Baggins and Sam Gamgee are wedded to very anti-heroic principles.

It is interesting to see how far the fundamentals of masculinity as defined over two centuries survive today: has the anti-hero such as Eion Colfer's Artemis Fowl any such codes? Has there been a trickle-down effect of the amorality of James Bond to, for example, the 'Alex Rider' or 'Young James Bond' books, or are the values of the old codes still implicit? The young James Bond first appears in Charlie Higson's *Silverfin* (2005):

> He was a new boy; tall for his age and slim, with pale, grey-blue eyes and black hair that he had tried to brush into a perfect, neat shape but, as usual, failed. One stray lock dropped down over his right eye like a black comma.[26]

Anthony Horowitz's Alex Rider is described at the beginning of *Stormbreaker* (2005): 'Alex was fourteen, already well-built, with the body of an athlete. His hair, cut short apart from two thick strands hanging over his forehead. His eyes were brown and serious.'[27] Both of these characters would be at home on one of Ballantyne's sea voyages – and the centrality of efficient violence to this construction of masculinity has not changed. In May 2007, the British Government's Education Department launched a £750,000 project to distribute books to schools for boys to read: as *The Times* headline (16 May 2007) reported, the book list contained books full of 'blood, guts and class heroes'.

Of course, the social engineering element of children's literature being what it is, there are plenty of examples of the 'new' man/boy, in touch with his feminine nature – from Hazel (the male-hero rabbit) in Richard Adams's *Watership Down* (1972) to Shrek – and it has been argued that even in neo-realistic texts like Burgess's *Doing It* which portray macho (or would-be macho) male behaviour there is a sympathetic portrayal of friendship and interdependence.

Female Repression and the Subversive

The construction of the female in children's literature might seem at first to be almost as straightforward: after all, there seems to be little difference between the timidity, subservience and domesticity of Mrs Fairchild's daughters in Mrs Sherwood's *History of the Fairchild Family* (1818) and the timidity, subservience and domesticity of Anne in Enid Blyton's 'Famous Five' series of the 1950s, or the characteristics of Bella Swan in Stephenie Meyer's 'Twilight' sequence (2005–8). However, possibly because of the 'double otherness' of the female child, as constructed in opposition to the adult male, and the association of the female with fantasy (actual escape from subservience not being likely) in the nineteenth century, there are many examples of covert rejection of societal gender norms in children's literature for girls. (Again, this discussion must be under the caveat that there are always exceptions – R. M. Ballantyne's 1885 *The Island Queen* and other South Sea Islands books feature strong females.)[28]

Such was the dominance of the male ethos that, when stories for girls were written after 1918, when the social position of women was beginning to change:

> new narrative and character models [for girls] were not easy to set up. A century of writing for girls had established the norm of the domestic tale, in which the trials of the heroine were involved with the learning of discipline, the internalisation of the feminine values of self-abnegation, obedience, and submission.[29]

What did this position involve? The female may have been the heart of the family, but it was a position that brought with it piety and immobility and a kind of self-immolation. Late nineteenth-century girls' books are populated by injured angels of the house. Margaret May in Charlotte Yonge's *The Daisy Chain* (1856), and a sequence of American selfless characters, from Katy Carr in *What Katy Did* (1872) through to Eleanor Porter's ever-glad Pollyanna (1912), at once provided a constricting role model for girls, but also (it is more and more frequently argued) the site of a proto-feminism. The key book for this argument is Louisa May Alcott's *Little Women* (1868; and its second part, published in the UK as *Good Wives* in 1869), for many years commonly regarded as a domestic idyll, with characters who are models of and for American young womanhood. Revisionist readings suggest that the book is, rather, a portrait of repression, with all the female characters trapped by the absent male power, to which they are answerable. Together, the March girls embody many of the nineteenth-century gender roles for the female, all of which incur punishment: Meg's pride is humbled, Jo's unfeminine wildness is starched into a 'strong, helpful, tenderhearted woman'[30] as her father calls her, Amy is married respectably and conventionally, and Beth dies a pious death.

The comparative freedom of behaviour of the characters in *Little Women* compared with their British sisters (a point made in an episode in the novel) accounted in some part for the book's popularity in Britain – which perhaps gives an insight into the tensions between real girls and girls-as-gendered in British society and fiction. However, it was some time before the strong, 'feisty' female role models, such as Anne Shirley in L. M. Montgomery's *Anne of Green Gables* (1908), were replicated in British fiction. As Shirley Foster and Judy Simons point out, the importance of *Anne of Green Gables* is not only the strength of Anne's character but that, at the end, 'the pattern of her later life seems less determined [...] Anne will of course have to grow up, but the text refuses to formulate the inevitabilities which await her.'[31]

These tensions within what might appear to be conventional domestic stories are paralleled – and emphasised – in other genres of writing for girls. The decline of the father as a reliable family figure in 'realistic' novels (which we will look at in connection with religion in Part Four: 'Children's Literature and Ideology') was paralleled by a rise in the power of the wise woman or fairy godmother in fantasy. Significantly enough, these strong females exist largely in non-realistic settings, but their importance as role models and subversive figures is inescapable. Thus the mystic Irishwoman/Mrs Doasyouwouldbedoneby in Kingsley's *The Water Babies* (1863) and Princess Irene's godmother in George MacDonald's *The Princess and the Goblin* (1872) dominate books in which the gender roles are otherwise conventional. (The powerful latent sexuality – not to say eroticism – of Kingsley's female characters and MacDonald's harridan North Wind should not be overlooked.)[32] Possibly the most important and characteristic of the subversive characters of fantasy in this period is Lewis Carroll's 'Alice' – and it is no accident that the 'Alice' books have generated a good deal of controversy over sexuality and gender roles. Alice is an independently minded girl, who spends two books confronting the madness of the adult world – and symbolically overcoming it as she sweeps away the apparently all-male jury with the hem of her skirt, towards the end of *Alice's Adventures in Wonderland* (1865). However, some of the characters that she encounters are demented or lazy women, and, above all, both books are only dreams. In the end, for all her fantasies, Alice is returned to her constricted role, a little girl whose fantasies can be explained away (as at the end of *Alice's Adventures in Wonderland*) or a Victorian girl in 'luxurious captivity' – sitting inside, watching through the window 'the boys getting in sticks for the bonfire [...] only it got so cold, and it snowed, so they had to leave off'[33] (as at the end of *Through the Looking Glass*, 1872); and perhaps above all, always being the object of the authorial (and male-societal) gaze.

At much the same time as the Alice books were shifting, if only slightly, gender possibilities in fiction, the *Girl's Own Paper* (1880–1956) was showing itself to be a far more ambiguous affair than its brother, the *Boy's Own Paper* (1879–1967). The content of the two magazines was, perhaps, predictable – action and independence, science and survival for the boys, 'affective relationships', domesticity, needlework and face creams for the girls. Whereas the *Boy's Own Paper* had a clear attitude to gender – including the idea that femininity was 'an inferior counterpart' to masculinity – the *Girl's Own Paper* had a reformist agenda:

> Girls were not incited to reject traditional feminine characteristics; purity, obedience, dependence, self-sacrifice and service are all presented as desirable qualities for the magazine's readers. However, the image of feminine womanhood was expanded to incorporate intelligence, self-respect and, when necessary, the potential to become financially independent. Thus it is possible to see articulated in this early periodical the kind of contradictory tendencies characteristic of femininity: reason and desire, autonomy and dependent activity, psychic and social identity.[34]

There was a similarly dual focus – of the strong female ultimately becoming subservient (or was she?) to weaker males, in a highly complex and debatable fashion – in the works and lives of two of the most influential female writers of the period, Frances Hodgson Burnett and Edith Nesbit. Burnett was a highly successful international author using fairy-tale and romance elements grafted onto the waif novel. In *A Little Princess* (1904), Sara is an ideal female child and, although she ultimately triumphs, her fate is dominated by males (and evil females). However, *The Secret Garden* (1911) is much less Romantic and a much more complex portrayal of the feminine. Mary Lennox moves from being everything a female child should not be (ugly, spoilt, self-willed), to a powerful life force, transforming the lives of the neglected Colin and his emotionally shrivelled father. It is true that her guru is the nature-boy, Dickon, but Burnett emphasises that many of Dickon's characteristics are feminine – and that the real centre of the book is Dickon's mother (or earth-mother). The fact that, at the end of the book, the focus shifts to Colin has been taken to indicate that Burnett could not, in the male-dominated society, allow Mary to triumph. However, it may be worth considering Adrian Gunther's analysis (especially in relation to books for girls over the next hundred years):

> To regret that it is not Mary winning the race, holding forth berating the group and striding back into the great house, is to accept such patriarchal concepts of power on their own terms. Burnett has a much more subversive and subtle agenda [...] In terms of the quest archetype, a key state in the journey is transcendence of ego [...] [Mary's] behaviour in the last section of the book is characterised by an unselfish compassion, and a total absence of egocentric concern. Colin, however, in true masculine mode, remains intrinsically self-centred up to the very last line [...] He remains 'blocked'.[35]

The World of Girls and the Radical Female

The turn of the twentieth century was clearly a time of change. Kimberley Reynolds has noted that at this point in history the girl/boy readership divide was far from simple – girls read boys' books, with all the exposure to worldly knowledge that they contained. Strategies for control were needed:

> One way of doing this was to incorporate appropriate models for girls into suitable boys' adventure stories [...] which gave rise to those depictions of late-Victorian and Edwardian family life which have become 'classics' [...] Such books (typified in the works of Mrs Ewing, Frances Hodgson Burnett and E. Nesbit) replace the ethos of confidence, mastery and independence based on masculine superiority with one based on class.[36]

Writers for girls were caught between catering to the aspirations of their audience, while acknowledging older norms of motherhood and spirituality. At the point at which the boys' school story was fading – as we have seen, its *raison d'être* had been undercut by the war – the girls' school story came into its own. By 1920 'the schoolgirl [...] was a well-defined image in its own fictional context', although the genre 'at its lowest level [...] incorporated the pot-boiling elements of tawdry sentiment and far-fetched melodrama'.[37] In these stories, girls were increasingly portrayed as being groomed for an independent and productive life after school, although not as much as for their future roles as wives and mothers. With the Girl Guide Movement, however, which was initially imperialistic and reactionary, moving in the 1920s and 1930s towards an emphasis on outdoor activities, female power was, as it were, smuggled into the texts. The problems encountered over sexuality in girls' school stories can be seen in the progress from the more realistic novels of Dorita Fairlie Bruce to the mildly sexually suggestive caricatures of Ronald Searle's 'St Trinian's' series of cartoons – and the way in which Searle's ideas were treated in the films made between 1954 (*The Belles of St Trinian's*) and 2009 (*St Trinian's II: The Legend of Fritton's Gold*).

If Arthur Ransome was bound by Victorian codes of family, he seems to have tried hard to portray an egalitarian world in gender terms. Thus, although Mrs Walker in *Swallows and Amazons* (1930) is, like Mrs Fairchild, the agent through which the father's will is transmitted, she is 'other' – Australian, and a sailor in her own right.

Similarly, although her eldest daughter Susan is, as we have seen, always number two (cook, housekeeper, nurse) to her brother John, the very viability of the expeditions run by the boys and the quasi-boys (the 'Amazons', Nancy and Peggy Blackett) always depends on her. In *Pigeon Post* (1936) the Amazons' mother, Mrs Blackett, wondering whether to allow the children to camp away from home, says:

> 'It would be all very well if you were all Susans [...] You see how it is, Susan. It all comes down to depending on you. [...] And you too, John,' she added. John grinned. It was kind of her to say it, but he knew she did not mean it. On questions of milk and drinking-water and getting able-seamen to bed in proper time, Susan was the one the natives trusted.[38]

Of the other female characters, Titty, the mystic self-portrait of Ransome, stands outside the norms of gender stereotypes (although the unfortunate Dorothea, Ransome's self-portrait as a writer, does not), while it can be debated whether the sailing twins, Port and Starboard, or the tomboys Nancy and Peggy (who do not want to be girls) favour a feminist cause.

Possibly the most familiar derivative of Ransome's Susan is Anne in Enid Blyton's 'Famous Five' series (1942–63). Although Anne is generally seen as the ultimate in the caricatured repressed feminine, forced to use the same dependency device as Susan does, David Rudd argues persuasively that the gender patterns in Blyton are not what they seem. Throughout Blyton's books (and even in the 'Malory Towers' series), 'the persistent message to readers is that [a] state of freedom is more desirable than a return to the Patriarchal Fold.' (Rudd also cautions us against the too easy correlation between what is, and what was, 'PC'.)[39]

In children's books in general, then, the implicit subservience of the female to the male lingered well into the twentieth century, although there was an increasing number of exceptions, among which W. E. Johns's female action hero Worralls of the WAAF

(Women's Auxiliary Air Force) (1941–50; who will not be patronised by men) and P. L. Travers's *Mary Poppins* (1934; who is more a cosmic force than a nanny) stand out.

In the decades immediately following the Second World War – which, like the first, had a decisive effect on gender portrayal – there were some striking examples of female heroes who were not following the previously accepted agenda, notably Arrietty Clock in Mary Norton's 'The Borrowers' series (1955–82) and Joan Aiken's Dido Twyte (in *The Wolves of Willoughby Chase*, 1963 and sequels). However, possibly the most forceful discussion of gender roles was by the American fantasy writer Ursula Le Guin, whose first three 'Earthsea' books – *A Wizard of Earthsea* (1968), *The Tombs of Atuan* (1972) and *The Farthest Shore* (1973) – were rooted in conventional hero tales. She rectified this with a fourth volume, *Tehanu* (1990), in which the achievements of the central female character (rather than female hero), powerless and deformed, owe nothing to any male heroic norms – and cannot be measured in terms of 'conventional' achievements. As Le Guin wrote in *Earthsea Revisioned*:

> The deepest foundation of the order of oppression is gendering, which names the male normal, dominant, active, and the female other, subject, passive. To begin to imagine freedom, the myths of gender, like the myths of race, have to be exploded and discarded.[40]

Since then, there has been no shortage of books that have deliberately subverted or inverted female gender roles, such as Babette Cole's *Princess Smartypants* (1986) and Robert N. Munsch's *The Paper Bag Princess* (1982) or Gene Kemp's *The Turbulent Term of Tyke Tiler* (1977). However, there is some evidence to suggest that children whose sense of self has already been established in bi-polar terms may resist such manipulation (if manipulation it is).[41] Equally, and in a postmodern society in which gender has been highly commodified, and in which readers are (or are assumed to be) self-aware, we may be entering a new era in terms of the relationship of text to life, where power is at last shifting to the reader via an irony shared with the narrator. For example, in Terry Pratchett's fantasy *Only You Can Save Mankind* (1993) the reluctant hero, Johnny, is being interviewed by the captain of a space-fleet (who happens to be a crocodile – and female), about the gender mores on Earth:

> *'What is sexist?'*
> 'Oh, that [said Johnny]. It just means you should treat people as people and, you know [...] not just assume girls can't do stuff. We got a talk about it at school. There's lots of stuff most girls can't do, but you've got to pretend they can, so more of them will. That's all of it, really.'
> *'Presumably there's, uh, stuff boys can't do?'*
> 'Oh, yeah. But that's just girls' stuff,' said Johnny. 'Anyway, some girls go and become engineers and things, so they can do proper stuff if they want.'[42]

Gender, Commodification and Criticism

In 1997, in her evangelically feminist analysis of writing for children, *Waking Sleeping Beauty: Feminist Voices in Children's Novels*, Roberta Seelinger Trites asserted that:

> no organised social movement has affected children's literature as significantly as feminism [...] The majority of novels about girls no longer focus so pointedly on socializing girls into traditional femininity as books like *Charlotte's Web* (1952) did.[43]

She then produces a formidable list of books to prove her case, by writers such as Mildred Taylor and Patricia MacLachlan.

Opinion varies as to whether the trend Trites describes has been sustained in the light of 'third-wave' feminism, 'which recognizes identity as plural (rejecting essentialist notions of female identity) and conceptualizes masculinity and femininity as relational, rather than oppositional'.[44] Lissa Paul felt positive about this in 2004:

> The end of feminism has not meant a plunge into the dark ages. It has opened up a kind of criticism that, in its best forms, is informed by the insights of feminist theory – and the joy.[45]

However, the huge sales to young girls in Britain of such traditionally gender-marked series as Janey Louise Jones's 'Princess Poppy' series and Daisy Meadows's 'Rainbow Magic' has suggested to some, such as Joan Smith, that:

> a generation of teenage girls has missed out on feminist ideas and is having to deal with an increasingly exploitative culture without the tools to look beyond the surface glitter.[46]

Even Roberta Seelinger Trites (in a personal communication) has lamented that she now finds her presentation of the situation of feminism in *Waking Sleeping Beauty* absurdly optimistic, and that the past ten years have seen serious regression in terms of attitudes to gender in general, and especially as expressed in children's literature.

One reason for this supposed regression may be the commodification of childhood – the hard selling of a limited range of packaged attitudes, to which simplistic gender stereotypes lend themselves. Many of these stereotypes are derived from folk and fairy tales, in which females are depicted as witch or angel, demonised or idealised. A classic example is Roald Dahl's *Matilda* (1988) where the two major female characters are the grotesque and brutal Miss Trunchbull, and the virtuous Miss Honey. A. A. Milne said that, in describing character for children, writers should use tar or whitewash, and Dahl certainly does. Miss Trunchbull:

> was above all a formidable female [...] Looking at her, you got the feeling that this was someone who could bend iron bars and tear telephone directories in half. Her face, I'm afraid, was

neither a thing of beauty nor a joy for ever. She had an
obstinate chin, a cruel mouth and small arrogant eyes [...] She
looked, in short, more like a rather eccentric and bloodthirsty
follower of the stag-hounds than the headmistress of a nice
school for children.

In contrast:

Miss Honey [...] had a lovely pale oval madonna face with
blue eyes and her hair was light-brown. Her body was so slim
and fragile one got the feeling that if she fell over she would
smash into a thousand pieces, like a porcelain figure.[47]

This may be seen (as Dahl claimed to see it) as harmless farce, but
many critics have detected a disturbing underlying eroticism, a
throwback to the misogyny and sadism of earlier generations. This
can be seen in the demonised woman encountered in the form of the
White Witch in C. S. Lewis's *The Lion, the Witch and the Wardrobe*
(1950):

She was covered in white fur up to her throat and held a long
straight golden wand in her right hand and wore a golden
crown on her head. Her face was white – not merely pale, but
white like snow or paper or icing-sugar, except for her very red
mouth.[48]

This image was replicated in the film (2005). Once again, questions
of power and influence, both inside and outside the children's book,
reassert themselves problematically, focusing on the question of
gender.

Notes

1   M. O. Grenby, *Children's Literature* (Edinburgh: Edinburgh University Press, 2008), p. 8.
2   Perry Nodelman, *The Hidden Adult: Defining Children's Literature* (Baltimore, MD: Johns Hopkins University Press, 2008), p. 173.
3   Mary Jane Kehily and Heather Montgomery, 'Innocence and Experience: A Historical Approach to Childhood and Sexuality', in Mary Jane Kehily (ed.), *An Introduction to Childhood Studies* (Maidenhead: Open University Press, 2004), p. 57.
4   Nodelman, *Hidden Adult*, p. 176.
5   Mary Cadogan and Patricia Craig, *You're a Brick, Angela!: The Girls' Story 1839–1985* (London: Gollancz, 1985), p. 373.
6   Beverly Cleary, *Fifteen* (Harmondsworth: Peacock, 1962), pp. 5, 175; Judy Blume, *Forever* (London: Pan, 1986), pp. 5, 154.
7   Elaine Millard, *Differently Literate: Boys, Girls and the Schooling of Literacy* (London: Falmer Press, 1997), pp. 37, 181.
8   John Goldthwaite, 'Notes on the Children's Book Trade: All Is Not Well in Tinsel Town', in Sheila Egoff, G. T. Stubbs and L. F. Ashley (eds), *Only Connect: Readings on Children's Literature*, 2nd edn (Toronto: Oxford University Press, 1980), pp. 389–404, pp. 396, 398.
9   Cadogan and Craig, *You're a Brick, Angela!*, p. 228.
10   Lynne Vallone, *Disciplines of Virtue: Girls' Culture in the Eighteenth and Nineteenth Centuries* (New Haven, CT: Yale University Press, 1995); Christine Wilkie-Stibbs, *The Feminine Subject in Children's Literature* (New York and London: Routledge, 2002); John Stephens, *Ways of Being Male: Representing Masculinities in Children's Literature and Film* (London and New York: Routledge, 2002); Kenneth Kidd, 'Boyology in the Twentieth Century', *Children's Literature*, 28 (2000), pp. 44–72.
11   Quoted in Patricia Demers and Gordon Moyles (eds), *From Instruction to Delight: An Anthology of Children's Literature to 1850* (Toronto: Oxford University Press, 1982), p. 104.
12   Sarah Fielding, *The Governess, or, the Little Female Academy* (London: Oxford University Press, 1968), pp. 87–8.
13   See Ann Alston, *The Family in English Children's Literature* (London: Routledge, 2008), pp. 12–13.
14   Peter Hunt (ed.), *Children's Literature. An Anthology, 1801–1902* (Oxford: Blackwell, 2000), pp. 52–4.

15   Kimberley Reynolds, *Children's Literature in the 1890s and the 1990s* (Plymouth: Northcote House/British Council, 1994), p. 31.
16   R. M. Ballantyne, *The Coral Island* (Oxford: Oxford University Press, 1990), p. 7.
17   Quoted in Guy Arnold, *Held Fast for England: G. A. Henty: Imperialist Boys' Writer* (London: Hamish Hamilton, 1980), p. 35.
18   Jeffrey Richards (ed.), *Imperialism and Juvenile Literature* (Manchester: Manchester University Press, 1989), pp. 5–6.
19   Joseph A. Kestner, *Masculinities in British Adventure Fiction, 1880–1915* (Farnham: Ashgate, 2010), p. 10.
20   Richard Jefferies, *Bevis: The Story of a Boy* (Oxford: Oxford University Press, 1989), pp. 261, 400.
21   Quoted in Peter Hunt, *Children's Literature: A Guide* (Oxford, Blackwell, 2001), p. 301.
22   Quoted in Hunt, *Anthology*, p. 139.
23   Hunt, *Anthology*, pp. 221, 339.
24   Mark Girouard, *The Return to Camelot: Chivalry and the English Gentleman* (New Haven, CT: Yale University Press, 1993), pp. 70–1.
25   Geoffrey Trease, *Tales out of School: A Survey of Children's Fiction*, 2nd edn (London: Heinemann, 1964), pp. 80, 81.
26   Charlie Higson, *Silverfin* (London: Penguin [Puffin], 2005), p. 17.
27   Anthony Horowitz, *Stormbreaker* (London: Walker, 2005), pp. 7–8.
28   See Claudia Marquis, 'Romancing the Home: Gender, Empire and the South Pacific', in Beverly Lyon Clark and Margaret R. Higonnet (eds), *Girls Boys Books Toys: Gender in Children's Literature and Culture* (Baltimore, MD: Johns Hopkins University Press, 1999), pp. 53–67.
29   J. S. Bratton, 'British Imperialism and the Reproduction of Femininity in Girls' Fiction, 1900–1930', in Jeffrey Richards (ed.), *Imperialism and Juvenile Literature* (Manchester: Manchester University Press, 1989), pp. 195–215, p. 197.
30   Louisa May Alcott, *Little Women* (London: Penguin, 1953), p. 286.
31   Shirley Foster and Judy Simons, *What Katy Read: Feminist Re-Readings of 'Classic' Stories for Girls* (London: Macmillan, 1995), pp. 169–70.
32   See Marina Warner, *From the Beast to the Blonde: On Fairy Tales and Their Tellers* (London: Chatto and Windus, 1994).
33   Lewis Carroll, *Alice's Adventures in Wonderland and Through the Looking Glass*, ed. Peter Hunt (Oxford: Oxford University Press, 2009), p. 125.
34   Kimberley Reynolds, *Girls Only? Gender and Popular Children's Fiction in Britain, 1880–1910* (Hemel Hempstead: Harvester Wheatsheaf, 1990), pp. 140–1.

35   Adrian Gunther, '*The Secret Garden* Revisited', *Children's Literature in Education*, 25:3 (1994), pp. 159–68, p. 160.

36   Reynolds, *Girls Only?*, p. 94.

37   Cadogan and Craig, *You're a Brick, Angela!*, pp. 180, 205.

38   Arthur Ransome, *Pigeon Post* (London: Cape, 1936), pp. 54, 55.

39   David Rudd, *Enid Blyton and the Mystery of Children's Literature* (Basingstoke: Macmillan, 2000), p. 131.

40   Ursula Le Guin, *Earthsea Revisioned* (Cambridge, MA: Children's Literature New England in association with Green Bay Publications, 1993), p. 24; and see David Pringle (ed.), *The Ultimate Encyclopedia of Fantasy* (London: Carlton, 2006), pp. 183–4.

41   See Bronwyn Davies, *Frogs and Snails and Feminist Tales: Preschool Children and Gender* (Sydney: Allen and Unwin, 1989).

42   Terry Pratchett, *Only You Can Save Mankind* (London: Corgi, 1993), p. 83.

43   Roberta Seelinger Trites, *Waking Sleeping Beauty: Feminist Voices in Children's Novels* (Iowa City, IA: University of Iowa Press, 1997), p. ix.

44   Victoria Flanagan, 'Gender Studies', in David Rudd (ed.), *The Routledge Companion to Children's Literature* (London and New York: Routledge, 2010), pp. 26–38, p. 30.

45   Lissa Paul, 'Feminism Revisited', in Peter Hunt (ed.), *International Companion Encyclopedia of Children's Literature*, 2nd edn, vol. 1 (London and New York: Routledge, 2004), pp. 140–53, p. 150.

46   *The Times*, 14 August 2008, quoted in *IBBYLink*, 23 (2008), issue on the theme of 'Gendered Reading', ed. Pat Pinsent, p. 1.

47   Roald Dahl, *Matilda* (London: Puffin, 1988), pp. 83, 66.

48   C. S. Lewis, *The Lion, the Witch and the Wardrobe* (Harmondsworth: Penguin, 1956), p. 10.

Children's Literature and Ideology

After Ursula Le Guin wrote *Tehanu*, the 'revisioning' of her 'Earthsea' trilogy, she reflected on what she had been doing:

> if we discard the axiom what's important is done by men, with its corollary what women do isn't important, then we've knocked a hole in the hero-tale, and a good deal may leak out [...] To begin to imagine freedom, the myths of gender, like the myths of race, have to be exploded and discarded. My fiction does that by these troubling and ugly embodiments.
>
> Oh, they say, what a shame, Le Guin has politicized her delightful fantasy world, Earthsea will never be the same.
>
> I'll say it won't. The politics were there all along, the hidden politics of the hero-tale, the spell you don't know you're living under till you cast it off.[1]

One of the most resilient myths about children's literature is that it is, and should be, innocent. For many, children's books are an amalgam of *The Tale of Peter Rabbit*, *Winnie-the-Pooh* and *The Wind in the Willows*, simple, rural worlds of peace, play and food, or else they are satisfying fantasy, like the 'Harry Potter' books, or jolly farce, like Roald Dahl's *Matilda*. This image tends to ignore uncomfortable facts, such as the death joke on the second text page of *Peter Rabbit*: 'don't go into Mr McGregor's Garden: your Father had an accident there; he was put in a pie by Mrs McGregor';[2] or that half of the characters in *Winnie-the-Pooh* are misanthropes – notably Rabbit and Eeyore; or that *The Wind in the Willows* is arguably not a children's book at all, but the retreatist fantasy of a disillusioned middle-aged man. Not to mention the terrors and violence of Harry Potter, or the (alleged) misogyny of Dahl, notably in *The Witches* (1983), when he was accused by the cultural commentator Catherine Itzin of having 'womanhatred' at the core of his writing.[3]

Children's books – even those that try to – cannot stand apart from the world: nothing exists outside of ideology, and children's texts are as much the product of their culture as any other text. Children's literature, however, because it is aimed at inexperienced readers, is a special case: adult readers (although not all, as we shall see in discussing censorship) may be aware of dominant cultural ideologies, or the unexamined assumptions of an author, but, as Peter Hollindale points out in discussing *The Adventures of Huckleberry Finn*:

> You cannot appreciate the book as an anti-racist text unless you
> *know how to read a novel*. In modern children's writing the
> consciously didactic text rarely displays such confidence in its
> readers, with the unhappy result that reformist ideological
> explicitness is often achieved at the cost of imaginative depth.
> The inference is clear: in literature as in life the undeserved
> advantage lies with *passive* ideology.[4]

Our engagement with past ideological positions is complex. Nineteenth-century imperial fiction for children was often overtly racist, although at the time the negative concept of racism was scarcely an issue. In contrast, Helen Bannerman's *Little Black Sambo* (1899), about an Indian child, and Florence and Bertha Upton's *The Adventures of Two Dutch Dolls and a Golliwogg* (1895), which 'stars' the amiable and heroic golliwog, had, as far as can be established, no racist intent, although they became reviled symbols of racism and colonialism. *Little Black Sambo* has been partially rehabilitated by a new version by Julius Lester and Jerry Pinkney, *Sam and the Tigers* (1996) and its British reissue in 1998, and both books are now available in several editions.[5]

Since the 1970s, children's books have increasingly dealt with hitherto taboo subjects, and the power relationship within the form being what it is, often with revisionist intent. There seems little that is out of bounds. A glance at publishers' lists in the UK for 2009–10 reveals, among the hundreds of cloned epic trilogies and vampire novels, topics including: life in Nazi-ruled Berlin during the Second World War (Paul Dowswell, *Ausländer*); a first-person account of the degeneration of a southern African family whose mother has died of AIDS (Sally Grindley, *Torn Pages*); a boy with schizophrenia being treated to electro-convulsive therapy by a German doctor in 1939 (Julie Hearn, *Rowan the Strange*); city secondary-school feuds, including knife crime (Gillian Philip, *Crossing the Line*); an account of violence and life in a young offender's institution (J. A. Jarman, *Inside*); and a novel about cultural tensions between Indian and English families, including a character abused by his father who has seen his mother being drowned (Sharon Dogar, *Falling*).

Words like 'tragic', 'horrific', 'unremitting' and 'grim' pepper the review pages: perhaps most telling in terms of the way in which children's texts have become 'issue-driven' is that it was possible for a scholarly book, *Children's Fiction about 9/11*, to appear, only eight years after the event.[6] Books for the very youngest readers deal with topics such as ADHD (attention deficit hyperactive disorder; Jack Gantos, *Joey Pigza Swallowed the Key*, 1998); the 'No Outsiders' project explores ways of challenging homophobia in primary schools, using books such as Linda de Haan and Stern Nijland's *King and King* (2002); and the 'In the Picture' project promotes the inclusion of disabled children in early-years picture books.

Thus confronting 'questionable' areas has not been confined to 'young adult' texts: there have been dozens of picture books about childbirth, generally sanitised, but Jenni Overend and Julie Vivas's *Hello Baby!* (1999), with its explicit pictures, broke new ground.

246

Similarly, death has usually been treated through stories of animals, such as Susan Varley's *Badger's Parting Gifts* (1984). A notable exception is Tessa Wilkinson's *The Death of a Child* (1991); in that case, the author wanted to produce a colour picture book, but publishers were reluctant to produce a stand-alone picture book, and so the picture book was packaged with a long essay addressed to bereaved families and their helpers. The horrors of nuclear war have been depicted in Toshi Maruki's *Hiroshima no Pika* (1982), the Holocaust in Roberto Innocenti's *Rose Blanche* (1985) and depression in *Michael Rosen's Sad Book* (2004), which describes Rosen's reaction to the death of his son.

These examples raise serious questions about how books are used, and what should be made freely available to the young: it is a question not only of the protection of the young, but of the protection of concepts of childhood. It is often argued that many of these topics are irrelevant to children, or should be introduced to them through less emotional, powerful and evocative means than fiction. Yet there is perhaps still force in Edward Ardizzone's view that:

> I think we are possibly inclined, in a child's reading, to shelter him too much from the harder facts of life. Sorrow, failure, poverty, and possibly even death, if handled poetically, can surely all be introduced without hurt [...] if no hint of the hard world comes into these books, I'm not sure we are playing fair.[7]

Writers have struggled with the implications of this; how are the harder facts actually to be mediated to children? Ursula Le Guin describes the problem:

> But what, then, is the naturalistic writer for children to do? Can he [sic] present the child with evil as an *insoluble* problem [...] To give the child a picture of [...] gas chambers [...] or famines or the cruelties of a psychotic patient, and say, 'Well, baby, this is how it is, what are you going to make of it' – that

is surely unethical. If you suggest that there is a 'solution' to these monstrous facts, you are lying to the child. If you insist that there isn't, you are overwhelming him with a load he's not strong enough yet to carry.[8]

This chapter examines some of the complexities of these positions, and some of the major themes that children's books have grappled with, or been influenced by.

Postcolonialism, Race and Multiculturalism

In 1918, when Britain annexed German and Turkish territories, the British Empire ruled about 600 million people, or about one third of the world's population, so it is hardly surprising that it had a huge influence on its literature – and, symbiotically, that the literature fed the empire. G. A. Henty sold 25 million copies of his empire-building books between 1871 and 1906, and a Dutch commentator, R. van Eehen, in *The Captain* in May 1908, noted:

> There is no doubt that the immortal Henty and his host of imitators have made the British nation the most conceited people on this earth. It is the plotless trash of authors who shelter themselves behind the section in the library catalogue entitled 'Books for Boys' which has given the average young Englishman that very excellent opinion of himself which he now enjoys. [...] It is quite easy to see the harm the authors of these volumes cause by the exaggeration of the deeds and opinions of their *invraisemblables* heroes. After fourteen or fifteen years' perusal of 'piffle' written apparently for his education, the young Englishman leaves home and country with the very firm idea in his head that he, personally, is equal to two or more Frenchmen, about four Germans, an indefinite number of Russians, and any quantity you care to mention of the remaining scum of the earth.[9]

Colonial texts, as Clare Bradford notes, 'are by and large organised through such binary oppositions as self and other, civilised and savage, white and black'. Postcolonial texts are far more ambiguous, but whether postcolonialising or postcolonised, texts continue to struggle with conscious and subconscious issues of power, race and language. Bradford, writing in 2001, asserted that 'colonialism is never over and done with';[10] in contrast, Salman Rushdie, writing in 1997, argued that fifty years on from Indian independence marked the end of the postcolonial phase, and that India is now better understood in postmodern terms.[11]

The British imperialist ethos of racial superiority and arrogance, and the divine right of colonisation and exploitation, can easily be interpreted as running through the twentieth century in Kipling, Tolkien and Ransome, to W. E. Johns, C. S. Lewis and Enid Blyton. The characters seem to be in situations of conquest or quasi-colonisation, often with the implication (even in domestic settings) that they are dealing with inferior people. Not until the 1960s, with the Civil Rights Act of 1964 in the United States, and when the first generation of the children of the West Indian and South Asian immigrants of the 1950s were born in Britain, did multiculturalism start to become a fact, and children's literature start to become aware of its colonial legacy.

However, a slightly less condemnatory view might be that children's writing which was not specifically intended to recruit for the defence of the nation (such as W. E. Johns's work or the *Girl's Own Paper*, which admired the Hitler Youth in the 1930s) provided a subversive challenge to the colonialist mindset, although maintaining certain codes of behaviour. How deeply embedded the imperial codes were in boys' psyches was demonstrated in Kipling's *Stalky and Co.* (1899), when a visiting speaker at the school, the 'jelly-bellied flag flapper', exhorts the boys to patriotism:

> Now the reserve of a boy is tenfold deeper than the reserve of a maid [...] With a large and healthy hand [the speaker] tore down these veils, and trampled them under the well-

intentioned feet of eloquence. In a raucous voice he cried aloud little matters, like the hope of Honour and the dream of Glory, that boys do not discuss even with their most intimate equals [...] He pointed them to shining goals, with fingers that smudged out all radiance on all horizons. He profaned the most secret places of their souls with outcries and gesticulations. [...] Their years forbade them even to shape their thoughts clearly to themselves. They felt savagely that they were being outraged by a fat man who considered marbles a game.[12]

Elsewhere in Kipling, however, we can find the beginnings of another tradition, one that considers the end of empire: the values that this tradition espouses are less militaristic and far more inclusive than before. *Puck of Pook's Hill* (1906) is an elegiac view of empire, set in an idyllic, nostalgic England and discussing the parallels between the decline of the Roman and British empires. Kipling emphasises that the development of democratic England (upon which the empire rests) was essentially a synthesis: Sir Richard the Norman and Sir Hugh the Saxon come to work together under the eye of the Norman knight, de Aquila, who thinks not for Normans and Saxons, but for England. The law is forged by the Kadmiel, the Jewish money lender, who is the ultimate outsider, an aristocrat who despises those he manipulates for their own good. In themselves, these characters are not empire builders. Kadmiel, having broken the power of the king, retires to obscurity:

> 'And you? Did you see the signing of the Law at Runnymede?' said Puck, as Kadmiel laughed noiselessly.
> 'Nay. Who am I to meddle with things too high for me? I returned to Bury and lent money on the autumn crops. Why not?'[13]

These men are individualists, new thinkers, and, if they are present in the context of an unchanging England, in the symbolic form of the elemental, amoral, unjudgemental Puck, and the eternal poachers, hedgers, labourers and craftsmen represented by the Hobdens, they also acknowledge the diminution of craft, the loss of traditional power. Even the young 'Roman' soldiers (as Pertinax says, 'I'm one of a good few thousands who have never seen Rome except in a picture', p. 85) fighting on the Roman Wall are essentially their own men in their valuing of friendship over power, of integrity over imperialism, of home over empire.

An indication of the change in attitude to empire can be seen in Frances Hodgson Burnett's *The Secret Garden* (1911). The British Empire is only mentioned very briefly, in the opening chapter, but Burnett, from an American outsider's point of view, condemns it for its corrupting effect on its children, and mocks its racism and class snobbery. Mary returns to England as

> the most disagreeable-looking child ever seen. [...] Her hair was yellow and her face was yellow because she had been born in India and had always been ill in one way or another.

Burnett also takes the opportunity to satirise the English on the question of race. Martha, the Yorkshire maid, acknowledges that things must be different in India:

> 'I dare say it's because there's such a lot o' blacks there instead o' respectable white people. When I heard you was comin' from India I thought you was a black too.'
> Mary sat up in bed furious.
> 'What!' she said. 'What! You thought I was a native. You – you daughter of a pig!'
> Mary stared and looked hot.
> 'Who are you callin' names? [...] That's not the way for a young lady to talk. I've nothin' against th' blacks. When you read about 'em in tracts they're always very religious. You always read as a black's a man and a brother.'[14]

Burnett is referring to the motto on the emblem of a kneeling slave produced for the Society for the Effecting of the Slave Trade (1787) – 'Am I not a man and a brother.'

Few British writers were as critical, but the general acknowledgement of the decline of empire can be traced in the retreatist work of Arthur Ransome: although his main characters are mapping their world, they are not conquering or enslaving. Ransome, who believed that there were 'no lower orders' in the Lake District, ensures that the 'Natives' are superior to the 'colonising' children – only playing their games when it is sensible to do so. At the end of *Swallows and Amazons*, Mr Dixon will not allow the hay bags to be burnt on a celebratory bonfire, and the charcoal burners ignore the children's protestations that they cannot give Captain Flint a message because they are at war with him. These timeless inhabitants of the Lake District are more likely to absorb the incomers than be colonised by them. Thus Ransome's books are a recreation of a childhood that emphatically does not value imperialism (even if the father figure is a naval officer). Even in Tolkien's epics, the heroes are anti-heroes, and the expanding empire is quintessentially evil.

If attitudes to colonialism have changed, the move to racial inclusiveness has been painfully slow. It was not until the 1960s in the United States that readers first showed black children and white children together – Macmillan's 'Bank Street Readers'. In Enid Blyton's first 'Noddy' books, in the early 1950s, not only are the golliwogs the threatening villains, but they live in a grimy industrial town, rather than the tree-lined market town inhabited by Noddy and his friends. Thus racism and imperialism overlap with class, as in Margery Sharp's *The Rescuers* (1959) in which Miss Bianca, the superior white mouse, lives literally on a higher plane than the common mice.

In 1965, Nancy Larrick pointed out in an article in the *Saturday Evening Post*, 'The All White World of Children's Books', that fewer than 1 per cent of American children's books contained non-white characters. By the 1980s that figure had risen to around 15 per cent, and children's books have gradually come to reflect the minority balance of adult culture. However, in 2006, Arts Council England organised a conference, 'Diversity Matters', which concluded that:

> nothing much has changed since the seventies [...] There is a dearth of ethnic minority writers and illustrators [...] major bookshop chains are not very keen to stock multi-cultural books [...] [and] [...] dual-language picture books are selling badly.[15]

There is no question that poets such as John Agard or novelists such as Malorie Blackman are making important contributions to contemporary British children's literature. However, the fact that they are routinely singled out as 'other' suggests that the struggle for diversity, equality, mutual respect or whatever may be the possible end of three centuries of colonialist thinking is far from being resolved. Terry Pratchett, ever alert to any form of sexism and racism, pinpoints the problem: one of Johnny Maxwell's friends, in *Only You Can Save Mankind*, is Yo-less:

> Yo-less was called Yo-less because he never said 'Yo'. He'd given up objecting to the name now [...] He pointed out that Johnny was white and never said 'YerWhat'? [...] and anyway, you shouldn't make jokes about racial stereotyping.[16]

In *Johnny and the Dead*, Yo-less encounters an arrogant (white) chairperson at a public inquiry:

> 'I've got a question,' said Yo-less, standing up.
> The Chairman, who had her mouth open, hesitated. Yo-less was beaming at her, defying her to tell *him* to sit down.
> 'We'll take the question from the other young man, the one in the shirt – no, not you, the – she began.
> 'The black one,' said Yo-Less helpfully.[17]

Religion

Given that on the best estimates fewer than 10 per cent of the British population, of all religious faiths, regularly attend a place of worship or otherwise actively practice their religion, it is perhaps not surprising that religion does not figure greatly in children's fiction. There is no shortage of religious books, most notably picture books for young readers: characteristic titles are Rukhsana Khan and Patty Gallinger's *Muslim Child: Understanding Islam Through Stories and Poems* (2002) and Fiona Watt and Rachel Wells's *The Nativity* (2005) in Usborne's 'Touchy-Feely' series. Religious publishers such as Lion and Kingsley Press have extensive catalogues.

Religious publishing, however, has become a specialist, niche, industry: in the past 200 years, mainstream children's books have moved from a position where the vast majority were religiously driven, to a literature that celebrates humanistic, non-redemptory values. Very often, religious activity is actually feared, or not understood, or has become an empty cultural gesture. All of this has left both a philosophical and a sociological void, perhaps uneasily filled by myth and fantasy.

This progress, from religious to secular, can be traced through the decline of the figure of the Father, which, like the idea of family, has become corrupted from something admirable and powerful to something unreliable and fragmented. Thus, in 1818 we find Mr Fairchild, God's representative, in Mrs Sherwood's *The History of the Fairchild Family*, lovingly beating his children in order to save their souls; in 1990, in Gillian Cross's award-winning *Wolf*, the father is a terrorist prepared to kill his daughter to retrieve some plastic explosive. The association of 'father' with 'God' is no longer a positive one.

Different social contexts have modulated these changes. When the errant Henry Fairchild refuses to learn his Latin lesson, his father beats him and explains:

I stand in the place of God to you, whilst you are a child; and as long as I do not ask you to do any thing wrong, you must obey me: therefore, if you cast aside my authority, and will not obey my commands, I shall not treat you as I do my other children. From this time forward, Henry, I have nothing to do with you: I shall speak to you no more, neither will your mamma.[18]

Henry has to repent in order to be saved. In the American 'equivalent', Catharine Sedgwick's *Home* (1835), Mr Barclay's punishment of his impetuous son has a different emphasis:

Go to your own room, Wallace [...] You have forfeited your right to a place among us. Creatures who are slaves of their passions are, like beasts of prey, fit only for solitude [...] till, sir, you can give me some proof that you dread the sin and danger of yielding to your passions.

When Wallace has mastered his temper, he is accepted back into the family, and Mr Barclay reflects that 'There is no telling [...] how much good may be done by a single right action, nor how much harm by a single wrong one.'[19]

The Romantic idea of the pure, innocent and therefore religiously influential child was reinforced by a series of nineteenth-century bestsellers, such as Mary Louisa Charlesworth's *Ministering Children* (1854). In the first story, the nearly starving Ruth has been visiting a child even poorer and hungrier than herself:

But one cold November day, when she came into the house from school [...] the poor child's mother came crying from the room and said to her, 'Oh I am so glad you are come! [...] [M]y poor child's dying , and she keeps asking for you!' Ruth went in and stood by the bed, and the dying child said, 'Dear Ruth, I am quite happy [...] and I want you to sing about – "Those great drops of blood Jesus shed at even-tide"' [...]

Ruth sang it two or three times, and then she stopped; and the poor child had shut her eyes and seemed asleep, but she soon opened them again, and said, 'Oh, do sing about "Jesus, let me to Thy bosom fly!"', and while Ruth sang, and the mother stood weeping by, the little child fell asleep, and died [...]

But now the child's poor mother said she wanted Ruth to comfort her up, as she had done her dying child; and she begged Ruth to read to her and tell her those beautiful stories out of the Bible. [...] And so Ruth became a ministering child to the poor, childless widow.[20]

It is noticeable that in this story there is an absence of fathers – which became something of a trend: they are either unreliable or, as in the case of Mr March in *Little Women* (1868), choose to be elsewhere, or in the case of the father in Nesbit's *The Railway Children*, are forced to be elsewhere. In *Good Wives* (1869), the structure of the family is very similar to that of the Fairchilds, but there is a pragmatic shift of tone, of which Mrs Sherwood would not have approved:

Now, if [Jo] had been the heroine of a moral story-book, she ought at this period of her life to have become quite saintly, renounced the world, and gone about doing good in a mortified bonnet, with tracts in her pocket. But, you see, Jo wasn't a heroine; she was only a struggling human girl, like hundreds of others, and she just acted out her nature, being sad, cross, listless, or energetic as the mood suggested.[21]

In a historical era of doubt as well as faith, the pragmatic children's book, especially for girls, became conflicted between narrative traditions of the past (the ministering child, the pious death) and the realities of life. This can be seen no more vividly than in Ethel Turner's *Seven Little Australians* (1894). Not only is the father savage and unreliable, but, when it comes to death, there is no longer any religious comfort. Judy, the lively, rebellious central character, dies in the arms of her sister Meg, fearful of a lonely afterlife without her sister. Turning to Meg for comfort, Judy asks her to 'say something [...] hymns – anything!' Meg's Sunday-school lessons provide no comfort, however. She manages to say 'Come unto Me, ye weary, And, I will give your rest ...', to which Judy's answer is 'I'm not weary, I don't want to rest ...'[22] There has been a complete dissociation from religion, and, in mainstream English-language children's literature of the twentieth century, this has become the norm.

In the 1920s, John Masefield, who in *The Box of Delights* (1935) has the Dean and Chapter of Tatchester Cathedral kidnapped, regards religion as no more than part of the kaleidoscope of English myth. On the rare occasions that religious figures do appear in twentieth-century children's novels, they are generally sinister and frightening, as in Susan Cooper's *The Dark Is Rising* (1973), or positively weak and malign, as in Robert Cormier's revisioning of the school story, *The Chocolate War* (1974). Novels which take a sympathetic view of religion in general (and Christianity in particular) are rare – William Mayne takes the role of the Church in English life either as normal (as in his sequence set at Canterbury Cathedral Choir School, beginning with *A Swarm in May*, 1955), or as something to be taken seriously in a discussion of fantasy in *It* (1977) and *Cuddy* (1994). Yet books that discuss Christianity seriously in a contemporary context, such as Aidan Chambers's *Now I Know* (1987), are extremely rare.

There are, of course, exceptions, but these are hardly uncontentious. C. S. Lewis's partly allegorical 'Narnia' sequence (1950–6) – which employs characters symbolic of figures from Christian faith, notably the self-sacrificing Lion, Aslan – is probably the most famous, and has polarised religious views. A writer on the 'religious right', Michael D. O'Brien, in a chapter titled 'The Restoration of Christian Storytelling', regards the books as:

> rich theological treatises that teach truth without falling into the tedious habit of preaching to children [...] The attempted

psychological seduction of the young questers in *The Silver Chair* is especially well done and could be read as a description of what is occurring right now in our own culture. [...] There can be no doubt that Lewis was a Christian evangelist of outstanding genius. [...] The scope of his contribution to religious thought, to the defence of the Christian teachings, and to the development of the Christian imagination is practically unparalleled.[23]

This is probably the majority view; however, there is a growing body of opinion that questions Lewis's position. John Goldthwaite takes the extreme view that, as a fervent Protestant, Lewis ridicules other faiths, speaks 'for God' and takes a misogynistic view of his female characters:

It is everywhere painfully clear in *The Chronicles* that if girls are to be of any use, either in this world or in the New Jerusalem, they must learn to conform to the code as set out in boys' adventure novels. [...] Once you have granted yourself licence to say the snide thing, you are only a smirk away from the wicked one. In *Prince Caspian* appears what may well be the vilest passage ever to poison a children's book [when Aslan scourges the school].[24]

Christianity or, indeed, any religion has become a minor, specialist area in terms of children's books; it has been replaced by at best a vague humanism; at Hogwarts School, they celebrate Christmas, but it is a secular, cultural–commercial occasion with no significance beyond holiday and presents. In the recent past, no apologist for any religion has made any impression on a secular children's fiction market. Ultimately, as in Philip Pullman's 'His Dark Materials' trilogy (1995–2000), we have arrived at the death of God. The success of Pullman's book suggests that religion and children's books have once more become intertwined, in a highly paradoxical way: those critics who have a strong faith seem to have developed doubts about the validity of fiction, and those who champion fiction seem to have lost faith.[25]

War

There are certain aspects of children's fiction that might give the impartial observer pause, and the apparent preoccupation with war is one of these. The reasons given by authors for writing about conflicts are clear. H. Rider Haggard, author of *King Solomon's Mines*, observed that:

> Personally, I hate war and all killing [...] but when the battle-clouds bank up I do not think that any can be harmed by reading of heroic deeds or of frays in which brave men lose their lives.[26]

Barbara Harrison in her pioneering study of books about the Jewish Holocaust noted both the principal reason for writing about war, and the principal difficulty:

> War is an ever-present reality for vast numbers of children; we who can choose to keep our children ignorant are a minority. [...] Although there is now greater candour in literature for the young than ever before, the one characteristic which adults are reluctant to see diminished in any way is hope, traditionally the animating force in children's books. Many adults cannot endure the thought that during the Holocaust, hope [...] was swept into the ovens.[27]

However, the presentation of situations where adults are disempowered and there is no hope has proved difficult for some adult readers, who find, for example, the end of Gudrun Pausewang's *The Final Journey* (1998; originally published as *Reise im August* in 1992), in a gas chamber, unacceptably bleak:

The heavy iron door slammed shut.

Alice tipped back her head. Soon, soon, water would pour down over her from the nozzle up there. The water of life. It would wash her clean of the dirt and horror of the journey, would make her as clean as she had been before. She raised her arms and opened out her hands.[28]

Equally, some might question the very act of fictionalising such a situation at all. Jane Yolen, in an epilogue to her time-slip novel *The Devil's Arithmetic* (1988), 'What Is True about This Book', writes:

To witness. To remember. These were the only victories of the camps. Fiction cannot recite the numbing numbers, but it can be that witness, that memory. A storyteller can attempt to tell the human tale. [...] And can remind us that the swallows still sing around the smokestacks.[29]

Even more questionable might be the writing of a comedy about Second World War bombers; in Andrew Davies's *Conrad's War* (1978), the war-mad boy Conrad keeps finding himself in the war – with his dad and his dog. It may be a cautionary tale, but are horror and tragedy appropriate backdrops, and is the fact that at the end of the book Conrad is 'a bit tired of war and army and killing'[30] a sufficient justification for the device?

One view is that of those who, like Yolen, argue for the ability of fiction to allow readers to cope with otherwise unimaginable horrors:

Events on a grand scale, mass sufferings, catch the imagination and arouse compassion only incompletely and in an abstract way. We need a specific example to arouse our love or fear. We are so made that the face of a weeping child touches us more than hearing that a whole province has died of starvation.[31]

The opposite view is that the subject of war brings us close to the limits of fiction and masks the reality behind the fiction, falsifying and trivialising. It raises questions about the desensitising of the audience: the 'packaging' of war must have some impact on the way the world is perceived.

A rare discussion of the issues involved occurs in Terry Pratchett's *Only You Can Save Mankind* (1993), when streetwise teenagers are considering the use of 'smart' bombs in the Gulf War of 1990–1:

> 'I mean – the whole world seems kind of weird right now. You watch the telly, don't you? How can you be the good guys if you're dropping clever bombs right down people's chimneys? And blowing people up just because they're being bossed around by a looney [...]'
>
> '[...] There was a man on [the television] saying that the bomb-aimers were so good because they all grew up playing computer games [...]'
>
> 'See?' said Johnny. 'That's what I mean. Games look real. Real things look like games [...] We always turn [war] into something that's not exactly real. We turn it into games and it's not games. We really have to find out what's *real*!' (pp. 115, 116, 117)

In short: does fiction about war actually contribute to the understanding of what is real?

It is also possible, however, to detect a certain optimism in critics who write on this subject:

> In the treatment of the two world wars in recent novels and picture-books [...] young readers are invariably urged to examine the nature of violence and suffering, persecution and endurance, hatred and loyalty, selfishness and sacrifice. They are asked to share the writers' condemnation of war and the repugnant beliefs which lead to conflict, and to feel compassion for the anguish imposed upon the innocent many by the powerful few.[32]

Terry Pratchett's teenagers might question this, as they are momentarily reduced to horrified silence by the discovery that in the First World War there were such things as 'Pals' Battalions':

> 'It says here [said Yo-less] what a Pals' Battalion was. It says, people all from one town or even one street could all join the Army together if they wanted, and all get sent to [...] the same place [...]'
>
> 'They all died,' said Johnny eventually. 'Four weeks after the picture was taken. All of them [...]'
>
> 'They all marched off together because they were friends, and got killed,' said Yo-less.
>
> 'Except for [one],' said Johnny. 'I wonder what happened to him?'
>
> 'Perhaps he came back from the war and moved away somewhere else,' said Yo-less.
>
> 'It'd be a bit lonely around here, after all,' said Bigmac.
>
> They looked at him.
>
> 'Sorry,' he said. (*The Dead*, pp. 63–4)

It may be that the most successful books are those in which war is a background – almost a distant background, such as Nina Bawden's *Carrie's War* (1973), about children evacuated to a Welsh valley. On the children's last day, Carrie, the teenage female hero, reflects on the 'thought of bombs falling, of the war going on all this year they'd been safe in the valley; going on over their heads like grown-up conversation when she'd been too small to listen'.[33]

Other novels which successfully portray war from a child's perspective are Judith Kerr's 'Out of the Hitler Time' trilogy, beginning with *When Hitler Stole Pink Rabbit* (1971), and the similar trilogy by Irene Watts, who was a child rescued from Nazi Germany by the *Kindertransporten*, beginning with *Goodbye Marianne* (1998). The limits of what both adults and children understand are tested by Robert Westall's *The Machine Gunners*

(1975), in which the social tensions that existed before the war are magnified.

It can be argued that the best writers, as Agnew and Fox put it, all

> share a passionate belief that children must be made aware of the evils of the past and the courage with which that evil has often been met; and also that young readers need narratives which explore the nature and experience of war if they are to make sense of the world they have inherited and the future they confront.[34]

Censorship

Children's literature, at least up to the point that it is read, is controlled by adults: when it deals with the kinds of subjects that we have been discussing, censorship of various kinds appears to be inevitable. However, whether the various controls inherent in the process of writing, or commissioning and writing, marketing, buying, selecting, and transmitting and mediating texts to children amount to censorship is a matter for debate.

Famous, high-profile cases of censorship tend to overshadow the many small decisions made by authors, publishers, retailers, librarians and parents – they also emphasise the fact that children's literature is considered disproportionately influential, and a matter of simple cause and effect. There have been rather more examples of direct action being taken against books in the United States than in the UK.[35] One of the earliest formal measures in the UK was the Children's and Young Person's (Harmful Publications Act) of 1955, a response to the gratuitously gruesome horror comics that were then being imported. Fifty years on, however, the act is redundant, as far more graphic material is readily available.

Cultural sensitivities change with the years. Anne Higonnet, writing about published images of children, points out that in

Victorian times photographs, such as those by Lewis Carroll, were trying to capture childhood innocence, but in fact they forced (and force) viewers 'to see what our ideals deny, just as they expressed what their makers could not admit'. A hundred years ago, such images might have been acceptable; today, however, the situation is different:

> erotically suggestive images of children – perhaps deliberately erotic – now pervade all media, appearing with increasing frequency in spectacles ranging from fashion photography to Disney movies [...] All the difficulties of Romantic childhood have surfaced. While we look at troubling images of children we not only see abstract meanings, but dread real consequences.[36]

Censorship, then, is a protective phenomenon, often concerned with the possible consequences of viewing certain images. In picture books, Beatrix Potter was persuaded by her publisher, Frederick Warne, to alter a picture of a rat drinking what looked like alcohol, in *The Tailor of Gloucester* (1903). However, when it came to *The Tale of Tom Kitten*, she refused to change the line 'Moppet and Tom descended after her; the pinafores and all the rest of Tom's clothes came off on the way down.'[37] Warne had wanted it to read 'nearly all'. This squeamishness about naked children (or kittens) has been encountered by illustrators as disparate as Maurice Sendak (*In the Night Kitchen*, 1970) and Jan Ormerod (*Sunshine*, 1981).

Local mores make a considerable difference: Julie Vivas's *The Nativity* (1986) was considered unacceptable by readers in some southern states of the United States because of the eccentric portrayal of angels and the Holy Family. Humorous approaches to bodily functions have now become so common that the local censorship of Babette Coles's *Mummy Laid an Egg* (1993), with its pictures of improbable coital positions and sperm swimming across the endpapers, are forgotten. It has become rather more difficult to 'ban' books on the grounds of vulgarity since, with adult collusion, masterpieces of bad taste, such as Werner Holzwarth and Wolf Erlbruch's *The Little Mole Who Knew It Was None of His Business* (translated in 1994) and William Kotzwinkle, Glen Murray and Audrey Coleman's 'Walter the Farting Dog' series (2001–), have become bestsellers.

The motives behind censorship, then, range from protecting children from inappropriate knowledge to shielding them from material that is physically or spiritually dangerous. In terms of physical danger, Alan Garner reported some editorial objections to his story *Tom Fobble's Day* (1977), part of 'The Stone Book Quartet':

> There was also the matter of sledging at night. I was told that it was dangerous. I said that I was relating an activity, not promoting it. The argument got nowhere. It seemed that the editor was so concerned for child-safety that the dramatic and structural force of the sledging incident [...] had not been noticed. So I asked why – and the answer scared me, and still does: [...] they were incidents that teachers and librarians might object to, which in turn might damage the sales potential of the book.[38]

Religious matters are taken very seriously. The response to the 'Harry Potter' books in the context of religion has demonstrated some complex sociological phenomena: the books have become the most banned or 'challenged' books in the United States. The primary arguments against them rest not simply upon an apparently naïve understanding of the link between text and effect, but on the subject matter: those who would ban or burn the books fear the depiction of the occult as a tenet of belief. This might be seen as curious, for the books are the product of an age that (generally) understands the fictionality of fiction. If you do not believe in the supernatural, you cannot be corrupted by witchcraft because for you it does not exist – in the sense that people do not have occult or supernatural powers. Rowling herself is reported as being 'truly bemused' by suggestions that she was advocating the occult. The idea that stories are a psychological necessity, or that fantasy requires the reader to think metaphorically, seems to have been lost.

Objections to books on the grounds of race have led to many books being edited to suit the mood of the times. Hugh Lofting's Prince Bumpo of the Jollijinki tribe, a comic African who wants to become white in *The Story of Dr Dolittle* (1922), has been edited out of later editions. Even Roald Dahl was forced to concede that the colour of the original Oompa-Loompas, the black pygmy slaves in *Charlie and the Chocolate Factory* (1964), would be better changed to pink – this despite the fact that throughout they are the voices of (in the novel's terms) good sense, good morals and good behaviour. Many of Enid Blyton's books have been modified with regard to the frightening black faces of the generally ill-behaved golliwogs in the 'Noddy' novels. It is, however, interesting to note that the world authority on Blyton, David Rudd, points out that the golliwog changes are racist in themselves, based on a racist assumption – because there are actually more bad teddy bears than bad golliwogs.[39] In the United States, the centralised school book-buying of some large states allowed pressure groups to exert a good deal of influence. Mel and Norma Gabler's organisation, Educational Research Analysts, based in Texas, remained powerful into the first decade of the twenty-first century. At the other end of the political spectrum, the Council on Interracial Books for Children succeeded in having books that presented African Americans or Africans badly – such as *Little Black Sambo* and *Mary Poppins* – withdrawn from libraries. The American Library Association publishes lists of 'challenges' to books: since the beginning of the twenty-first century, Robert Cormier's *The Chocolate War* has been third on the list, while possibly the longest-running 'challenged' book, still restricted in many states after thirty-five years, is Judy Blume's *Forever* (currently at number 8). In the UK, such challenges are increasingly rare and, whereas in the past they were likely to damage sales of a book, the reverse is now the case, as Anne Fine's vitriolic attack on *Doing It* demonstrated.[40] Whatever the logic of censorship, it illustrates the power that the children's book is accorded, and the expanding range of its subject matter.

Notes

1   Ursula Le Guin, *Earthsea Revisioned* (Cambridge, MA: Children's Literature New England in association with Green Bay Publications, 1993), pp. 13, 24.

2   Beatrix Potter, *The Tale of Peter Rabbit* (London: Warne, 1902), p.10.

3   Jeremy Treglown, *Road Dahl: A Biography* (London: Faber and Faber, 1994), pp. 226–7.

4   Peter Hollindale, 'Ideology and the Children's Book', *Signal*, 55 (1988), pp. 3–22, p. 12 (original emphasis).

5   See Jan Susina, 'Reviving or Revising Helen Bannerman's *The Story of Little Black Sambo*: Postcolonial Hero or Signifying Monkey?', in Roderick McGillis (ed.), *Voices of the Other: Children's Literature and the Postcolonial Context* (New York: Garland, 2000), pp. 237–52.

6   Jo Lampert, *Children's Fiction about 9/11* (New York and London: Routledge, 2009).

7   Edward Ardizzone, 'Creation of a Picture Book', in Sheila Egoff, G. T. Stubbs and L. F. Ashley (eds), *Only Connect: Readings on Children's Literature*, 2nd edn (Toronto: Oxford University Press, 1980), pp. 289–98, p. 293.

8   Ursula Le Guin, *The Language of the Night, Essays on Fantasy and Science Fiction*, rev. edn (New York: HarperCollins, 1992), pp. 64–5 (original emphasis).

9   Quoted in C. C. Eldridge, *The Imperial Experience: From Carlyle to Forster* (London: Macmillan, 1996), pp. 68–9.

10 Clare Bradford, 'The End of Empire? Colonial and Postcolonial Journeys in Children's Books', *Children's Literature*, 29 (2001), pp. 197, 216.

11 Salman Rushdie, 'India at Five-O', *Time*, 11 August 1997, pp. 22–4, quoted by Victor J. Ramraj, 'Afterword: the Merits and Demerits of the Postcolonial Approach to Writings in English', in Roderick McGillis (ed.), *Voices of the Other* (New York and London: Garland, 2000), pp. 263–7.

12 Rudyard Kipling, *Stalky and Co.* (Harmondsworth: Puffin, 1987), pp. 175–6.

13 Rudyard Kipling, *Puck of Pook's Hill* (Oxford: Oxford University Press, 1993), p. 173.

14 Frances Hodgson Burnett, *The Secret Garden* (Oxford: Oxford University Press, 2011), pp. 5, 23.

15   Shereen Pandit, 'Diversity Matters', *Books for Keeps*, 160 (2006), pp. 8–9.
16   Terry Pratchett, *Only You Can Save Mankind* (London: Corgi, 1993), p. 27.
17   Terry Pratchett, *Johnny and the Dead* (London: Corgi, 1993), p. 120.
18   Mary Sherwood, *The History of the Fairchild Family* (London: J. Hatchard, 1818), p. 269.
19   Catharine Sedgwick, *Home*, in Peter Hunt (ed.), *Children's Literature: An Anthology* (Oxford: Blackwell, 2001), pp. 34–6.
20   Mary Louisa Charlesworth, *Ministering Children*, in Hunt, *Anthology*, p.115.
21   Louisa May Alcott, *Good Wives* (*Little Women, Part II*) (London: Puffin, 1978), pp. 244–5. See Angela M. Estes and Kathleen Margaret Lant, 'Dismembering the Text: The Horror of Louisa May Alcott's Little Women', *Children's Literature*, 17 (1989), pp. 98–123.
22   Ethel Turner, *Seven Little Australians*, in Hunt, *Anthology*, pp. 411–12.
23   Michael D. O'Brien, *A Landscape with Dragons: The Battle for Your Child's Mind* (San Francisco, CA: Ignatius, 1998), pp. 127–8.
24   John Goldthwaite, *The Natural History of Make Believe* (New York: Oxford University Press, 1996), pp. 227, 228, 229; and see also Philip Pullman, 'The Dark Side of Narnia', the *Guardian*, 1 October 1998.
25   See William Gray, *Death and Fantasy: Essays on Philip Pullman, C. S. Lewis, George MacDonald and R. L. Stevenson* (Newcastle: Cambridge Scholars Press, 2008), pp. 85–102.
26   Henry Rider Haggard, *The Days of My Life*, 2 vols (London: Longman, 1926), vol. 1, p. 105.
27   Barbara Harrison, 'Howl Like the Wolves', *Children's Literature*, 15 (1987), pp. 87, 69–70.
28   Gudrun Pausewang, *The Final Journey* (London: Penguin, 1998), p. 154.
29   Jane Yolen, *The Devil's Arithmetic* (London: Barn Owl, 2001), p. 167.
30   Andrew Davies, *Conrad's War* (London: Penguin, 1980), p. 144.
31   Joseph Kessel quoted in Claude Gutman, *The Empty House* (South Woodchester: Turton and Chambers, 1991), p. 5.
32   Kate Agnew and Geoff Fox, *Children at War: From the First World War to the Gulf* (London: Continuum, 2001), p. 53.
33   Nina Bawden, *Carrie's War* (London: Gollancz, 1988), p. 134.
34   Agnew and Fox, *Children at War*, p. 179.
35   See, for example, Mark I. West, *Trust Your Children: Voices against Censorship in Children's Literature* (New York: Neal-Schuman, 1988).

36   Anne Higonnet, *Pictures of Innocence: The History and Crisis of Ideal Childhood* (London: Thames and Hudson, 1998), pp. 10, 11; and see also James R. Kincaid, *Child-Loving: The Erotic Child and Victorian Culture* (London: Routledge, 1992).

37   Beatrix Potter, *The Tale of Tom Kitten* (London: Warne, 1907), p. 38.

38   Cited in Nancy Chambers (ed.), *The Signal Approach to Children's Books* (Harmondsworth: Kestrel, 1980), p. 326.

39   David Rudd, *Enid Blyton and the Mystery of Children's Literature* (Basingstoke: Macmillan, 2000), p. 152.

40   Anne Fine, 'Filth, Which Ever Way You Look at It', the *Guardian*, 29 March 2003.

The Future of Children's Literature

Of all the chapters in this book, this is the most likely to become out of date, for reasons that most of its readers may find exciting: texts for children are changing! In 1993, in a book on childhood, *Children's Cultural Worlds*, David Buckingham wrote:

> It is now impossible to understand contemporary childhood without taking account of the media. Indeed, it could be argued that children today are living 'media childhoods' – that children's experiences, and indeed the *meanings* of childhood itself, are largely defined and determined by the electronic media.[1]

Since then, technology has become more sophisticated and more available – to the extent that, in 2010, a Nielsen survey of American children concluded that six- to eleven-year-olds spend on average 54 hours and 25 minutes per week – 7 hours and 46 minutes per day – watching television or engaged in activities involving electronic media, including texting.[2]

As children's literature, however defined – fiction, poetry, drama, picture books, narratives, stories, entertainment for children – has always been bound up with and perhaps defined symbiotically by childhood, what does this radical change in childhood mean for children's literature? Equally, what does the change in medium from fixed print on a page to variable and physically interactive electronic screens imply for the way stories are told, for the way narrative works?

New Ways of Reading

If we are to include new media in our study of children's literature – and unless we are prepared to see it as a purely historical phenomenon, we must do so – there are some serious questions to be asked:

- What is the effect of new media on the ways in which readers construct narratives and make meanings from texts?
- How has the traditional book responded in terms of language and style – and how, in turn, has this affected the literacy and literary skills of the child readers and the way we think and write about the texts?
- How has the form of the book adapted itself to compete with electronic media?

There are still over 8,000 new children's titles being published in the UK alone each year, so the book is far from dead or displaced. Yet there has been a change: primarily, there has been an increasing emphasis on the visual, notably with the graphic novel and manga. We are used to thinking of literature as being about print-based texts, but these texts have become increasingly influenced by, or have had to compete with, electronic media, or have become part of a multimedia experience. It is important, therefore, to think about the changes that have occurred in 'conventional' texts, and to look at the printed texts that inhabit the borderline between print and electronics, and to consider what these changes imply for our critical thinking.

   We are living in the greatest media revolution since the invention of moveable type, and, just as that meant a move from orality to text, and the development of new forms of storytelling – such as the novel – so the new media are producing new forms of storytelling. With the introduction of writing and printing, there were many quite fundamental changes to narrative, and hence to story; as Walter J. Ong put it: 'writing restructures consciousness.' The most obvious changes involve less dependence on memory, more subtle modes of imposing coherence, allusion, character development, more and different points of view and focalisation – and, perhaps above all, 'print encourages a sense of closure, a sense that what is found in a text has been finalised, has reached a state of completion.'[3]

The new media – the computer game, the Internet and so on – require step changes of a similar magnitude when we come to narrative; how do we deal with it? As long ago as 1999, Margaret Mackey, a Canadian critic, suggested that the teaching of literature in schools was becoming fundamentally out of step with life outside the classroom:

> Students who enter their secondary classrooms knowledgeable about the back-stories of many movies, familiar with the leisurely, non-linear appeal of *The Simpsons'* universe [...] at ease with circular and repetitive attraction of many different on-line forms of fiction, will often find their expertise is little valued in the academic forum. If they are truly unlucky, they will be taught about 'the' plot diagram and trained to think that there is only one way to write a valid story. Even in more enlightened classrooms, they may regularly wonder why their 'fit' with linear school stories is often so uneasy.[4]

What it means to be a skilled reader is changing, and criticism and educational attitudes may have to change too.

Traditional, printed narratives work to certain unconscious rules: the way a series of happenings or 'facts' are connected to make a story is governed by the medium; things happen in sequences which are made coherent by character, scene, atmosphere, theme or motif.

There are generic traditions – we expect Harry Potter to survive to the end of the book because he is the hero, whereas the survival of other characters – even Hermione or Ron – is not quite so assured. We know that, however desperate the villains in Enid Blyton's books, no physical harm will ever actually come to the Famous Five. We know that even in an imaginative world which contains magic, there are still rules: Gandalf cannot do just anything that he wants to. A 'realistic' novel for teenagers may well contain explicit sex, but we do not expect to find any in a novel about teenage secret agents. Readers assume that the character introduced first, or who is described most fully, or whose actions are followed most closely ('focalised') is the character we should take most notice of. If the story is told in the first-person 'I' form, we expect that 'I' to tell us the truth. Stories have a beginning, a middle and an end: we know that conventionally, books for younger readers will have a secure 'closure', where things are made safe – the children come home, or, in the Edwardian tradition exemplified by *The Secret Garden* or *The Railway Children*, Daddy comes home. Books for older children might have a more ambiguous ending – Jacqueline Wilson's *The Story of Tracy Beaker* ends: 'This started like a fairy story. And it's going to finish like one too. Happily ever after.'[5] Her *Lola Rose*, for older readers, ends a little more ambiguously: 'We're going to live happily ever after, Mum and Auntie Barbara and Kendall and me. Fingers crossed.'[6] A novel with a serious philosophical purpose such as Philip Pullman's *The Amber Spyglass* can have a much more 'open' ending, a mixture of sacrifice and optimism. Lyra and Will are separated, but for a purpose vital to the future: '[w]e have to be all those difficult things like cheerful and kind and curious and brave and patient, and we've got to study and think, and work hard, all of us, in all our different worlds, and then we'll build [...] the republic of heaven.'[7] In addition, the way a story ends depends upon the genre as much as on the age range: a popular romance for teenagers such as Stephenie Meyer's *Twilight* ends with closure – although perhaps with an appropriate *frisson*, as the hero leans down to 'press his cold lips once more' to the heroine's throat. Even relatively inexperienced readers know where they are. The new media, however, do not know these rules, which are, in themselves, culture-specific:

> Many cultures have stories [...] that are expressed chiefly in circular or spiral terms. There might be a 'beginning', but there is no real 'middle' or 'end'. Cumulative stories in some cultures do not have a climactic event that then triggers actions moving the story to a final conclusion.[9]

In some ways, the new media are like the very old medium – of oral storytelling – because in both cases it is not necessarily the sequence of the narrative that is vital. The act of narrating, the interactive building of mutual as well as personal meaning, seems to be at least as important. Similarly, the experience of both oral narratives and new-media narratives is not stable – the story changes with each performance, unlike the 'fixed' meanings of the book (although these will change with each reader's rereading). Thus our traditional modes of 'static' criticism and judgements of literary 'quality' are much more difficult to sustain.

In 1983 a computer specialist, Nigel Woodward, predicted that:

> even the literary work may be set to become less an isolated act by a single author, and more and more the product of a process in which the author is one of a group of several authors – a group that eventually includes the 'reader'.[10]

In the twenty-first century, shared authorship of a narrative event (such as using the social-networking site 'Twitter') is commonplace, just as the 'narrative events' whose structure (if there is one) is not obvious have little in common with the structures that are so valued in 'traditional' texts.

Equally, the reader's imagination is expected to do something different. Thus, however many times we read *Charlie and the Chocolate Factory*, Charlie will always be given the factory at the end.

What that factory looks like, however, is largely up to the images in our own heads. In contrast, computer 'games' offer landscapes, visualised characters, skills and challenges which result in an infinity of outcomes. Within multi-user domains, within virtual worlds with thousands of players, outcomes in the traditional sense – the resolutions, the happy endings, the closures that are basic to literature as we have known it – are no longer relevant.

Consequently, these new narratives are personal and involve 'shared authorship' and, at the same time, they are all unstable works in progress. Criticism, if it has a place at all, has to be an intervention, an interruption and an extension of the story itself. Just as the printed book was at first feared – and, of course, as censorship shows, continues to be feared – so the Internet has become an immense social and political force. Printing allowed fiction – especially the novel – to demonstrate its cultural power: the Internet is doing the same for new forms of narrative and storytelling.

How the Book Has Responded: Form

Children's literature has, from the very beginning, been cross-media: as a 'popular' form it has always taken advantage of and sometimes pioneered developments in printing. Initially, chromolithography – invented in the 1830s in Britain – was expensive, and wood engraving survived well into the nineteenth century: the editions of Heinrich Hoffmann's *Struwwelpeter* from 1858 used wood engraving to enable mass production at low cost. A good example of a series that made use of chromolithography is Florence and Bertha Upton's *Adventures of Two Dutch Dolls and a Golliwogg* (1895). In the 1870s the picture book developed with major figures such as the printer Edmund Evans, and artists such as Kate Greenaway and Randolph Caldecott, and in 1874 the first comic was published in London – *Funny Folks*. It started an immensely successful trend, and with the development of cheap rotary printing, the juvenile market was flooded with dozens of titles, such as *Comic Cuts* – which developed often highly stylised conventions of interlinking words and pictures.

In the 1920s and 1930s, children's book illustrators made good use of the development of offset lithography, and the experimental work of this period remains seminal. Edward Ardizzone's *Little Tim and the Brave Sea Captain* (1935) integrated text and illustration in a way that is still imitated, while Jean de Brunhoff's *Babar the Elephant* (1931–) and Kathleen Hale's *Orlando the Marmalade Cat* (1938–) appeared in extravagantly brightly coloured large formats. From the 1950s the ability of colour photolithography to produce almost any image faithfully led to a flood of high-quality picture books (pioneered by artists such as Brian Wildsmith), and since then the form has developed to include references to virtually every art form and technique, from the surreal to bricolage.[11]

Books such as David Macaulay's *Black and White* (1990), which provides four simultaneous narratives in apparently random form, David McKee's *I Hate My Teddy Bear* (1982), which presents two mysterious narratives and fragments of dozens more, or Janet and Allan Ahlberg's *The Babies' Catalogue* (1982), which dispenses with narrative completely, were pioneering experiments.

There was also a tradition of illustrating novels and short-story collections, which lingered far longer in children's books than in adults' books – from Joyce Lankester Brisley's 'Milly-Molly-Mandy' stories (1928–67) to the work of artists such as Shirley Hughes and Victor Ambrus, and, perhaps most famously, Nick Sharratt's work with Jacqueline Wilson, and Quentin Blake's with Roald Dahl. This rich tradition of pushing at the boundaries of the book means that children's books are in a strong position when it comes to negotiating the boundaries between print media and electronic media.

The fact that children's books have also existed on the boundary between books and games was demonstrated forcefully with the success of the 'Choose Your Own Adventure' series published by Bantam, which sold over 250 million copies between 1979 and

1998. Another hugely successful series, 'Fighting Fantasy Gamebooks', consisted of 'single-player gamebooks' by Steve Jackson and Ian Livingstone, developed from the fashion for the games 'Dungeons and Dragons' (from 1974) and 'Warhammer' (from 1983). These books, which sometimes required dice and pencil and paper to 'play' them, invited readers' decisions at key points in the adventure/story (or trust to the roll of a dice). For example, in Jackson and Livingstone's *The Warlock of Firetop Mountain* you might arrive at this scene:

168

You open the door to a large room. A large chair behind a solid-looking table suggests to you that someone, or some*thing*, of rank uses this room. A chest in the centre catches your eye. In a corner of the room stands a man-sized creature with a warty face, standing over a smaller creature of similar race. With the whip in his hand, the ORC CHIEFTAIN has been beating his servant, who is whimpering beneath him. Will you:

Attack them both?	Turn to 372
Spring at the Chieftain in the hope that his servant will aid you?	Turn to 65
Leave the room and head back for the Junction?	Turn to 293[12]

Given the technological constraints of the book, these texts obviously have severe limitations in comparison with the computer games that followed. Some of them also had a not-very-hidden agenda, of rewarding certain choices and actions (heroism), and punishing others (cowardice). Their importance in changing the very nature of narrative, however, cannot be underestimated. This is a major step in shifting control to the reader, as well as relegating the importance of the prose to a poor second place after the events. (After a steady decline in popularity in the face of competition from computer games, some of these titles have now been adapted as electronic games for iPhone and iPod.)

There have also been more 'literary' attempts to rethink the linearity of narratives – not in direct response to new media, but rather as a response to the concepts of postmodernism (of which the intellectual moves and consequences of electronic media are an integral part). Some, like Aidan Chambers's *Breaktime* (1978) and Peter Hunt's *Backtrack* (1986) – described by *The Times* as the 'first postmodernist' children's book – disrupt the 'invisibility' of the text by incorporating (fictional) extracts from diaries, handbooks, manuscripts, cartoons, newspapers, letters and so on. At one point in *Breaktime*, when the hero is about to make love for the first time, Chambers famously (or notoriously) divides his pages into two columns: in the left-hand column alternate lines give a first-person account of what is happening, and (each alternate line in italics) a transcription of the hero's internal monologue; the right-hand column is an extract from Dr Benjamin Spock's *A Young Person's Guide to Life and Love*, describing intercourse in clinical terms.[13] At the end of *Breaktime*, Chambers leaves the reader to decide whether the events in the book 'happened', or whether they are fictional adventures invented by fictional characters; Hunt, in *Backtrack*, presents the reader with several different versions of the 'same' events, without indicating which 'actually' happened. Gillian Cross's *Wolf* (1990) blurs the distinction between dream and 'reality', and while ostensibly telling the story of a girl being pursued by her terrorist father, presents the reader with an encyclopedic study of wolves and their habits.

Radical as they are, each of these three books retains a form of coherent narrative: just as the 'Choose Your Own Adventure' books built in resolutions (of success or failure), so it is possible to retell each of these books as a sequence of events (or several sequences). They are, like the picture books, one or two steps away from the almost complete freedom (or anarchy) that electronic, multimedia storying affords.

The other major influence on changes in print-based books is that the book is only part of the experience of the narrative. Books come with DVDs, films are issued with 'tie-in' books; fans have websites where stories are expanded or changed, characters are developed, scholarship is exchanged. The 2006 paperback edition of Stephenie Meyer's *Twilight* contains not only the first two chapters of the sequel, *New Moon* (extending the lure of the world of the books), but an advertisement for the DVD/Blu-Ray disc of the film. The DVD's special features are of a kind that has now become common-place – audio commentary by actors, 'The Journey from Page to Screen', 'Catherine Hardwicke's Vampire Kiss Montage', deleted and extended scenes with 'director introduction', remixes of soundtrack songs and so on. The book is only part of the complete multimedia experience, and the fact that many critics have lamented its stylistic deficiencies (it has the 'pillowy quality distinctly reminiscent of internet fan fiction')[14] is hardly relevant to its universe of possibilities.

Young readers now acquire and process knowledge in ways that were not possible in the 1980s. Information is accessible in small units, and associations can be made instantaneously. The very meanings of 'plot' or 'coherence' are changing. In *Aspects of the Novel* (1927), E. M. Forster made a distinction between 'story' and 'plot':

> We have defined a story as a narrative of events, the emphasis falling on causality. 'The king died and then the queen died,' is a story. 'The king died and then the queen died of grief' is a plot.

He then went on to make a rather severe value judgement:

> A plot cannot be told to a gaping audience of cave men [...] or to their modern descendant the movie-public. They can only be kept awake by 'and then – and then –' they can only supply curiosity. But a plot demands intelligence and memory also.[15]

The changes in media are so radical, and require such a shift in mindset, that Forster's distinctions and conclusions no longer hold.

Therefore, as far as new and old mindsets are overlapping, it is vital to consider what critical resources may be relevant to this situation.

Criticising the Visual

In the face of texts with a large visual content, we need a vocabulary, a metalanguage, with which to talk about them; since the early 1980s, a great deal of progress has been made in theorising the visual, and especially the picture book. There is nothing new about the combination of visuals and words – picture books have been available in vast numbers since the 1950s and comics since the 1880s; what is different is the blending of media, and the sophistication and complexity of the texts. As Robin Brenner has pointed out:

> Not only do graphic novels entail reading in the traditional sense, they require reading in a new way. To read a comic requires active participation in the text that is quite different from reading prose: the reader must make the connections between the images and the text and create the links between each panel and the page as a whole. This is generally referred to as 'reading between the panels', and this kind of literacy is not only new but vital in interacting with and succeeding in our multimedia world. If you've ever struggled to make the connections in reading a graphic novel while a teen reader whizzes through it, you've experienced how different this type of literacy is.[16]

Before looking at those differences, it is useful to examine the key strategies that authors and illustrators have adopted in the picture book, and with which our critical thinking needs to deal.

For inexperienced or pre-readers (or, increasingly in the electronic age, non-readers), the picture book/film/video game, that is the texts where images come first and words, if at all, second, has a particular power. The need for verbal literacy is dramatically reduced, although a certain kind of visual literacy is required: as Perry Nodelman pointed out in a 7,000-word discussion of the first picture from John Burningham's *Mr Gumpy's Outing*, almost everything about even a wordless picture has to be learnt: relative sizes, perspectives, the symbolism of dots for eyes, hatched lines for sky or clouds and so on.[17] Nevertheless, the picture book (and its electronic siblings) can empower the child reader. The classic example of this is Pat Hutchins's *Rosie's Walk* (1968); the thirty-two words of the text simply list the places that Rosie, a hen, visits on her walk around the farmyard, while the pictures show a fox repeatedly attempting to attack her, and repeatedly getting his comeuppance. In the adult-reading-to-pre-verbally-literate-child scenario (implied by the text) the words, which are the adult element, are blind or stupid, whereas anyone can see the fox. However, this is perhaps a romantic scenario, suggesting a present adult for the child to react against; whether the same would apply to an isolated child in front of a screen brings in other considerations.

The visual – picture book or film – also relies on allusion to make meaning. The *Shrek* franchise is a classic example: you need to know the fairy tales that it is lampooning. In print form, Janet and Allan Ahlberg's *The Jolly Postman, or Other People's Letters* (1986) stands in the tradition of the novelty book and the pop-up book (itself a genre with a distinguished history, and its own discipline of 'paper-engineering'). The eponymous postman delivers letters to various nursery-rhyme and folk-tale characters, such as the three bears, the witch in the gingerbread bungalow, Jack's giant and Goldilocks, and each letter can be removed from its built-in envelope. The whole book is a texture of allusion: the letter to the wolf, for example, is from Meeny, Miny, Mo & Co., Solicitors:

> We are writing to you on behalf of our client, Miss Riding-Hood, concerning her grandma. Miss Hood tells us that you are presently occupying her grandma's cottage and wearing her grandma's clothes without this lady's permission.

Please understand that if this harassment does not cease, we will call in the Official Woodcutter, and – if necessary – all the King's horses and all the King's men.

On a separate matter, we must inform you that Messrs. Three Little Pigs Ltd. are now firmly resolved to sue for damages.[18]

It might be argued that a good deal of this material is 'double address', aimed at two audiences separately, especially as the images of several of the Ahlbergs' books, such as *Peepo* (1981), derive from the 1930s and 1940s. It is the intense visual and verbal intertextual reference, however, that is at the heart of this book, and many more since. Intertextuality lends itself to satire, for example Babette Cole's *Princess Smartypants* (1986), or to social commentary, as in Eugene Trivizas and Helen Oxenbury's *The Three Little Wolves and the Big Bad Pig* (1993), in which the timid wolves retreat to grimmer and grimmer houses, ultimately fortified with barbed wire and iron plates – which the pig blows up.

The Three Little Wolves sets its unsettling message in a completely conventional picture-book frame, unlike perhaps the most accomplished and influential of intertextually based books, Jon Scieszka and Lane Smith's *The Stinky Cheese Man and Other Fairly Stupid Tales*. Clearly the deconstruction of tales such as 'Chicken Licken' (the title page falls on his head) or 'The Really Ugly Duckling' (who grows up to be a really ugly duck) depends on a knowledge of the originals. The real innovation, however, lies in the way the authors manipulate the idea of the book. It begins on the front endpaper with the narrator trying to deal with a noisy Little Red Hen ('Wait a minute. Hold everything. You can't tell your story right here. This is the endpaper. The book hasn't even begun yet') and ends on the back cover with the Little Red Hen objecting to the barcode ('What is this doing here? This is ugly! Who is this ISBN guy? Who will buy this book anyway? Over fifty pages of nonsense and I'm only in three of them').[19]

This is perhaps as far as the print book can be taken without exploding, but the success of books in the same vein, such as Emily Gravett's *Little Mouse's Big Book of Fears* (2007), which takes the form of a scrapbook, or Lauren Child's explorations of the relation between fiction and reality, *Beware of the Storybook Wolves* (2000) and *Who's Afraid of the Big Bad Book?* (2002), suggests that this play on the borders of the print medium may have a great deal of ingenious life left. (See also the discussion of Maurice Sendak's *Where the Wild Things Are* in Part Three: 'Picture Books'). This richness is often enhanced by intertextual reference to other artists and artworks – a classic example is Anthony Browne's referencing of Magritte and other surrealists in *Through the Magic Mirror* (1976). (In 1997, the Magritte estate required Browne to delete such references in his book *Willy the Dreamer*.)

There has been a good deal of research since the 1980s into the structures of the pictures in picture books, so that we can construct a metalanguage for their criticism. Equally, there has been debate as to whether the experience of apprehending a picture can legitimately be paralleled with reading words. As Sarah Toomey put it:

> There is a feeling of uncertainty that surrounds the vocabularies used to talk about the visual, and, while some critics refuse to use a term like 'visual literacy', others want to ally the visual with the verbal by reclaiming concepts which have come to be associated with language [...] [But] is a picture [...] really nothing more than a text whose codes need to be cracked, and its languages deciphered?[20]

Toomey rejects the efforts of semioticians such as Gunther Kress and Theo van Leeuwen in their attempts to codify the elements of visual images[21] in favour of examining specific responses in specific cultural contexts. A similar motive is behind the work of Arizpe and Styles: their extensive and intensive work with children of differing verbal skills and social backgrounds demonstrated that picture books both rewarded and 'demanded highly interactive reading'.[22] Perry Nodelman, in contrast, in another seminal book, suggested the necessity, if not the primacy, of words:

> Pictures can communicate much to us [...] but only if words
> focus them [...] In a sense, trying to understand the situation a
> picture depicts is always an act of imposing language upon it –
> interpreting visual information in verbal terms; it is not
> accidental that we speak of 'visual literacy', of the 'grammar' of
> pictures, of 'reading' pictures.[23]

One of the earliest attempts to define the elements of 'picture-book codes' was that of William Moebius in 1986, who noted that one of the most interesting features of the picture book is the relationship between word and image:

> Between text and picture, or among the pictures themselves,
> we may experience a sort of semic slippage, where word and
> image seem to send conflicting, perhaps contradictory
> messages about the 'who' or 'what' of the story. Here is a kind
> of 'plate tectonics' of the picturebook, where word and image
> constitute separate plates sliding and scraping along against
> each other.[24]

We are in deeper waters than it may seem here: do the pictures illustrate the words – and what can that possibly mean? Every illustration is an interpretation. Given even the simplest named object, an illustration must pick a style, a viewpoint, a tone ... Do pictures complement the words – add to or contradict them? Do words provide narrative while pictures provide the substance? Do pictures actually limit the readers' imagination by specifying what the words only imply? Moebius invites us to categorise the elements of a picture in terms of codes of position and size, perspective, frame, line and capillarity, and colour[25] – but many other taxonomies could be, and have been, suggested.

Once we move out of the traditional critical comfort zone of the printed text, to comics, manga, video, computer game, different skills are required. In his groundbreaking theorisation of the comic (in comic-strip form) Scott McCloud defined the comic as 'sequential art' – which requires yet another vocabulary.[26]

How the Book Has Responded: Language

As Ludwig Wittgenstein famously wrote in his *Tractatus Logico-Philosophicus* (1922), 'Die grenzen meiner sprache sind de grenzen meiner welt' ['The limits of my language are the limits of my world'], and there has been much concern in literacy circles about the damage that the new media are doing to children's use of language – and to a lesser extent to their stylistic sensitivity. Styles of prose naturally change, but the acceleration of change since the 1980s has been remarkable. Most notably, the style of what might broadly be called 'quality', or 'mainstream' or 'literary' fiction has moved closer to that of 'popular' fiction: the very concept of 'good style' has changed. It seems to some observers that the style of children's fiction in general has become less subtle, less suggestive, less allusive (in certain ways), less original and less reflective: content now dominates over form. What is being said is more important than how it is being said – the texture of language is no longer valued. 'Writerly' texts – those which require input from the reader, which require and allow ranges of interpretation – have commonly been assumed to produce a richer literary experience. 'Readerly' texts, where only a limited response is required – telling rather than showing the reader – have been more common in children's literature for obvious reasons of power and education, and they seem to be on the increase. This is despite the support for 'literary' texts from educationalists such as Lawrence R. Sipe:

> [Literature] [...] actually expands our view of what literacy is. This [...] includes literary understanding as an integral part of literate behaviour. Children with developed literary understanding are alive to the force and power of multiple

interpretations of what they read and know how to engage in a critical exchange of views with their peers. They are children who know how to pleasurably surrender to the power of the text [...] while also using their analytical skill to heighten their pleasure. They are children who know that literature can be an informing and transforming force in their lives.[27]

'Literary' literacy – that is, engaging in sophisticated dialogue with sophisticated text – is in retreat. This tendency has also involved commodification; Jack Zipes observes that the process of simplifying texts is inevitable:

> For children's and young adult literature, the increase in production and the decrease in quality have been highly visible, but it is not so much this phenomenon that is of concern. Rather it is the way reading and viewing are framed by the [...] culture industry that configures children and teenagers into its calculations as consumers and as saturated nodal points of mass information.

In these circumstances, 'simply put, a book for children is a commodity, not the holy grail nor the salvation of civilised society.'[28]

Of course this is a difficult thesis to prove because of the problem of comparing like with like. However, we might compare short extracts from two bestselling books. Here is the first: '[it] was about five o'clock and a very lovely evening. They met nobody at all, not even a slow old farm cart. [...] There seemed a curious silence and loneliness everywhere. Miles and miles of countryside, set with cornfields, pasture land, tall hedges and glimpses of winding lanes; heather was out on some of the hills, blazing purple in the sun; and, gleaming in the distance was the dark blue brilliance of the sea ...'[29] And the second: '[the] market was dazzling. There were watermelons bigger than babies, and green bananas and yellow ones that were almost orange. There were piles of nuts heaped on barrows, and pineapples and peppers and freshly caught fish and fish that had been dried.'[30] The first example, written in 1953, is from a much reviled author, infamous for the allegedly corrupting simplicity of her language, but this little purple passage is far from 'simple'. It is characterised by a leisurely pace, matching the action; the judgements ('lovely', 'curious') represent a quite subtle use of free indirect discourse or 'mind style' (when it is not clear whether these are the ideas of the narrator);[31] there is the elision of the verb in the sentence beginning 'Miles and miles'; ingenious atmosphere building by focusing on a carefully qualified absence ('not even a *slow old*') as well as conventional devices such as assonance – 'blazing', 'blue brilliance'.

In contrast, in the second extract, the author uses familiar words ('tugging', 'delicate', 'leather'), repetitive listing ('there were'), a neutral narrational voice, imprecise images ('animals', 'piles [...] heaped') and one image that might seem rather discordant ('bigger than babies'). None of this is to criticise this writer, rather to point out that, although in comparison with the first extract it is linguistically unadventurous, the book is described on its cover as 'A warm-hearted, well-written and absorbing adventure' (*Independent on Sunday*) and 'The most perfect children's book of the year [...] captivatingly told, funny and moving' (Nicolette Jones, *Sunday Times*), and it won several awards (Gold Medal, Smarties Book Prize, 2001; runner-up, Whitbread Children's Book of the Year, 2001; Guardian Children's Fiction Award, 2001).

Stylistically, times are changing. Action clichés that one might have expected to find in 'popular' writing now crop up, unremarked, in 'quality' fiction. If you read: 'She felt a thrill of fear. There was only one thing this could mean ...' you might not expect to be reading one of the most famous and serious children's novels of the twentieth century, a book described by another award-winning author, Jan Mark, as 'beautifully written'.[32] Pullman, of course, is well aware of the difficulties; as he has remarked: 'For me, prose should be a plain glass window, and not a fanciful mirror – not that you need make it so workmanlike that it's drab.'[33]

The kind of unconscious changes to language demonstrated here can be well summed up by comparing an original text with an adaptation designed as part of a multimedia experience. Edith Nesbit's *Five Children and It* was first published in 1902 with forty-six monochrome illustrations by H. R. Millar. Here, in the original, is the episode in which the Psammead grants the children another wish. Millar did not provide an illustration for this scene: the words, and the imagination of the readers, have to do the work:

Anthea said: 'I wish we all had beautiful wings to fly with.'

The Sand-fairy blew himself out, and next moment each child felt a funny feeling, half heaviness and half lightness, on its shoulders. The Psammead put its head on one side and turned its snail's eyes from one to the other […]

The wings were very big, and more beautiful than you can imagine – for they were soft and smooth, and every feather lay neatly in its place. And the feathers were of the most lovely mixed changing colours, like the rainbow, or iridescent glass, or the beautiful scum that sometimes floats on water that is not at all nice to drink.

'Oh – but can we fly?' Jane said, standing anxiously first on one foot and then on the other.

'Look out!' said Cyril; 'you're treading on my wing.'

'Does it hurt?' asked Anthea with interest; but no one answered, for Robert had spread his wings and jumped up, and now he was slowly rising in the air. He looked very awkward in his knickerbocker suit – his boots in particular hung helplessly, and seemed much larger than when he was standing in them. But the others cared but little how he looked – or how they looked, for that matter. For now they all spread out their wings and rose in the air. Of course you all know what flying feels like, because everyone has dreamed about flying, and it seems so beautifully easy – only, you can never remember how you did it; and as a rule you have to do it without wings, in your dreams, which is more clever and uncommon, but not so easy to remember the rule for. Now the four children rose flapping from the ground, and you can't think how good the air felt running against their faces. Their wings were tremendously wide when they were spread out, and they had to fly quite a long way apart so as not to get in each other's way. But little things like this are easily learned.

All the words in the English Dictionary, and in the Greek Lexicon as well, are, I find, of no use at all to tell you exactly what it feels like to be flying, so I will not try. But I will say that to look *down* on the fields and woods, instead of *along* at them is something like looking at a beautiful live map, where, instead of silly colours on paper, you have real moving sunny woods and green fields laid out one after the other [...] They paused on their wings. I cannot explain to you how this is done, but it is something like treading water when you are swimming, and hawks do it extremely well.[34]

This is characteristic of its period: the narrator's friendly (if occasionally ironic) voice is part of the experience, there is a wide range of judgements, a discussion of the difficulties of narrative, an unpatronising vocabulary ('iridescent') and careful incidental detail. Such was the reading for children who had no competing media (apart from line drawings).

In 2004, John Stephenson's film *Five Children and It* was released, with a screenplay by David Solomons, starring Kenneth Branagh and Freddie Highmore; a book was produced to accompany it. The anonymous adaptation ('based on the Motion Picture Screenplay by David Solomons. Based on the original novel by E. Nesbit') has fifty-two colour photographs and reduces Nesbit's 75,000-word novel to around 3,000 words. This is perhaps the more remarkable because the screenplay introduces two subplots, one of which sets the book in the First World War and sends the children's father to France. Here is the equivalent scene, in which the children begin to fly.

Jane squealed. When Anthea and Cyril turned to look, they couldn't believe their eyes – Jane had sprouted a pair of wings!

Anthea was next to scream, as she too sprouted wings from her back, and then Cyril did the same.

'Robert!' growled Cyril. 'He must have made a wish!'

There was a beating noise at the window. It was Robert – and he was flying!

Cyril opened the window.

'You've done it again!' he yelled. 'What were you thinking?'

Robert hovered just outside the window.

'I'm going to France,' he said. 'Dad said he wished he could fly to us. Well, he can't, so we'll fly to him. Come on!'

He flew off.

'France?' cried Cyril. 'No, Robert, NO!'

He looked at Anthea, helplessly. They climbed out of the window and flew after their brother.

Robert flew as hard as he could, way out ahead of the others.[35]

The point here is not the spareness of the language, which has virtually none of the attributes of the original (although certain literacy teachers and language enthusiasts may be depressed by the contrast). Quite clearly, the words are functioning differently: if the totality of the experience of the reader/viewer is assumed to be equivalent in the original and the new versions, then in the 2004 version the words and the book are, perhaps, only an *aide-mémoire* to the experience of having seen the film. Very little resides in the words themselves: there is plenty to say about the text linguistically (as with all texts) but, in terms of traditionally accepted values, and traditionally accepted triggers for discussion, this text is alien. It has all the clichés, the limited vocabulary, the lack of narrative contract that mark an 'undesirable' text in 'old' critical terms – but is that relevant to the text in its multimedia context? In one sense, ironically, this is the ultimate 'writerly' text – it is all gaps – but the difference is that writerly texts were valued for the fact that readers generated the missing information by a combination of interaction with the words, and their own imaginations. In this kind of text, the overall effect is achieved by slotting material supplied by and gathered from another part of the information universe.

The 2004 version of *Five Children and It* is therefore not an impoverished version of the original text, but a legitimate product of its times and context which just happens to be using old technology so that it looks like a book. Thus, while it is not surprising that the linguistic texture of books that are designed as books reflects the changes in language in the wider world, in 'books' on the intermedia margins we can find much more radical changes.

Writing about Children's Texts: The Future

Do we accept this step change in literacy, in narrative, and in the style and form of 'fiction'? If we do not, how do we convince a readership brought up with the new mental set that texts created for a previous mental set can offer them an interesting or valid experience? If we do accept the changes, how do we, as critics, commentators, arbiters, gatekeepers, fit into the act of creation of literature, which is becoming a process, rather than a static, completed act: how do we intervene while the text is being written?

Children's literature, as a set of texts, has always been pioneering. It may seem that it merely follows adult ideologies and literary and cultural trends, but because it has always spoken to the marginalised and silenced (if only to attempt to dominate them) it has been constantly subversive, and constantly experimental. As Walter Ong presciently put it in 1983:

> Electronic technology has brought us into the age of 'secondary orality'. This new orality has striking resemblances to the old in its participatory mystique, its fostering of a communal sense, its concentration on the present moment.[36]

To study and to write about children's literature now is to join in this participation at an exciting and challenging moment.

Notes

1   David Buckingham, 'Multimedia Childhoods', in Mary Jane Kehily and
     Joan Swann (eds), *Children's Cultural Worlds* (Chichester: John Wiley,
     2003), p. 184.
2   The Daily Green, 'Kids Spend Nearly 55 Hours a Week Watching TV,
     Texting, Playing Video Games ...', accessed from
     www.thedailygreen.com on 26 January 2011, n.p.
3   Walter J. Ong, *Orality and Literacy* (London: Methuen, 1982), p. 132;
     see also pp. 78–115.
4   Margaret Mackey, 'Playing in the Phase Space', *Signal*, 88 (1999),
     pp. 16–33, p. 30.
5   Jacqueline Wilson, *The Story of Tracy Beaker* (London: Corgi, 1992),
     p. 158.
6   Jacqueline Wilson, *Lola Rose* (London: Doubleday, 2003), p. 288.
7   Philip Pullman, *The Amber Spyglass* (London: Scholastic, 2001), p. 548.
8   Stephenie Meyer, *Twilight* (London: Atom, 2006), p. 434.
9   Anne Pellowski, 'Culture and Developing Countries', in Peter Hunt
     (ed.), *International Companion Encyclopedia of Children's Literature*,
     2nd edn, 2 vols (London: Routledge, 2004), vol. 2, pp. 858–71, p. 864;
     and see Carol Fox, *At the Very Edge of the Forest: The Influence of
     Literature on Storytelling by Children* (London: Cassell, 1993),
     pp. 68–83.
10   Nigel Woodward, *Hypertext and Hypermedia* (Wilmslow: Sigma Press,
     1983), p. 8.
11   See 'Developments in Printing Technology', in David Lewis (ed.),
     Picturing Text: The Contemporary Children's Picturebook (London:
     RoutledgeFalmer, 2001), pp. 138–44.
12   Steve Jackson and Ian Livingstone, *The Warlock of Firetop Mountain*
     (Harmondsworth: Penguin, 1982), segment 168.
13   Aidan Chambers, *Breaktime* (London: Bodley Head, 1978), pp. 122–6.
14   Lev Grossman, 'Is Stephenie Meyer a New J. K. Rowling?', *Time*, 24
     April 2008.
15   E. M. Forster, *Aspects of the Novel* (Harmondsworth: Penguin, 1962),
     pp. 93–4.
16   Robin Brenner, 'Graphic Novels 101: FAQ', *Horn Book Magazine*,
     March–April 2006, quoted in Ann Lazim, '"Reading" Graphic Novels',
     IBBYLink, 16 (2006), p. 8.

17   Perry Nodelman, 'Picture Books and Illustration', in Hunt (ed.),
      International Companion Encyclopedia, vol. 1, pp. 154–65.
18   Janet and Allan Ahlberg, *The Jolly Postman, or Other People's Letters*
      (London: Heinemann, 1986), n.p.
19   Jon Scieszka and Lane Smith, *The Stinky Cheese Man and Other Fairly
      Stupid Tales* (London: Puffin, 1993), n.p.
20   Sarah Toomey, *Embodying an Image: Gender and Genre in a Selection of
      Children's Responses to Picturebooks and Illustrated Texts* (Newcastle:
      Cambridge Scholars Press, 2009), pp. 5–6.
21   Gunther Kress and Theo van Leeuwen, *Reading Images: The Grammar
      of Visual Design* (London: Routledge, 2000).
22   Evelyn Arizpe and Morag Styles, *Children Reading Pictures:
      Interpreting Visual Texts* (London: RoutledgeFalmer, 2003), p. 223; see
      also Victor Watson and Morag Styles (eds), *Talking Pictures: Pictorial
      Texts and Young Readers* (London: Hodder & Stoughton, 1996); Maria
      Nikolajeva, 'Word and Picture', in Charles Butler (ed.), *Teaching
      Children's Fiction* (Basingstoke: Palgrave, 2006), pp. 106–51; Jane
      Doonan, *Looking at Pictures in Picture Books* (South Woodchester:
      Thimble Press, 1993); and Maria Nikolajeva and Carole Scott, *How
      Picture Books Work* (New York and London: Garland, 2001).
23   Perry Nodelman, *Words about Pictures: The Narrative Art of Children's
      Picture Books* (Athens, GA: University of Georgia Press, 1988), p. 211.
24   William Moebius, 'Introduction to Picturebook Codes', in Peter Hunt
      (ed.), *Children's Literature: Critical Concepts in Literary and Cultural
      Studies*, 4 vols (London and New York: Routledge, 2006), vol. 1, pp.
      249–63, p. 252.
25   Moebius, 'Introduction to Picturebook Codes', pp. 249–63.
26   Scott McCloud, *Understanding Comics: The Invisible Art* (New York:
      HarperCollins, 1994), p. 9; see also Bridget Carrington and Jennifer
      Harding, *Going Graphic: Comics and Graphic Novels for Young People*
      (Lichfield: Pied Piper, 2010); Roger Sabin, *Comics, Comix and Graphic
      Novels: A History of Comic Art* (London: Phaidon, 2001).
27   Lawrence R. Sipe, 'Children's Literature, Literacy, and Literary
      Understanding', in Hunt (ed.), *Children's Literature: Critical Concepts*,
      vol. 2, pp. 92–109, p. 104.
28   Jack Zipes, *Relentless Progress: The Reconfiguration of Children's
      Literature, Fairy Tales, and Storytelling* (New York: Routledge, 2009),
      pp. 5, 31.
29   Enid Blyton, *Five Go Down to the Sea* (London: Hodder Headline,
      1982), p. 21.

30   Eva Ibbotson, *Journey to the River Sea* (London: Macmillan Children's
      Books, 2001), p. 25.
31   See Katie Wales, *A Dictionary of Stylistics* (London: Longman, 1990),
      pp. 191–2.
32   Philip Pullman, *Northern Lights* (London: Scholastic, 1996), p. 273.
33   Cited in James Carter, *Talking Books* (London: Routledge, 1999),
      p. 184.
34   E. Nesbit, *Five Children and It* (Oxford: Oxford University Press,
      1994), pp. 72–3.
35   *Five Children and It* (London, HarperCollins Children's Books, 2004),
      p. 41.
36   Ong, *Orality*, p. 136.

Part Five
References and Resources

Timeline

	Historical Events and Key Literary Works	Children's Literature Publications
1484		William Caxton, *Aesop's Fables*
1644	John Milton, *On Education*	
1658		Comenius, *Orbis Sensualium Pictus*
1671–2		James Janeway, *A Token for Children*
1678	John Bunyan, *The Pilgrim's Progress*	
1686		John Bunyan, *Book for Boys and Girls* (also called *Country Rimes for Children* or *Divine Emblems*)
1692	Countess d'Aulnoy, *Les contes des fées* [*Fairy Tales*]	
1693	John Locke, *Some Thoughts Concerning Education*	
1697	Charles Perrault, *Histoires ou contes du temps passé* [*Tales of Mother Goose*]	
1706–8	First English translation of *Arabian Nights Entertainments*	

	Historical Events and Key Literary Works	Children's Literature Publications
1719	Daniel Defoe, *Robinson Crusoe*	
1726	Jonathan Swift, *Gulliver's Travels*	
1744		John Newbery, *A Little Pretty Pocket-Book*
1749		Sarah Fielding, *The Governess*
1762	Jean-Jacques Rousseau, *Émile*	
1786		Sarah Trimmer, *Fabulous Histories: The History of the Robins*
1789–94	William Blake, *Songs of Innocence and of Experience*	
1792–6		John Aikin and Anna Laetitia Barbauld, *Evenings at Home*
1796		Maria Edgeworth, *The Parent's Assistant*
1798	Invention of lithography (Alois Senefelder)	
1812	The Brothers Grimm, *Kinder- und Hausmärchen* [*Children's and Household Tales*]	
1814		Johann David Wyss, *The Swiss Family Robinson*
1822	Mechanical typesetting	
1840	Dalziel Brothers, wood engravers, established	
1841	Captain Frederick Marryat, *Masterman Ready*	
1845	Heinrich Hoffmann, *Struwwelpeter*	
1846	Edward Lear, *A Book of Nonsense*	

Timeline

	Historical Events and Key Literary Works	Children's Literature Publications
1847	Charlotte Brontë, *Jane Eyre*	
1857		Thomas Hughes, *Tom Brown's Schooldays*
1858		R. M. Ballantyne, *The Coral Island*
1859	Charles Darwin, *On the Origin of Species*	
1863		Charles Kingsley, *The Water Babies*
1865		Lewis Carroll, *Alice's Adventures in Wonderland*
1868		Louisa May Alcott, *Little Women*
1870	Elementary Education Act: universal elementary education	
1872		Susan Coolidge, *What Katy Did*
1883	Married Women's Property Act	R. L. Stevenson, *Treasure Island*
1884	National Society for the Prevention of Cruelty to Children (NSPCC) founded	
1885	Age of consent raised to sixteen	R. L. Stevenson, *A Child's Garden of Verses*
1888	Lawsuit by Frances Hodgson Burnett leads to change in International Copyright Law	
1894		Ethel Turner, *Seven Little Australians*
1901	Net Book Agreement introduces fixed prices for books in the UK	
1902		Edith Nesbit, *Five Children and It*; Beatrix Potter, *The Tale of Peter Rabbit*

	Historical Events and Key Literary Works	Children's Literature Publications
1907	Creation of first 'Teddy Bear' toy, named after President Theodore Roosevelt	
1908		Kenneth Grahame, *The Wind in the Willows*
1911		Frances Hodgson Burnett, *The Secret Garden*; J. M. Barrie, *Peter and Wendy*
1913		Walter de la Mare, *Peacock Pie*
1914–18	First World War	
1918	School-leaving age raised to fourteen	
1924		A. A. Milne, *When We Were Very Young*
1928	'Steamboat Willie', the first Walt Disney animated cartoon	
1930		Arthur Ransome, *Swallows and Amazons*
1930s	Commercial use of offset-photolithography	
1934		Geoffrey Trease, *Bows against the Barons*
1935		Laura Ingalls Wilder, *Little House on the Prairie*
1936	Carnegie Medal established, for best Children's Book of the Year	Noel Streatfeild, *Ballet Shoes*
1937		Eve Garnett, *The Family from One End Street*; J. R .R. Tolkien, *The Hobbit*
1939–45	Second World War	

Timeline

	Historical Events and Key Literary Works	Children's Literature Publications
1941	Penguin Books establish Puffin Picture Books	
1942		Enid Blyton, *Five on a Treasure Island*
1944	Education Act separates primary, secondary and further education	
1946	First children's television programme *For the Children* (BBC)	
1950		C. S. Lewis, *The Lion, the Witch and the Wardrobe*
1951	J. D. Salinger, *The Catcher in the Rye*; GCE school examinations introduced; creation of the British Children's Film Foundation	
1954		Rosemary Sutcliff, *The Eagle of the Ninth*
1955	Kate Greenaway Medal established for picture books	
1958		Philippa Pearce, *Tom's Midnight Garden*
1959	Iona and Peter Opie, *The Language and Lore of Schoolchildren*	
1960	Philippe Ariès, *L'Enfant et la Vie Familiale sous l'Ancien Régime* [*Centuries of Childhood*]	
1962		Ezra Jack Keats, *The Snowy Day*; Brian Wildsmith, *A.B.C.*
1963		Maurice Sendak, *Where the Wild Things Are*

	Historical Events and Key Literary Works	Children's Literature Publications
1964		Louise Fitzhugh, *Harriet the Spy*; Roald Dahl, *Charlie and the Chocolate Factory*
1965		Susan Cooper, *Over Sea, Under Stone*
1967		Alan Garner, *The Owl Service*; S. E. Hinton, *The Outsiders*
1968		Ursula Le Guin, *A Wizard of Earthsea*
1969		Eric Carle, *The Very Hungry Caterpillar*
1972	School-leaving age raised to sixteen	Richard Adams, *Watership Down*
1974		Bernard Ashley, *The Trouble with Donovan Croft*; Michael Rosen, *Mind Your Own Business*; Robert Cormier, *The Chocolate War*
1975		Robert Westall, *The Machine Gunners*; Judy Blume, *Forever*; Virginia Hamilton, *M. C. Higgins, the Great*
1976	Bruno Bettelheim, *The Uses of Enchantment*	
1977		Gene Kemp, *The Turbulent Term of Tyke Tiler*; John Burningham, *Come Away from the Water, Shirley*; Shirley Hughes, *Dogger*
1978		Jan Needle, *My Mate Shofiq*; Raymond Briggs, *The Snowman*; Aidan Chambers, *Breaktime*
1983		Anthony Browne, *Gorilla*
1984	Creation of first British MA in Children's Literature, at the University of Reading	

Timeline

	Historical Events and Key Literary Works	Children's Literature Publications
1986		Diana Wynne Jones, *Howl's Moving Castle*; Janet and Allan Ahlberg, *The Jolly Postman*
1991		Jacqueline Wilson, *The Story of Tracy Beaker*
1992	First pilot scheme by children's book charity Bookstart	
1995		Philip Pullman, *Northern Lights*; Benjamin Zephaniah, *Talking Turkeys*
1996		Anne Fine, *The Tulip Touch*; Melvin Burgess, *Junk*
1997	National Literacy Strategy introduced for primary schools; Net Book Agreement abolished, allowing booksellers to heavily discount books	J. K. Rowling, *Harry Potter and the Philosopher's Stone*
1998		David Almond, *Skellig*
1999	First Children's Laureate, Quentin Blake	Julia Donaldson and Axel Scheffer, *The Gruffalo*
2000		Anthony Horowitz, *Stormbreaker*
2002		Lauren Child, *Who's Afraid of the Big Bad Book?*
2004		Robert Muchamore, *The Recruit*
2005	Seven Stories, the Centre for Children's Books, opens in Newcastle	Stephenie Meyer, *Twilight*
2008		Patrick Ness, *The Knife of Never Letting Go*
2009		Anna Perera, *Guantanamo Boy*; Justine Larbalestier, *Liar*
2010		Malorie Blackman, *Boys Don't Cry*

Further Reading

General Reference

Carpenter, Humphrey, and Mari Prichard, *The Oxford Companion to Children's Literature* (Oxford: Oxford University Press, 1984)

> Comprehensive, readable and reliable reference, although becoming dated

Chevalier, Tracy (ed.), *Twentieth Century Children's Writers*, 3rd edn (Chicago and London: St James Press, 1989)

> Although dated, an invaluable source of bibliographical details

Grenby, M. O., and Andrea Immel (eds), *The Cambridge Companion to Children's Literature* (Cambridge: Cambridge University Press, 2009)

> Urbane and wide-ranging non-technical essays on the major areas of discussion in children's literature, including chapters on constructions of childhood, difference, retellings, canons and animal stories

Grenby, M. O., and Kimberley Reynolds, *Children's Literature Studies: A Handbook for Research* (Basingstoke: Palgrave Macmillan, 2011)

> This practical guide covers a range of skills for literary-critical study of children's literature, including guidelines on using libraries and archives, advice on approaching children's literature research and a useful list of other resources

Hunt, Peter (ed.), *International Companion Encyclopedia of Children's Literature*, 2nd edn, 2 vols (London: Routledge, 2004)

> A collection of 119 specially commissioned essays, most of around 6,000 words, from leading authorities such as Iona Opie, Maria Nikolajeva, Margaret Meek and Anne Pellowski. They cover all aspects of the theory and practice of children's literature; forty-six essays deal with individual countries, continents or regions

—, *Children's Literature: Critical Concepts in Literary and Cultural Studies*, 4 vols (London and New York: Routledge, 2006)

> These four volumes bring together the ninety-nine most significant English-language statements on all aspects of theory and children's literature

Mikenberg, Julia, and Lynne Vallone (eds), *The Oxford Handbook of Children's Literature* (New York: Oxford University Press, 2011)

> An interdisciplinary handbook, with substantive critical essays exemplifying critical approaches and theoretical perspectives

Rudd, David (ed.), *The Routledge Companion to Children's Literature* (London: Routledge, 2010)

> A combination of extensive essays on subjects such as gender studies, narratology, media, race and ethnicity, and a detailed reference section on critical and theoretical terms. Comprehensive timeline and bibliography

Watson, Victor (ed.), *The Cambridge Guide to Children's Books in English* (Cambridge: Cambridge University Press, 2001)

> A comprehensive reference book, with an emphasis on contemporary writing and on English-speaking countries across the world

Zipes, Jack (ed.), *The Oxford Encyclopedia of Children's Literature*, 4 vols (New York: Oxford University Press, 2006)

> Four volumes, with an emphasis on biographies of authors

Anthologies

Demers, Patricia (ed.), *A Garland from the Golden Age: An Anthology of Children's Literature, 1850–1900* (Toronto: Oxford University Press, 1983)

> Extremely useful selection of illustrations and extracts, grouped thematically

—, *From Instruction to Delight: An Anthology of Children's Literature to 1850*, 3rd edn (Toronto: Oxford University Press, 2008)

> Collection of essential extracts, with biographical and critical headnotes and illustrations. Takes into account the most recent research

Hunt, Peter (ed.), *Children's Literature: An Anthology, 1801–1902* (Oxford: Blackwell, 2000)
> Over a hundred poems, stories and extracts from novels; each item is introduced with a contextualising and critical headnote

Salway, Lance (ed.), *A Peculiar Gift: Nineteenth Century Writings on Books for Children* (Harmondsworth: Kestrel [Penguin], 1976)
> Unique collection of the earliest critical essays on children's literature, including writers such as Dickens, Thackeray, Stevenson, Conrad and Ewing

Zipes, Jack, Lissa Paul, Lynne Vallone, Peter Hunt and Gillian Avery (eds), *The Norton Anthology of Children's Literature: The Traditions in English* (New York: Norton, 2005)
> Nearly 2,500 pages, featuring 170 writers and illustrators and 40 complete books including *A Child's Garden of Verses* and Aidan Chambers's *The Present Takers*

Theory and Criticism

Collections of Essays

Avery, Gillian, and Julia Briggs (eds), *Children and Their Books: A Celebration of the Work of Iona and Peter Opie* (Oxford: Clarendon Press, 1989)
> Scholarly essays, with some unusual topics, such as William Godwin, Arthur Hughes, Henry James, Walter de la Mare and William Mayne

Hunt, Peter (ed.), *Children's Literature: The Development of Criticism* (London: Routledge, 1990)
> A selection of early essays on children's literature by, for example, Ruskin, Chesterton and Ransome, followed by the most important critical/theoretical essays of the 1970s and 1980s, including Lissa Paul on feminist theory, Hugh Crago on response and John Rowe Townsend on standards of criticism

—, *Understanding Children's Literature*, 2nd edn (London and New York: Routledge, 2005)

> Key essays from the *International Companion Encyclopedia of Children's Literature*, covering topics such as the theory of children's literature, picture books, bibliography and bibliotherapy

—, *Literature for Children: Contemporary Criticism* (London: Routledge, 1992; Kindle edn: 2007)

> Landmark essays including Hollindale on ideology, Geoff Moss on illustration, Lissa Paul on fractal geometry and Sarah Gilead on closure in fantasy fiction

Maybin, Janet, and Nicola J. Watson (eds), *Children's Literature: Approaches and Territories* (Basingstoke: Palgrave Macmillan/Open University, 2009)

> A good introduction to critical issues in children's literature, including new and important previously published essays. Themes include 'Purposes and Histories', 'Publishing, Prizes and Popularity', 'Poetry' and 'Storytelling, Stage and Screen'

Meek, Margaret, Aidan Warlow and Griselda Barton (eds), *The Cool Web: The Pattern of Children's Reading* (London: Bodley Head, 1977)

> One of the earliest collections of academic essays and extracts from professional and popular journalism, ostensibly concerned with literacy, but in fact ranging entertainingly across all aspects of children's reading

Montgomery, Heather, and Nicola J. Watson (eds), *Children's Literature: Classic Texts and Contemporary Trends* (Basingstoke: Palgrave Macmillan/Open University, 2009)

> A wide-ranging collection of essays on key texts and authors, including Louisa May Alcott, J. M. Barrie, Arthur Ransome, J. K. Rowling, Philip Pullman and Beverley Naidoo

Reynolds, Kimberley (ed.), *Modern Children's Literature: An Introduction* (Basingstoke: Palgrave Macmillan, 2005)

> A handbook based on a course at Roehampton University; each chapter examines a group of key texts in detail, and summarises relevant theory and key terms. The fifteen topics include feminism, youth culture, autobiography, and time and memory

Monographs

Beckett, Sandra L., *Crossover Fiction, Global and Historical Perspectives* (New York and London: Routledge, 2009)

> Comprehensive exploration of fiction written for, or adopted by, adult and child audiences

Chambers, Aidan, *Booktalk: Occasional Writing on Literature and Children* (London: Bodley Head, 1985)

> Essays on literature, theory, education, literacy, from a liberal-humanist position, by a well-respected author of groundbreaking fiction. Contains the seminal essays 'The Reader in the Book' and 'Tell Me: Are Children Critics?'

—, *Reading Talk* (South Woodchester: Thimble Press, 2001)

> Essays and talks on children's literature; topics include Anne Frank, Huckleberry Finn, Talbot Baines Reed and Penguin Books

Clark, Beverly Lyon, *Kiddie Lit: The Cultural Construction of Children's Literature in America* (Baltimore, MD: Johns Hopkins University Press, 2003)

> An exploration of the marginalisation of children's literature (and children's literature studies) in American culture and academia

Hollindale, Peter, *Signs of Childness in Children's Books* (South Woodchester: Thimble Press, 1997)

> Important exploration of how we recognise the characteristics of, or essences of, the child, or childhood, in children's literature

Inglis, Fred, *The Promise of Happiness: Value and Meaning in Children's Fiction* (Cambridge: Cambridge University Press, 1981)

> Engaging liberal-humanist examination of modern children's writers, with an emphasis on social and cultural effects of literature

Kidd, Kenneth B., *Making American Boys: Boyology and the Feral Male* (Minneapolis, MN: University of Minnesota Press, 2004)

> A review of 'boy culture' in the twentieth century, with examples of its literary manifestations

Further Reading

Lesnik-Oberstein, Karín, *Children's Literature: Criticism and the Fictional Child* (Oxford: Clarendon Press, 1994)

> Argues that the concept of children as an audience is a purely adult creation, and that children's literature criticism is concerned solely with matching books to these theoretical children

McGillis, Roderick, *The Nimble Reader: Literary Theory and Children's Literature* (New York: Twayne, 1996)

> An introduction to more traditional forms of criticism and their application to children's literature; topics include formalism, myth and archetype, psychoanalytic criticism, structuralism, poststructuralism and reader response

Nodelman, Perry, *The Hidden Adult: Defining Children's Literature* (Baltimore, MD: Johns Hopkins University Press, 2008)

> The most comprehensive and accessible book on the theory of children's literature

—, and Mavis Reimer, *The Pleasures of Children's Literature*, 3rd edn (London: Allyn and Bacon, 2002)

> An introduction to studying and teaching children's literature, covering a variety of disciplinary approaches, including literary theory, cultural and media studies, pedagogy and psychology. Includes sections on children's books in the marketplace, picture books, poetry and fairy tales

O'Sullivan, Emer, *Comparative Children's Literature* (London and New York: Routledge, 2005)

> Erudite introduction to this subject, with accessible sections on translation and cultural differences

Reynolds, Kimberley, *Radical Children's Literature: Future Visions and Aesthetic Transformations in Children's Literature* (Basingstoke: Palgrave Macmillan, 2007)

> Reynolds rejects the position taken by Jacqueline Rose and argues that children's literature can be both radical and transformative, enabling children to take an active role in shaping narratives for the future

Rose, Jacqueline, *The Case of Peter Pan or the Impossibility of Children's Fiction*, rev. edn (London: Macmillan, 1994)

> A detailed study of the development and criticism of *Peter Pan*, but highly influential because of its theorising that children's literature is an entirely adult-controlled construct (like childhood) and consequently manipulative

Rustin, Margaret, and Michael Rustin, *Narratives of Love and Loss: Studies in Modern Children's Fiction*, rev. edn (London and New York: Karnac, 2001)

> Pioneering use of psychological criticism/analysis with children's books. Texts include *Tom's Midnight Garden*, the 'Narnia' books, *Five Children and It* and *Carrie's War*

Stephens, John, *Language and Ideology in Children's Fiction* (London: Longman, 1992)

> Although it has been overtaken by Stephens's own theoretical work, this book has been highly influential. It focuses on the ideologies pervading texts and the ideological relationship between adult author and child reader, and uses detailed analyses to demonstrate how language functions as an ideological tool

Trites, Roberta Seelinger, *Disturbing the Universe: Power and Repression in Adolescent Literature* (Iowa City, IA: University of Iowa Press, 2000)

> An in-depth discussion of young adult literature; Trites argues that young adult novels are fundamentally concerned with power and with adolescent experiences of negotiating power structures in society

Wall, Barbara, *The Narrator's Voice: The Dilemma of Children's Fiction* (London: Macmillan, 1991)

> Seminal work on style, tone and point of view. Wall distinguishes three common modes of address of narrator to child reader – single, double and dual – and explores their use through the history of children's literature

Waller, Alison, *Constructing Adolescence in Fantastic Realism* (New York and London: Routledge, 2008)

> Scholarly exploration of the way in which models of adolescence are found symbolically in fantastic tropes such as time-slip and hauntings. Establishes a new critical term: young adult fantastic realism

Wilkie-Stibbs, Christine, *The Feminine Subject in Children's Literature* (New York and London: Routledge)

> A highly theoretical discussion of *l'écriture féminine* and children's literature, drawing on the work of Cixous, Irigary, Lacan and others. Includes close analysis of works by Margaret Mahy and Gillian Cross

Zipes, Jack, *Sticks and Stones: The Troublesome Success of Children's Literature from Slovenly Peter to Harry Potter* (New York and London: Routledge, 2001)

> Opinionated essays on contemporary issues, such as 'the contamination of the fairy tale' and the Harry Potter phenomenon

History

General

Alston, Ann, *The Family in Children's Literature* (New York and London: Routledge, 2008)

> A comprehensive history; argues that the basic aims and motivations of the nuclear family have not changed, despite the ways in which fiction reflects reality

Avery, Gillian, *Behold the Child: American Children and their Books* (London and Baltimore, MD: Bodley Head and Johns Hopkins University Press, 1994)

> Still the only extended history of American children's literature. Very readable

Briggs, Julia, Dennis Butts and M. O. Grenby (eds), *Popular Children's Literature in Britain* (Aldershot: Ashgate, 2008)

> In-depth discussion of topics from Robin Hood, chapbooks and pantomime, Angela Brazil and religions tracts to Blyton, Dahl and Rowling

Butts, Dennis, *Children's Literature and Social Change: Some Case Studies from Barbara Hofland to Philip Pullman* (Cambridge: Lutterworth Press, 2010)

> Elegant literary history, including essays on Henty, Rider Haggard, flying stories and lesser-known authors such as Amy Le Feuvre

Carpenter, Humphrey, *Secret Gardens: The Golden Age of Children's Literature* (London: Allen and Unwin, 1985)

> Pioneering, readable and sometimes controversial study of the work of Kingsley, Carroll, Grahame, Nesbit and others, interpreting their books in terms of their lives

Darton, F. J. Harvey, *Children's Books in England: Five Centuries of Social Life*, rev. Brian Alderson, 3rd edn (Cambridge: Cambridge University Press, 1982; reissued: London and New Castle, DE: British Library and Oak Knoll Press, 1999)

> The first substantive history of children's literature has become a classic, although it is not always clearly organised and only takes the history to about 1910

Grenby, M. O., *Children's Literature* (Edinburgh: Edinburgh University Press, 2008)

> A succinct historical survey of children's literature from the eighteenth century to the present day, arranged by genre. Comprehensive and useful

Griswold, Jerry, *Audacious Kids: Coming of Age in America's Classic Children's Books* (New York: Oxford University Press, 1992)

> Entertaining discussion of *The Wizard of Oz*, *Little Lord Fauntleroy*, *Tarzan of the Apes*, *Little Women* and others

Hilton, Mary, Morag Styles and Victor Watson (eds), *Opening the Nursery Door: Reading, Writing and Childhood, 1600–1900* (London and New York: Routledge, 1997)

> Essays inspired by the 'home-made library' of Jane Johnson; primarily eighteenth- and nineteenth-century topics

Hunt, Peter, *An Introduction to Children's Literature* (Oxford: Oxford University Press, 1994)

> Brief history, now slightly dated, with a discussion of some of the basic issues in children's literature criticism

— (ed.), *Children's Literature: An Illustrated History* (Oxford: Oxford University Press, 1995)

> Extensively illustrated history, with chapters on the United States, Canada, Australia and New Zealand

Marcus, Leonard S., *Minders of Make Believe: Idealists, Entrepreneurs, and the Shaping of American Children's Literature* (Boston: Houghton Mifflin, 2008)

> Lively history of the publishers, educationalists, librarians and writers who influenced twentieth-century children's literature publishing in the United States

Thacker, Deborah Cogan, and Jean Webb, *Introducing Children's Literature from Romanticism to Postmodernism* (London: Routledge, 2002)

> Selective history, which looks in detail at two representative texts from each of five periods – Romantic, nineteenth century, *fin de siècle*, modernist and postmodernist – and sets them in the context of adult literature

Townsend, John Rowe, *Written for Children: An Outline of English-Language Children's Literature*, 5th edn (London: Bodley Head, 1995)

> For many years the standard popular history. Last updated in 1995, it remains valuable

Eighteenth Century

Summerfield, Geoffrey, *Fantasy and Reason: Children's Literature in the Eighteenth Century* (Athens, GA: University of Georgia Press)

> Opinionated and forceful account

Nineteenth Century

Foster, Shirley, and Judy Simons, *What Katy Read: Feminist Re-Readings of 'Classic' Stories for Girls* (London: Macmillan, 1995)

> Feminist readings of *The Wide, Wide World*, *The Daisy Chain*, *Little Women*, *What Katy Did* and others

Gubar, Maria, *Artful Dodgers: Reconceiving the Golden Age of Children's Literature* (Oxford: Oxford University Press, 2008)

> Challenging study that questions accepted ideas of the innocence of childhood and examines the 'beautiful child' cult

McCulloch, Fiona, *The Fictional Role of Childhood in Victorian and Early Twentieth Century Children's Literature* (Lampeter: Edwin Mellen Press, 2004)

> Wide-ranging and very incisive reassessments of major texts

McGavran, James Holt (ed.), *Literature and the Child: Romantic Continuations, Postmodern Contestations* (Iowa City, IA: University of Iowa Press, 1999)

> Essays on the persistence of the idea of the Romantic child in society; includes essays on postmodern poetry, Milne and Disney

Reynolds, Kimberley, *Girls Only? Gender and Popular Children's Fiction in Britain, 1880–1910* (Hemel Hempstead: Harvester, 1990)

> Explores the expansion of reading in this period and its effect on gender identities, gender difference and social practices

Thiel, Liz, *The Fantasy of Family: Nineteenth-Century Children's Literature and the Myth of the Domestic Idea* (New York and London: Routledge, 2008)

> A detailed reassessment of an accepted tradition

Twentieth/Twenty-First Century

Beckett, Sandra L. (ed.), *Reflections of Change: Children's Literature since 1945* (Westport, CT: Greenwood, 1997)

> Themed essays on theory, postmodern trends, boundaries between children's and adult literature, with essays on Germany, Taiwan, Russia and elsewhere

Bradford, Clare, Kerry Mallan, John Stephens and Robyn McCallum, *New World Orders in Contemporary Children's Literature: Utopian Transformations* (Basingstoke: Palgrave Macmillan, 2008)

> Exploration of postcolonial futures, utopias and dystopias, and the posthuman world, linked to critical and cultural theory

Lenz, Millicent, and Carole Scott (eds), *His Dark Materials Illuminated: Critical Essays on Philip Pullman's Trilogy* (Detroit, MI: Wayne State University Press, 2005)

> Fifteen academic essays, with excellent material on intertextuality, theology and Pullman's polemic

Reynolds, Kimberley, and Nicholas Tucker (eds), *Children's Publishing in Britain since 1945* (Aldershot: Scolar Press, 1998)

> An invaluable guide to different aspects of children's publishing in the twentieth century, covering publishing history, children's book prizes and children's books in different media

Genres

Adventure Stories and Boys' Stories

Bristow, Joseph, *Empire Boys: Adventures in a Man's World* (London: HarperCollins, 1991)

> Definitive account of the social and cultural background of the genre

Jones, Dudley, and Tony Watkins (eds), *A Necessary Fantasy? The Heroic Figure in Children's Popular Culture* (New York and London: Garland, 2000)

> Essays on many aspects of heroism, from pony stories, Nancy Drew and Robin Hood to Action Man and Dr Who

Stephens, John (ed.), *Ways of Being Male: Representing Masculinities in Children's Literature and Film* (New York and London: Routledge, 2002)

> Wide-ranging academic essays on (as well as much else) the representation of masculinity, cross-dressing, gendering bodies and behaviours, and stereotypes

Colonialism and Postcolonialism

Kutzer, M. Daphne, *Empire's Children: Empire and Imperialism in Classic British Children's Literature* (New York and London: Routledge, 2000)

> Considers the imperial legacy in Kipling, Burnett, Nesbit, Lofting, Milne and Ransome

Logan, Mawvena Kossí, *Narrating Africa: George Henty and the Fiction of Empire* (London and New York: Routledge, 1999)

> Detailed analysis of Henty's major novels, with a survey of pre-Henty novels about Africa

McGillis, Roderick (ed.), *Voices of the Other: Children's Literature and the Postcolonial Context* (New York: Garland, 2000)

> Pioneering collection of essays, including views from Canada, Australia and the UK

Fantasy

Butler, Charles, *Four British Fantasists: Place and Culture in the Children's Fantasies of Penelope Lively, Alan Garner, Diana Wynne Jones and Susan Cooper* (Oxford: Scarecrow Press, 2006)

> Incisive reassessment of four key figures of the 'golden age' of British fantasy

Gray, William, *Death and Fantasy: Essays on Philip Pullman, C. S. Lewis, George MacDonald and R. L. Stevenson* (Newcastle: Cambridge Scholars Press, 2008)

> Makes particularly interesting links between the authors, suggesting that Pullman has misread Lewis, just as Lewis misread MacDonald

Le Guin, Ursula, *Earthsea Revisioned* (Cambridge, MA: Children's Literature New England in association with Green Bay Publications, 1993)

> Important pamphlet explaining Le Guin's break with traditional, male-dominated forms of fantasy

Fairy and Folk Tales

Bettelheim, Bruno, *The Uses of Enchantment: The Meaning and Importance of Fairy Tales* (London: Thames and Hudson, 1976)
> Highly influential, but now much challenged, account of the psychological impact of fairy tales

Tatar, Maria, *Off with Their Heads! Fairy Tales and the Culture of Childhood* (Princeton, NJ: Princeton University Press, 1992)
> An analysis and history of the way in which fairy tales have been harnessed to the task of socialising children

Girls' Stories

Cadogan, Mary, and Patricia Craig, *You're a Brick, Angela!: The Girls' Story 1839–1985* (London: Gollancz, 1985)
> The definitive account of girls' school stories and other genres: witty and comprehensive

Picture Books

Carrington, Bridget, and Jennifer Harding, *Going Graphic: Comics and Graphic Novels for Young People* (Lichfield: Pied Piper, 2010)
> Explores the latest developments in theory and practice

Lewis, David, *Reading Contemporary Picturebooks: Picturing Text* (London: RoutledgeFalmer, 2001)
> Essential guide to theory, history and practice of picture books, including the interaction of word and picture

McCloud, Scott, *Understanding Comics: The Invisible Art* (New York: HarperCollins, 1994)
> Definitive book on the subject, presented brilliantly in comic-book form

Nikolajeva, Maria, and Carole Scott, *How Picture Books Work* (New York and London: Garland, 2001)
> Provides a new vocabulary for the examination and criticism of the picture book

Nodelman, Perry, *Words about Pictures: The Narrative Art of Children's Picture Books* (Athens, GA: University of Georgia Press, 1988)
> Seminal work that eloquently puts the case for the serious study of the form, and provides extensive theoretical underpinnings

Whalley, Joyce Irene, and Tessa Rose Chester, *A History of Children's Book Illustration* (London: John Murray with the Victoria and Albert Museum, 1988)
> The most extensive, thoroughly illustrated and well-balanced history of children's book illustration

Poetry

Chambers, Nancy (ed.), *Poetry for Children: The Signal Award 1979–2001* (South Woodchester: Thimble Press, 2009)
> Collection of the essays written for the *Signal* poetry award: both a record of two decades of publishing and a treasure-chest of opinions and theorising

Styles, Morag, *From the Garden to the Street: Three Hundred Years of Poetry for Children* (London: Cassell, 1998)
> The only comprehensive history, with profuse examples

—, Louise Joy and David Whitley (eds), *Poetry and Childhood* (Stoke on Trent: Trentham, 2010)
> Twenty-six essays from a British Library conference, featuring poets, critics, educators and historians. A comprehensive picture of contemporary attitudes

School Stories

Kirkpatrick, Robert J., *The Encyclopaedia of Boys' School Stories* (Aldershot and Burlington, VT: Ashgate, 2000)
> Comprehensive reference work

Musgrave, P. W., *From Brown to Bunter: The Life and Death of the School Story* (London: Routledge and Kegan Paul, 1985)
> Definitive, although rather dated, study

Sims, Sue, and Hilary Clare, *The Encyclopaedia of Girls' School Stories* (Aldershot and Burlington, VT: Ashgate, 2000)
> Comprehensive reference work

War

Agnew, Kate, and Geoff Fox, *Children at War: From the First World War to the Gulf* (London: Continuum, 2001)
> A general survey of children's books on war from 1914 to 2000, and specialist chapters on the First World War, and the Second World War in the UK, North America and mainland Europe

Edwards, Owen Dudley, *British Children's Fiction in the Second World War* (Edinburgh: Edinburgh University Press, 2007)
> Exhaustive account with a great deal of original material and extensive quotations from little-known books

Kokkola, Lydia, *Representing the Holocaust in Youth Literature* (New York and London: Routledge, 2002)
> Looks at the moral obligations of writers, especially for young readers, and includes an analysis of the appeal of Holocaust literature

Other Genres

Blount, Margaret, *Animal Land: The Creatures of Children's Fiction* (London: Hutchinson, 1974)
> The original study, which remains engaging and thorough, if outdated

Harding, Jennifer, Elizabeth Thiel and Alison Waller, *Deep into Nature: Ecology, Environment and Children's Literature* (Lichfield: Pied Piper, 2009)
> Important exploration of a rapidly developing critical area

Jackson, Anna, Karen Coats and Roderick McGillis (eds), *The Gothic in Children's Literature: Haunting the Borders* (New York: Routledge, 2007)
> Traces gothic elements in children's literature from the eighteenth century, and discusses the relationship between a genre typifying adult desire, and children

Keith, Lois, *Take Up. Thy Bed and Walk: Death, Disability and Cure in Classic Fiction for Girls* (London: Women's Press, 2001)
> Still the only extensive study of disability in children's literature, relating attitudes of nineteenth-century writers to persisting cultural attitudes

Kuznets, Lois R., *When Toys Come Alive: Narratives of Animation, Metamorphosis, and Development* (New Haven, CT: Yale University Press, 1994)
> A study of toy characters from Pinocchio and Winnie-the-Pooh to *The Mouse and His Child* and 'Calvin and Hobbes'

Lampert, Jo, *Children's Fiction about 9/11: Ethnic, Heroic, and National Identities* (New York and London: Routledge, 2009)
> Explores how far cultural change since 9/11 has been reflected in children's literature, largely in paradoxical ways

Mendlesohn, Farah, *The Inter-Galactic Playground: A Critical Study of Children's and Teens' Science Fiction* (Jefferson, NC: MacFarland, 2009)
> Quixotic and entertaining attempt to encompass the development of children's science fiction between 1950 and 2010, relating it to literary and cultural theory

Reynolds, Kimberley, Geraldine Brennan and Kevin McCarron, *Frightening Fiction* (London and New York: Continuum, 2001)
> Study of the commodification of horror, in the work of R. L. Stine, Robert Westall, David Almond and others

Teaching, Education, Literacy and Readers

Arizpe, Evelyn, and Morag Styles, *Children Reading Pictures: Interpreting Visual Texts* (London: RoutledgeFalmer, 2003)
> Report of research project, including detailed interviews and interviewing techniques

Butler, Charles (ed.), *Teaching Children's Fiction* (Basingstoke: Palgrave, 2006)
> Despite its title, an excellent general introduction to the key issues in children's literature, including historical, cultural and gender studies

Gamble, Nikki, and Sally Yates, *Exploring Children's Literature: Teaching the Language and Reading of Fiction* (London: Paul Chapman, 2002)
> A practical handbook for undergraduate teachers that enthusiastically goes far beyond its remit, and may be useful and informative for a very wide audience

Meek, Margaret, *How Texts Teach What Readers Learn* (South Woodchester: Thimble Press, 1988)
> Succinct introduction to the connections between literature and literacy

Associated Topics

Kehily, Mary Jane (ed.), *An Introduction to Childhood Studies*, 2nd edn (Maidenhead: McGraw Hill/Open University, 2009)
> Comprehensive and attractive linking of topics around childhood, including sociology, psychology, media, literature and law

—, and Joan Swann (eds), *Children's Cultural Worlds* (Chichester: John Wiley, 2003)
> Part of an Open University series, looks at connections between family, work, schooling and children's development

Lathey, Gillian (ed.), *The Translation of Children's Literature: A Reader* (Clevedon: Multilingual Matters, 2006)

> Classic essays, including theoretical approaches from different translators, with specific examples including the Grimms and Harry Potter

Useful Websites

www.carnegiegreenaway.org.uk/

> The official site for the Carnegie and Kate Greenaway Medals, awarded by the Chartered Institute of Library and Information Professionals to outstanding books for children. Includes a list of all past winners of the awards

http://comminfo.rutgers.edu/professional-development/childlit/

> This site by Kay Vandegrift of Rutgers University covers a whole host of topics relating to children's literature and includes pedagogical material on 9/11 and children, gender and culture, and feminism, along with links to other resources

www.ibby.org/

> The International Board on Books for Young People brings together people from a variety of fields who are interested in bringing books and children together. Their site includes information about their projects and activities, and links to the organisation's national sections

http://ion.uwinnipeg.ca/~nodelman/resources/resource.htm

> A companion site to Nodelman and Reimer's *The Pleasures of Children's Literature*, this updates the bibliography to the book and provides some teaching and study guides

www.irscl.com/

> The International Research Society for Children's Literature aims to promote scholarship in children's literature internationally. Their site includes a comprehensive list of journals in the field and information about current conferences

Further Reading

www.ncl.ac.uk/elll/about/childrensliterature/research.htm

The *Newcastle Check-List of Books on the History, Criticism and Theory of Children's Literature* contains around 1,400 items

www.sevenstories.org.uk/

Seven Stories, the Centre for Children's Books, is the only archive in the UK dedicated to original material relating to modern children's literature. The website includes access to the centre's online catalogue, an excellent starting point for research on original material

Index

Index

Index

fantasy 19–20, 22, 24, 26, 29, 33–5
  for adolescents 170, 182–3
  adventure stories and 90, 91–2, 105, 108–9
  dangers of 35–6
  Diana Wynne Jones books 50–8
  ideology and 48–50
  imaginative play 123–4
  Second World War and 44–5
  subversive female characters 232
  and the unconscious 47–8
Farrar, Frederick, *Eric, or Little by Little* 226
feminism 26, 159, 209, 238–9
Fielding, Sarah, *The Governess* 15, 222
film adaptations 37, 44, 125, 130, 137, 149, 240, 288–90
films 207
Fine, Anne 266
  The Tulip Touch 27–8
First World War (1914–18) 21, 41, 43, 101, 228, 262, 289, *see also under* world wars
Fisk, Nicholas, *A Rag, a Bone and a Hank of Hair* 25
Fitzhugh, Louise, *Harriet the Spy* 75–6
Fleming, Ian, 'James Bond' books 91, 106, 109, 110, 227
focalisation 272, 273
folklore 10, 12, 119, 197, 221
food 183, 212
Forster, E. M., *Aspects of the Novel* 279
foster care 75, 82, 85–6
Fox, Geoff 206
Funny Folks (first comic) 275

Gabler, Mel and Norma 266
Gaiman, Neil, *The Graveyard Book* 145
gangs 75, 92, 104, 107, 111, 157
Gantos, Jack, *Joey Pigza Swallowed the Key* 246
Garfield, James 227
Garner, Alan 24, 212
  The Owl Service 34, 176
  Red Shift 176, 177

Tom Fobble's Day 265
The Weirdstone of Brisingamen 43
Garnett, Eve, *The Family from One End Street* 70–1
gay and lesbian novels for children 221
The Gem 228
gender 49–50, 74, 82n, 197, 217–18
  adventure stories 95–6, 104, 107–8, 115
  commodification and 237–40
  early children's literature 221–3
  female repression 230–2
  feminism and 238–9
  heroes and 219, 220–1, 223–4, 226, 228–31, 236–8
  identity and 186–7
  masculinities 223–30
  nineteenth-century 225–6
  school stories 234–5
  sexism 59, 224, 238, 253
  subservient role of women 223, 230, 233, 236–7
  subversion 232–4, 237–8
gender studies 221
Georgiana, Duchess of Devonshire 13–14
Gesta Romanorum 10
Girl Guide Movement 235
Girl's Own Paper 233, 249
Girouard, Mark 228
Gleitzman, Morris, *Once* 77–8
Godwin, William 94
golden ages of children's literature
  first age 19–21, 24, 33
  second age 23–5, 33–4
  third age 29
'Goldilocks' 162, 281
Golding, William, *Lord of the Flies* 100n
Goldthwaite, John 206, 220, 258
golliwogs 245, 252, 266, 275
Grahame, Kenneth, *The Wind in the Willows* 17, 20, 33, 41, 202, 212, 244, 245
graphic novels 148, 271, 280

Index

Index

Index

Acknowledgements

Extracts from:

THE JOLLY POSTMAN by Janet and Allan Ahlberg (Viking, 1999) Copyright ©
Allan and Janet Ahlberg, 1986. Reproduced by permission of Penguin Books Ltd

The Trouble with Donovan Croft by Bernard Ashley (OUP, 2008), copyright © Bernard
Ashley 1974, reprinted by permission of the publisher

MATILDA by Roald Dahl, © 1988 by Roald Dahl (Jonathan Cape & Penguin Books
Ltd). Used by permission of Penguin Young Readers Group and David Higham
Associates. All rights reserved

SILVERFIN Copyright © Ian Fleming Publications Ltd 2005. Reprinted with the
permission of Ian Fleming Publications Ltd
www.ianfleming.com

STORMBREAKER by Anthony Horowitz and published by Walker Books. Text
copyright © 2000 Anthony Horowitz/Stormbreaker Productions Ltd. Reproduced by
permission of Walker Books Ltd, London SE11 5HJ and United Agents
(www.unitedagents.co.uk) on behalf of Anthony Horowitz

Journey to the River Sea by Eva Ibbotson (London: Macmillan Children's Books UK,
2001). Reprinted by permission of the publisher

The Warlock of Firetop Mountain by Steve Jackson and Ian Livingstone (Penguin,
1982). Reproduced by permission of Icon Books Ltd

The Ogre Downstairs (Harper Trophy, 2002), *The Tough Guide to Fantasyland*
(Gollancz, 2004), *The Lives of Christopher Chant* (Harper Trophy, 2001), *The Merlin
Conspiracy* (Collins, 2003), and *Howl's Moving Castle* by Diana Wynne Jones, © Diana
Wynne Jones. Permission to reproduce granted by the Author

'The Rowans' from *Red, Cherry Red* by Jackie Kay (London: Bloomsbury, 2007).
Reprinted by permission of the publishers

THE LION, THE WITCH AND THE WARDROBE by C. S. Lewis copyright ©
C. S. Lewis Pte. Ltd. 1950. Extract reprinted by permission

YORK NOTES **COMPANIONS**

Texts, Contexts and Connections from York Notes
to help you through your literature degree ...

✔ Medieval Literature
Carole Maddern
ISBN: 9781408204757 | £10.99

✔ Renaissance Poetry and
Prose
June Waudby
ISBN: 9781408204788 | £10.99

✔ Shakespeare and
Renaissance Drama
Hugh Mackay
ISBN: 9781408204801 | £10.99

✔ The Long Eighteenth
Century: Literature from
1660 to 1790
Penny Pritchard
ISBN: 9781408204733 | £10.99

✔ Romantic Literature
John Gilroy
ISBN: 9781408204795 | £10.99

✔ Victorian Literature
Beth Palmer
ISBN: 9781408204818 | £10.99

✔ Modernist Literature: 1890
to 1950
Gary Day
ISBN: 9781408204764 | £10.99

✔ Postwar Literature: 1950
to 1990
William May
ISBN: 9781408204740 | £10.99

✔ New Directions: Writing
Post 1990
Fiona Tolan
ISBN: 9781408204771 | £10.99

✔ Children's Literature
Lucy Pearson with Peter Hunt
ISBN: 9781408266625 | £10.99

✔ Gothic Literature
Sue Chaplin
ISBN: 9781408266663 | £10.99

✔ Postcolonial Literature
Wendy Knepper
ISBN: 9781408266656 | £10.99

✔ Nineteenth Century
American Literature
Rowland Hughes
ISBN: 9781408266632 | £10.99

✔ Twentieth Century American
Literature
Andrew Blades
ISBN: 9781408266649 | £10.99

Available from all good bookshops

For a 20% discount on any title in the series visit
www.yorknotes.com/companions and
enter discount code JB001A at the checkout!

The best books ever written

20% discount on your essential reading from
Penguin Classics, only with *York Notes Companions*

Alice's Adventures in Wonderland and Through the Looking Glass
Lewis Carroll
Edited by Hugh Haughton
Paperback | 400 pages | ISBN 9780141439761 | 27 Mar 2003 | £6.99

The Swiss Family Robinson
Johann D. Wyss
Edited with an Introduction and Notes by John Seelye
Paperback | 496 pages | ISBN 9780143104995 | 30 Aug 2007 | £7.99

Little Women
Louisa May Alcott
Edited with an Introduction by Elaine Showalter
Paperback | 544 pages | ISBN 9780140390698 | 26 Jan 1989 | £8.99

The Wind in the Willows
Kenneth Grahame
Edited with an Introduction by Gillian Avery
Paperback | 240 pages | ISBN 9780143039099 | 27 Oct 2005 | £5.99

Treasure Island
Robert Louis Stevenson
Edited with an Introduction by John Seelye
Paperback | 240 pages | ISBN 9780140437683 | 25 May 2000 | £5.99

The Secret Garden
Frances Hodgson Burnett
Edited with an Introduction by Alison Lurie
Paperback | 288 pages | ISBN 9780142437056 | 30 Jan 2003 | £6.99